RECOMBO DNA

THE STORY OF DEVO
OR HOW THE 60s BECAME THE 80s

KEVIN C. SMITH

RECOMBO DNA

THE STORY OF DEVO OR HOW THE 60s BECAME THE 80s
by **Kevin C. Smith**

For Joey

A Jawbone Book
Published in the UK and the USA by Jawbone Press
2a Union Court,
20–22 Union Road,
London SW4 6JP,
England
www.jawbonepress.com

ISBN 978-1-908279-39-2

EDITOR Tom Seabrook
DESIGN Paul Cooper

Printed by Regent Publishing Services Limited, China

1 2 3 4 5 17 16 15 14 13

CONTENTS

17 INTRODUCTION

19 PROLOGUE: 1969

22 PART 1: STRANGE PURSUIT, OR LIFE IN THE RUBBER CITY (1970–75)
23 CHAPTER 1: **1970–71**
62 CHAPTER 2: **1972–73**
79 CHAPTER 3: **1974**
101 CHAPTER 4: **1975**

116 PART 2: THE BEGINNING WAS THE END (1976–77)
117 CHAPTER 5: **1976**
143 CHAPTER 6: **JANUARY–JUNE 1977**
164 CHAPTER 7: **JULY–DECEMBER 1977**

193 PART 3: WIGGLY WORLD (1978–79)
194 CHAPTER 8: **JANUARY–MAY 1978**
222 CHAPTER 9: **JUNE–DECEMBER 1978**
258 CHAPTER 10: **1979**

282 EPILOGUE: THE 80s
292 ENDNOTES
303 BIBLIOGRAPHY
305 SELECTED DISCOGRAPHY
310 INDEX
317 ACKNOWLEDGEMENTS

CLOCKWISE FROM TOP LEFT: Robert Smithson's *Partially Buried Woodshed*, created as part of the 1970 Kent State Creative Arts Festival, in a later state of decay; a panel from a 1948 *Wonder Woman* comic book, featuring an "electronic evolutionizer," and the *Jocko-Homo Heavenbound* religious pamphlet from 1924, both of which would subsequently prove influential on Devo's choice of band name and their concept of Devolution; a broadside from the 1974 Kent State Creative Arts Festival, featuring a linocut by Zephyrus Image; Jerry Casale (second left) with 15-60-75, aka The Numbers Band, at Walters Cafe on South Water Street in Kent, Ohio, circa 1973.

OPPOSITE: Devo pose backstage at Max's Kansas City with a poster advertising their previous two nights at CBGB, May 25 1977; a poster for the gig at Max's, Devo's third show on consecutive nights of their first trip to New York City. The photograph used on the Max's poster was taken at Goodyear's World of Rubber museum in Akron before Jim Mothersbaugh left the group and Bob Casale and Alan Myers joined. **ABOVE:** Booji Boy holds court, August 1 1977. **BELOW:** Devo onstage at San Francisco's Mabuhay Gardens in their yellow HAZMAT suits, July 28 1977.

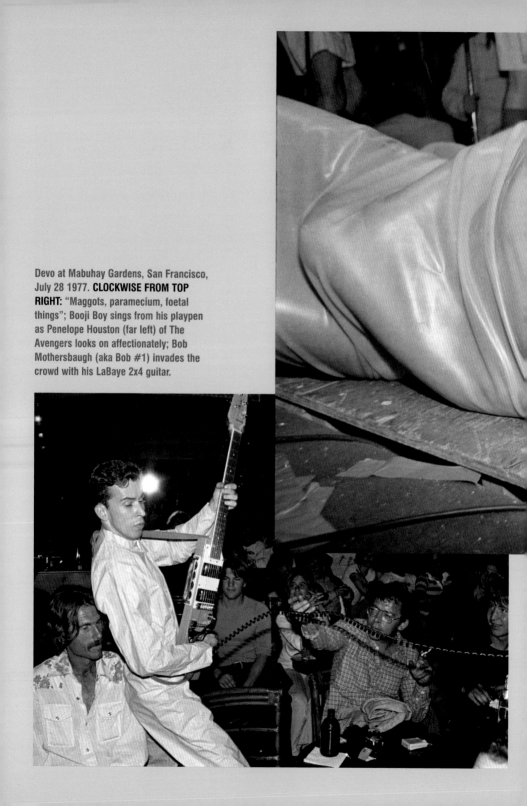

Devo at Mabuhay Gardens, San Francisco, July 28 1977. **CLOCKWISE FROM TOP RIGHT:** "Maggots, paramecium, foetal things"; Booji Boy sings from his playpen as Penelope Houston (far left) of The Avengers looks on affectionately; Bob Mothersbaugh (aka Bob #1) invades the crowd with his LaBaye 2x4 guitar.

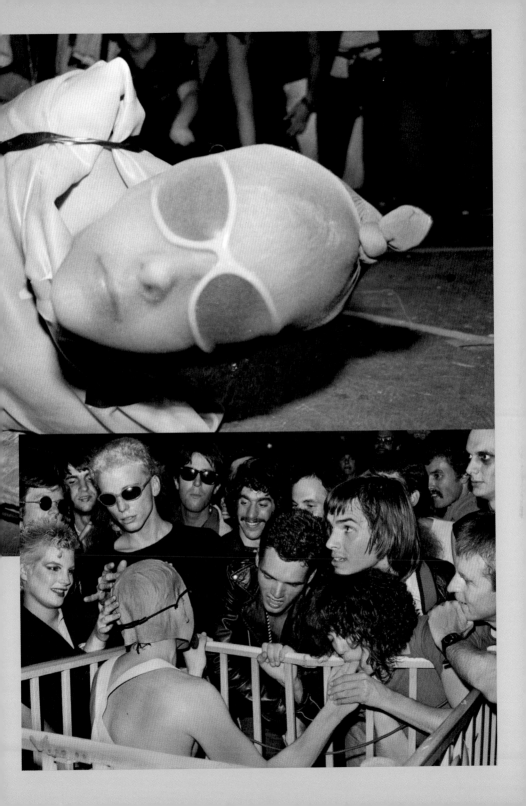

CLOCKWISE FROM TOP LEFT: backstage at the Mabuhay Gardens in Gurkha shorts and suspenders, with Jerry in his Chinaman glasses, September 11 1977; taking a break from filming the 'Satisfaction' video in downtown Akron, spring 1978, with Jerry holding his modified Gibson Ripper, which he dubbed the 'spudbass'; Devo in the 'Third Reich cowboy costumes' they wore for the 'Come Back Jonee' video, summer 1978; still on a break from the 'Satisfaction' video in downtown Akron.

BELOW: Devo on the beach in their adopted California, circa 1979. The coveralls and bulging deformities would also be seen in their video for 'The Day My Baby Gave Me A Surprize.' **OPPOSITE:** making an ill-fated appearance at the Knebworth Festival, with appropriate helmets, June 24 1978; performing 'Jocko Homo' on *Saturday Night Live*, with the stage covered in black plastic, October 14 1978.

LEFT: Jerry in 'leisure fashions' at the Agora Ballroom, Atlanta, July 27 1979. His custom-made bass body is attached to the neck of a Gibson EB-3. **BELOW:** Devo 'planking.' (Mark's neck brace is obscured in the photo.)

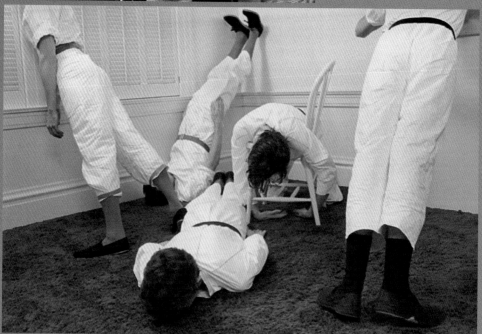

INTRODUCTION

Devo are a band who created their own mythology. While all bands of the rock era engage in this practice to some degree, Devo did so more blatantly and obviously—and with a lot more fun—than most, and could be said to have elevated the entire exercise to an art form in and of itself. While most bands would consider anything other than their music as an afterthought, Devo, in fact, reversed this process. Music was the last of the components of their overall worldview to fall into place. With a band so engaged in every aspect of their presentation—from music to short films and videos to writing to merchandising to their physical appearance and even the alternate cast of characters who figure into this world as well—it is virtually impossible to chronicle a comprehensive biography. Instead, this book focuses on one aspect of Devo's fascinating history. It explains how they went from being "free love, pot smoking hippie[s]" to a successful and slyly subversive multimedia entity who had not only renounced their former ideology but did everything in their power to dismantle it all within the span of a decade.[1] In doing so they pointed the way for a host of others to follow in their footsteps—the overwhelming majority of whom were not aware of (or did not understand) the band's initial impetus.

No matter how the press spun the story of rock music in the years immediately after their appearance, Devo have never been evaluated in their proper context, be it musical or social. This book is an attempt to trace the ideas, as well as the sounds, that Devo absorbed and in turn brought to prominence as unlikely rock stars in the late 70s and early 80s. Their idiosyncratic philosophy might not have always been consistent or even coherent (to those paying enough attention to notice) but it served as a deep well of inspiration across a

variety of mediums, and a source of fascination for their more dedicated fans.

Devo's innovations and accomplishments tend to be minimized in hindsight by the fact that they were so widely adopted as standard practice by most of the rock community within the space of a decade. Only by examining the band in relation to their peers can they be regarded as truly groundbreaking. They are also a sort of musical Zelig, crossing paths with a wide swath of musical genres from late 60s post-psychedelia, krautrock, punk rock, post-punk, and new wave without ever truly being a part of any of them.

While most rock biographies are content to simply document a band's or musician's history, few actually dig deeper to find their sources of inspiration and establish a continuity with other musicians' work. In Devo's case, however, many—if not most—of their influences were drawn from outside the realm of popular music. In an attempt to trace these inspirations we are led down a rabbit hole that takes in academic poetry, B-grade horror movies, performance art, obscure religious tracts, and political action. Though Devo meticulously crafted their image—consistently appearing in matching outfits and rarely being seen in ordinary street clothes, much like, in their own words, "a thinking man's Kiss"—they were not averse to engaging in press interviews. The clues to the genesis of their ideas are scattered throughout these dialogues, which span the time of the band's first releases in the late 70s to the present. This book, meanwhile, spans the years 1970 to 1979. Even though Devo did not perform regularly until the mid 70s, they managed to do a surprising amount of work in other media during the years prior to that. I believe all of this material—writing, visual art, performance art—is all of a piece with the band's music, and should all be considered under the umbrella of Devo. Indeed, much of this material would later resurface in different configurations and in different media. And although many of those ideas would find fruition in the corporate, conservative 80s, their seeds were planted in the radical underground of the 60s.

PROLOGUE: **1969**

The Cuyahoga River is an 85-mile stretch of shallow water that, with its tributaries, crisscrosses Northeast Ohio from Akron to Cleveland. The native Iroquois tribes gave the river its name, which means 'crooked river.' Connecticut lawyer and former Revolutionary War soldier General Moses Cleaveland arrived in 1796 to survey the land and founded the city that would be named after him. Settlement in the newly established city was slow. In the year of its founding, Cleveland's population numbered four; by the following year, it had only increased to fifteen. By 1800 it had dwindled to seven, on account of "the insalubrity of the locality."[1] Cleaveland himself was not among those counted in the census, having returned to Connecticut within six months of landing the expedition in Ohio.

In the intervening years the Cuyahoga River would come to be called many things besides the crooked river. By the late 19th century, Cleveland was discharging its untreated wastewater directly into the river, prompting Mayor Rensselaer R. Herrick to describe it, in 1880, as "a sewer that runs through the heart of the city." Despite his admonition, by 1897 Cleveland would still be pumping 50 million gallons of raw sewage into Lake Erie—into which the Cuyahoga feeds—every day. With the city's manufacturing boom in the late 1800s, the river became not just a sewer but a toxic dump. Factories, including numerous steel mills, discarded their refuse into the river with little to no regulation, resulting in a dangerous mix of floating oil and debris. The river would first catch fire in 1868 and then again in 1883, 1887, 1912, 1922, 1936, 1941, 1948, and 1952. The November 1952 fire burned for three days and caused $1.5 million of damage.

A Kent State University symposium convened in November 1968

19

found that "large quantities of black heavy oil floating in slicks, sometimes several inches thick are observed frequently. Debris and trash are commonly caught up in these slicks forming an unsightly floating mess. ... Animal life does not exist. ... The color changes from gray-brown to rusty brown as the river proceeds downstream. Transparency is less than 0.5 feet in this reach. This entire reach is grossly polluted."[2] Some of the waste floating in the river was fat and grease from slaughterhouses and rendering plants conveniently situated along the river, as well as acids used in steel mills or dyes from paint plants and the raw or partially treated sewage from the Cleveland–Akron area. But this wasn't all that wound up in the river. As someone involved in the river clean-up noted: "When spring floods would come, picnic benches, screen doors and automobile tires would come down and mix in with the industrial waste. ... The industrial got blamed, but it was like the old *Pogo* comic strip said: we have met the enemy—and it is us."[3]

Seven months later, on June 22 1969, the river caught fire again. The 30-minute fire caused $50,000 in damage. It was not the worst the river had seen, but it did generate the most press, with *Time* magazine noting: "No Visible Life. Some river! Chocolate-brown, oily, bubbling with subsurface gases, it oozes rather than flows. 'Anyone who falls into the Cuyahoga does not drown,' Cleveland's citizens joke grimly. 'He decays.' The Federal Water Pollution Control Administration dryly noted: 'The lower Cuyahoga has no visible life, not even low forms such as leeches and sludge worms that usually thrive on wastes.' It is also—literally—a fire hazard. A few weeks ago, the oil-slicked river burst into flames and burned with such intensity that two railroad bridges spanning it were nearly destroyed. 'What a terrible reflection on our city,' said Cleveland Mayor Carl Stokes sadly."[4]

The event spurred an interest in environmentalism and helped prompt the creation of the Environmental Protection Agency in 1970 and the Ohio Environmental Protection Agency in 1972, as well as the passage of the Clean Water Act that same year. (The 'crying Indian,' Iron Eyes Cody, would become a familiar face in 'Keep America Beautiful' Public Service Announcements on television.) Institutional change is notoriously slow, however, and as the beginnings of reform slowly wended their way through legislation, late night talk show hosts including Johnny Carson made Cleveland the butt of their jokes, with Northeast Ohio having developed a reputation as one of the most polluted parts of the country.

STRANGE PURSUIT OR LIFE IN THE RUBBER CITY (1970–75)

CHAPTER 1
1970-71

Things fall apart; the centre cannot hold;
Mere anarchy is loosed upon the world,
The blood-dimmed tide is loosed, and everywhere
The ceremony of innocence is drowned;
The best lack all conviction, while the worst
Are full of passionate intensity.
WILLIAM BUTLER YEATS

At the beginning of 1970, Jerry Casale was entering his final semester at Kent State University's Honors College. He had started at the university as a Liberal Arts major with a concentration in 20th Century Comparative Literature but was now due to finish with a double major in Fine Art (Painting and Printmaking). As part of his work/study program, one of his responsibilities was spending summers admitting new students, acting as a counselor to them, and guiding them through the curriculum.

Casale was born Gerald Vincent Pizzute in 1948 and does not remember his childhood in Kent, Ohio, fondly. He was by all accounts a bright student and something of an overachiever: he acted in school plays, served as the art editor for the school yearbook, and, perhaps most surprisingly, was vice president of the YMCA high school club, Hi-Y. Beneath his all-American veneer, however, Casale had a confrontational streak that had been manifesting itself since junior high.

"I was very angry about illegitimate authority," he later noted. "I grew up blue-collar and having to go to Catholic schools, and I was surrounded by mean people with lots of rules and lots of proclamations that were very offensive to a smart kid. You'd ask questions—because it didn't make sense—and you'd get punished for asking questions." He also witnessed firsthand the role that that status played in perception and treatment. "I saw how much class—that supposedly didn't exist in America—played a role in everything. There were *clear* class distinctions and class privileges and double and triple standards of justice and opportunity, and everybody acted like that didn't even exist. So you had that, and then you had the local cops, the mayor, the dean, the priests ... the bullies on the playground ... and they were *all* stupid shits. And that did it."[1]

Unsurprisingly for a smart kid with a rebellious streak, Casale also became interested in rock'n'roll. He was immediately drawn to the bass on records by Elvis Presley and eventually started playing the instrument "because of The Rolling Stones."[2] Then, toward the end of high school, he formed a band called The Satisfied Mind, which played "mostly Rolling Stones, Muddy Waters, John Lee Hooker and things like that."[3] He recalled growing up "listening to roots music, blues, and early R&B from stations out of Detroit, and I still love it. I think it's really some of the best stuff in the world, and what America's really about."[4]

Toward the end of his junior year of high school, Casale had a transformative experience when he bought the recently released Bob Dylan album *Bringing It All Back Home*. It was Dylan's last LP before infamously 'going electric' that summer at the Newport Folk Festival, and it also marked a shift from his earlier protest songs into stream of consciousness lyrics verging on the surreal. "I couldn't stop listening to it," he said. "It divided me from my college prep, pseudo Ivy League classmates and when I played it in poetry class in my Kent Roosevelt High School I was sent to the principal's office for making a joke of education."[5] When Casale was put in charge of the talent portion of the senior class assembly in 1966 he decided to play a version of Dylan's 'Rainy Day Women #12 & 35.' Four seniors had recently achieved notoriety, having been suspended from the football team for drinking beer, and Casale enlisted them to help sing the chorus of "everybody must get stoned." He had also hidden 'near beer' onstage in a bass drum, and on his signal the seniors pulled the contraband out and started imbibing. The gathered teachers were unimpressed and promptly pulled the plug on the performance. Casale was suspended and received his diploma by mail.

Casale's father was a machinist with a large family to support, so had never entertained the idea of sending his son to an out-of-state school. Instead, at a teacher's suggestion, Jerry applied to Kent State, a stone's throw from his high school, and entered the university that fall on a scholarship. Mike Lunine was the dean of the Honor's College at the time and described Casale as "spirited and creative" and a "raunchy undergrad."[6] One of the supposedly subversive acts that helped to cement his reputation came when he and his co-conspirators cooked up a huge pot of chicken soup and served it guerilla style at the Student Center. The 'Chicken Soup Rebellion' became front-page news on the *Kent Stater*. "Just by creating a 'disturbance' that had some kind of message or purpose [was] all it took to be labeled subversive and a troublemaker," Casale later noted, although he admitted his motivations weren't purely political. "The food was really rank."[7]

In hindsight, Casale would describe himself during this time as "a participant in pop culture … [I] was a bit of a hippie, and subscribed to that kind of apolitical 'love will conquer all' kind of feeling that was rampant."[8] He could have been describing the majority of his generation. Being born in 1948 placed him near the head of the baby-boomer generation. He was 15 when President Kennedy was assassinated, and when The Beatles first appeared on *The Ed Sullivan Show*; 19 when Martin Luther King Jr was killed; 20 when the draft lottery was instituted; and 21 when Woodstock took place.

Meanwhile, Bob Lewis grew up ten miles away in Akron, Ohio, but unlike Casale had no plans to stay in Ohio after high school. "I wound up at Kent by kind of a fluke," he recalled. Born Robert Curtis Lewis on March 4 1947, he had received a National Merit Scholarship and been accepted at Princeton University and the University of Chicago, but his high school girlfriend had only applied to Kent State, and he had no hesitation in following her. "By October of my freshman year she dumped me for a frat boy," he said. "So true love didn't turn out to be true but it put me in a situation I hadn't planned on. But I think actually being at Kent was kind of a magical place then."[9]

Lewis was an Anthropology major whose ambition at the time was to travel to Olduvai Gorge in the Serengeti and "dig up skulls."[10] Although he hadn't planned to stay so close to home, he soon found that Kent State was something of an island of culture in otherwise working class Ohio. It was this concentration of talent—both permanent and visiting—that would later prompt him to note: "Let me be plain about this: contrary to popular belief, Devo was not and is not a phenomenon of Akron, Ohio. It was rather a logical extension of a series of inexplicable forces that made Kent State University a mass culture nexus for a brief and shining moment."[11]

As the baby boomers attained college age, enrollment at Kent State increased in just a few short years from 8,000 to 20,000 students. The culture of the campus subsequently changed, too, from sleepy commuter campus to forward-thinking institution. Kent acted as a sponge, attracting many who made interstate pit stops between the East and West Coasts. "A constantly mutating parade of intellects created a cultural scene that seems unlikely in retrospective," he continued. "An acid dealer from New Jersey once told me he thought of Kent as the westernmost borough of New York City."

Although he became interested in music at an early age, later describing The Coasters' 1959 hit 'Charlie Brown' as "the first record I can think of that had an anti-establishment theme to it," Lewis did not seriously take up the guitar until he entered college.[12] He learned under the aegis of his friend and fellow Kent State student Joe Walsh, who would play with Kent bar band The Measles prior to joining The

James Gang in 1968 (and who was yet another example of the unexpected talent flowing through the area).

Lewis and Casale first met at Kent's Commuter's Cafeteria, a prosaically named gathering place that Lewis later claimed "served the same purpose as coffee houses in Greenwich Village, Paris, or *fin de siècle* Vienna, providing a place where highly caffeinated ideas could be exchanged." It was possibly the only place on campus where art students and anthropology majors alike—along with any others of a similarly inquisitive bent—could meet and cross-pollinate. "It was truly electric," Lewis recalled, "and underlying all of the academic discourse was rock'n'roll, Vietnam, and resistance to the state and its ill-advised war."[13] Casale's old friend Peter Gregg, whom he had befriended at Davey Junior High School in Kent, Ohio, was another regular, although Gregg never enrolled at the university. He, Lewis, and Casale would routinely get together for informal pot-fueled jam sessions.

Before that, Casale and Lewis got their first chance to work together on an issue of Kent State's literary magazine, *Human Issue* (formerly *Kent Quarterly*). Lewis contributed what he later described as "an epic-length poem entitled 'Space Man,' a pastiche of high and low poesy, quotes from *TV Guide* program descriptions, scenes from John Wayne movies … 'The fire-gutted Philippine freighter sank slowly in the convoy's wake,' and so forth."[14] Casale created a rubber stamp depicting a couple engaged in the missionary position (affectionately dubbed the 'fuck stamp') and not only hand-stamped the label of every envelope containing the magazine but also painstakingly added unique speech bubbles to each one.

While many of Casale and Lewis's generation were opposed to the Vietnam War and supported the civil rights movement, and occasionally marched to give voice to these opinions, others were not overtly political. By 1970, Casale had joined the local branch of Students for a Democratic Society (SDS), a radical student-activist group, which was involved in promoting a number of leftwing causes

27

on campus, most prominent among them ending the Vietnam War. If Kent State stood apart for the strength of its academic and cultural offerings at the time, the intensity of its politically radical faction would prove to be its equal. "Our SDS chapter's presence on campus at Kent was certainly an anomaly to mainstream Midwest culture and just as much an anomaly to a state university fueled by sports, fraternities, and curriculums favoring career opportunities in business and technology," Casale later noted. "Having said that, the intense and pioneering artistic/anti-war subcultural community at Kent State during the period of 1966 to 1972 was at least on par with those usually only attributed to famous A-list universities such as Columbia in New York and Berkeley in California. We may have been a small, land-locked group but we were harboring a powerhouse of unsung radical talent. Maybe we were outnumbered ten to one by marquee-name university students hogging the credit, but in any category—be it political speech making, radical organizing and demonstrations, musical performance art (before it was so-named), agit-prop paintings and posters, independent films, gay and lesbian activists, and yes, even hippie fashion shops and drug dealers—we had a local star that could stand with the best in the nation."[15] Although Casale would soon find that he was not entirely in step with the SDS message, he did agree with their general stance and became their go-to guy when any graphic design work was required.

By the late 60s, political protests had become commonplace on college campuses in the United States and abroad. Unfortunately, it was also not unheard of for protests to escalate to the point of violent confrontation. In April 1968, students at Columbia University demanded that the school sever its newly discovered ties with the Institute for Defense Analyses (IDA), a weapons research think-tank affiliated with the US Department of Defense. Columbia's branch of the SDS, led by its chairman Mark Rudd, eventually occupied four of the university's buildings (including the President's office) for seven days. Acting Dean Harry S. Coleman was held hostage in his own office for 26 hours along with two other administrators, while a photograph of student David Shapiro wearing dark sunglasses and sitting at University President Grayson Kirk's desk while smoking one of Kirk's cigars became famous when it appeared in *Life* magazine. (Ironically, Shapiro would later go on to teach at Columbia.) In the end, the occupiers were forcibly removed and more than 700 protestors were arrested. Approximately 150 people were injured, including 12 police officers.

In May 1968, what had begun as a discussion about discrimination and funding at a university in suburban Paris involving 150 students snowballed into the largest general strike the country had ever known, with more than one million people marching the streets and the French economy brought to a virtual standstill for two weeks. By the end of the month, President Charles de Gaulle had fled for Germany in an attempt to avert an attack on the Élysée Palace. The protests died down by July, and de Gaulle clung on to power after calling a new legislative election, but to anyone coming of age at the time, the events in France were inescapable and had a strong galvanizing effect. (A 22-year-old British art student named Malcolm McLaren was so inspired by the demonstrations that he attempted, unsuccessfully, to travel to Paris to take part. Undeterred, he and fellow student Jamie Reid helped stage a similar student occupation at their own Croydon Art School in London.)

Casale joined the Kent State SDS after listening to Mark Rudd speak there in the fall of 1968. After being expelled for his participation in the 1968 Columbia Student Revolt, Rudd had embarked on a speaking tour of around 75 college campuses. By 1969, Rudd had founded the Weathermen (or Weather Underground), which was named for a line from Dylan's 'Subterranean Homesick Blues,' and which he assembled from the more confrontational aspects of the SDS. Concerned that years of nonviolent resistance had had no effect in stopping the Vietnam War, the Weathermen would embark on a string of bombings between

1969 and 1975, usually targeting police departments, courthouses, military structures, and banks. They began modestly—almost comically—on October 7 1969 by bombing a Chicago statue commemorating police casualties incurred in the 1886 Haymarket Riot, in which anarchists threw a bomb at police dispersing a rally in support of workers striking for an eight-hour day. A new statue was unveiled on May 4 1970, on the anniversary of the riot—and coincidentally on the same day as the Kent State shooting—only to be blown up a second and then a third time. The Weathermen's activities quickly escalated to the point of bombing the home of the New York State Supreme Court Justice presiding over the trial of members of the Black Panther Party, and then to detonating bombs inside the Capitol Building and the Pentagon.

The Kent State chapter of the SDS was among the most radical. "It was not widely known that Kent State, a school that drew from the sons and daughters of Ohio tire and auto workers, had been one of the Weathermen's bases," Rudd later noted.[16] Established by Terry Robbins, who had previously set up SDS chapters at Kenyon College, Ohio, and in Ann Arbor, Michigan, it produced "dozens of Weather cadre," as Rudd put it—so much so that when Congress decided to study the SDS, it focused on two chapters: Columbia University and Kent State.

The Kent State chapter of the SDS had been involved in escalating confrontations with the university for months, prompting a string of rallies featuring nationally prominent speakers, among them 'yippie' leader Jerry Rubin, whose speech Casale attended. Less than a year earlier, Rubin had appeared at the 1968 Democratic National Convention in Chicago, which culminated in a "police riot." Many of these speeches were incendiary in nature, and the SDS had been circulating newsletters instructing protestors how to handle a confrontation, should one occur. On April 8 1969, the SDS had held a rally to demand the abolition of the Reserve Officers' Training Corps (ROTC) and the Kent State Law Enforcement School as well as the removal of the Northeast Ohio Crime Lab and Liquid Crystals Institute (partially funded by the Defense Department) from campus. Their stated aim was to "stop this university's ability to serve imperialism and racism, to challenge fundamentally some of the ways Kent State serves the ruling class."[17] The rally developed into a march through campus buildings and classrooms before finally wending its way to the administration building. The SDS estimated that 400 people attended the rally, while 200 went on the march, during which a scuffle broke out between protestors and campus police.

After the dust settled, seven individuals were suspended, and five of those seven were charged with assault and battery and ordered off campus for the next three weeks. Meanwhile, the SDS had its status as a recognized campus organization suspended, effectively banning it from Kent State, but ignored the ban and continued to hold rallies. It also added a further point to its list of demands: open and collective hearings for all those suspended. The university ignored this demand, as it had the others, and when a disciplinary hearing for one of those arrested, Colin Nieberger, was held on April 16, the SDS held another large-scale rally. By its own estimation, 2,000 people attended the rally, while 700 marched to the Music and Speech building where the hearing was being held.

After an hour of struggling to gain access to the building, around 100 protestors broke through and rushed the hearing room. After succeeding in disrupting the hearing, the protestors attempted to flee, but 58 of them—including Robbins—were arrested and charged with trespassing. Two days later, the charge of inciting a riot was added. Robbins was sentenced to three months in prison, ultimately serving six weeks in a Cleveland jail. (A year later, on March 6 1970, Robbins and two other members of the Weather Underground were killed when a bomb they were building exploded in a Greenwich Village townhouse.)

Even so, there was nothing to suggest that these relatively minor disturbances would lead to anything more serious. As a subsequent

31

Presidential report would put it: "Compared with other American universities of its size, Kent State had enjoyed relative tranquility … and its student population had generally been conservative or apolitical. … They are predominantly the children of middle class families, both white collar and blue collar, and in the main go on to careers as teachers and as middle-level management in industry."[18]

Mark Mothersbaugh was two years younger than Jerry Casale and grew up in the town of Cuyahoga Falls, roughly midway between Akron and Kent. Born on May 18 1950, he was a true baby boomer in that his father, Robert Mothersbaugh Sr, had served in World War II and would ironically later appear in many of Devo's short films and videos as 'General Boy' clad in an army service uniform and M1 helmet. Mark's early experiences were not dissimilar to those of many future artists. "I hated school," he later recalled. "I just really didn't fit in very well. K through 12 were awful years for me."[19] Some of his difficulties came as a result of his poor vision, undiagnosed until the second grade—at which point he was declared legally blind. His newly corrected 20/20 vision inspired a wave of creativity as he began drawing everything he saw, and the compliments he received from his art teacher were, he claimed, the first positive feedback he'd ever received from an authority figure. It was then that his career path was set. "I think I became an artist kind of because I got to save up on getting to see things until I was almost eight years old," he said.[20]

His obsession with drawing was not only a blessing but also a curse. He became an inveterate daydreamer, obsessed with filling notebooks with his drawings—a habit that would persist into college and beyond. "I would say: OK, this semester, I'm going to pay attention," he recalled. Before long, however, he would slip into his old ways. "I would look at my notebooks from that time period, and I saw that even through college, I would have really excellent notes the first couple of days, but already, before the first week of school was over, I would already be starting to draw pictures in the margin. And, by the time it got to the end of the notebook, they were all drawings. You'd maybe see, like, two words: 'Test on Monday. I'm fucked,' or something like that."[21]

Even before acquiring his first pair of glasses, Mark had been encouraged by his parents to study the organ. He began lessons at the age of six or seven, and perhaps surprisingly the first music he played was not classical or even contemporary pop music but a collection of TV theme songs. One that stuck in his mind was the swinging, horn-driven theme to *77 Sunset Strip* (even more ironically, given that his Mutato Muzika operation is currently located three blocks away from the fictional private detective agency on Sunset Boulevard).

Mark only became hooked on rock'n'roll at the age of 13 when he saw The Beatles on *The Ed Sullivan Show* on a little black-and-white television while eating dinner with his family. (Where Jerry was inspired to play music by The Rolling Stones, Mark was equally motivated by their rivals—a creative dichotomy that would continue to exhibit parallels throughout Devo's career.) Mark and an accordion-playing friend promptly bought sheet music of Beatles songs and practiced them for about two weeks. It was then that he reached the devastating conclusion that he'd spent his young life learning the wrong kind of organ. Watching The Beatles perform 'I'm Down' during their fourth appearance on *Ed Sullivan* on September 12 1965, just 19 months after their debut, he saw John Lennon sitting at what looked like a card table before realizing it wasn't a card table at all but a Vox Continental portable organ. He was impressed for two reasons: not only because it was red and black, unlike the "big dorky wooden box" in his parents' home, but also because the 'white' keys were black, and the 'black' keys were white.[22] When Lennon broke into an organ solo for which he employed his elbows as well as his hands, Mark was sufficiently inspired to put his keyboard skills to use in a rock band.

Mothersbaugh was playing in his first band by the time he was 12

33

and continued to play informally with his younger brothers, Bob and Jim, on guitar and drums respectively. He also spent a summer in a band led by an Akronite named Chrissie Hynde. The band was called Sat Sun Mat (short for 'Saturday Sunday Matinees'), and as Hynde later noted they already had a penchant for something that would become a Devo hallmark. "We played a few quirky covers, such as Traffic's '40,000 Headmen,' in a church hall," she recalled.[23] It would be the band's only public performance. They might have played more had Hynde's shyness not got the better of her. "We used to rehearse down in some guy's basement," she said, "and I was so shy that I wouldn't stay in the same room as the band to sing. I'd take the mike into the laundry room and shut the door."[24]

Upon graduation from high school, Mark was torn between his two interests—art and music—but was swayed against simply trying his luck in music by events in Vietnam. On December 1 1969, the United States Selective Service instituted the first draft lottery in 27 years—a televised event preempting the regularly scheduled broadcast of Andy Griffith's *Mayberry R.F.D.* Viewers watched as light-blue plastic capsules (not numbered ping-pong balls, as many remember) were drawn one by one from a giant glass jar. Within each capsule was a rolled-up slip of paper with a day and month printed on it, which was unfurled and placed on a board beside corresponding numbers ranging from 1 to 366. The earlier the date was drawn, the more likely it was that young men born on that day between 1944 and 1950 would be called to serve. Mark was at the tail end of the range, but by the time the lottery occurred he made sure he had a 2–S, or student deferment, by being enrolled at Kent State as a graphic design major.

"I loved Kent State, actually," he later recalled. "I really disliked all my school years until I got to Kent. I loved the idea that the school was so big. I could be anonymous. I didn't have to get into confrontations and fights every day."[25] While he enjoyed the anonymity that the school afforded him, he also took full advantage of the art facilities—often to the detriment of any kind of social life. At the end of the school day, when others would begin their socializing, Mark would usually stay in the studio and continue his studies on his own. He would remain there until the early hours of the morning before heading home for a few hours' sleep and then returning to repeat the process the next day. By the end of his first year he had discovered the process of silk-screening, which had also become Andy Warhol's method of choice earlier in the decade, and which enabled Mark to quickly and cheaply produce as many copies of an image as he wanted as well as a choice of how to deliver it. "I could come up with an idea for a piece of art and burn a screen," he recalled, "and then print it on a T-shirt or on a poster, or on a sticker, and then stick it up somewhere like graffiti."[26] It was precisely this practice that would eventually lead Mothersbaugh to meet his long-term musical partner.

Although Mark had been playing the organ for over a decade, in 1970 he was exposed to another instrument that would change the course of his life. The Kent State Creative Arts Festival had begun in 1967, and although it prominently featured poetry (the university having cultivated a reputation for hosting readings by poets including William Butler Yeats, Robert Frost, and Langston Hughes in the 30s and 40s) it also included art in other media. The 1970 festival would feature electronic music pioneer Morton Subotnick and conceptual artist Allan Kaprow (who had coined the term 'happening' to describe the art he was making), both of whom arrived fresh from opening the California Institute of the Arts (CalArts) on the outskirts of Los Angeles a year earlier; and land artist Robert Smithson, shortly to complete his most renowned work, *Spiral Jetty*, a 1,500-foot-long spiral of earth extending into Utah's Great Salt Lake.

Subotnick was noteworthy for having recorded the first electronic work commissioned by a record company, 1967's *Silver Apples Of The Moon* (named for a line in Yeats's poem 'The Song Of Wandering Aengus'). He had also designed, in collaboration with Don Buchla, one of the first synthesizers, the Buchla Series 100. Buchla's premier synth was released just months after Robert Moog's appeared on the market but his design arguably predates Moog's. (The two would maintain a friendly rivalry for decades—Buchla, the Berkeley hippie who had jammed with the Grateful Dead and had steadfastly refused to outfit his synthesizers with keyboards and Moog, the engineering Ph.D. who, not being a musician himself, deferred to what his customers wanted and gave them the piano-like keyboards they requested.)

Subotnick led workshops during the arts festival, one of which was attended by the teenage Mark Mothersbaugh, who would later recall that it was the first time he had seen a synthesizer in action. What Subotnick remembers most vividly about his time at Kent, however, was not the workshop but the overwhelming tension at the university. "I don't think this is just hindsight," he said. "I've never quite experienced anything like it—you could almost smell the tension in the air that was within the university."[27] Subotnick's colleague Kaprow led his own workshops and also created *Graft*, which involved the hanging of hothouse greenery and dollar bills (of the same value as the greenery) on the bare branches of trees on a winter day. Devo would later acknowledge the influence not just of Subotnick but of Kaprow, too, particularly his all-encompassing view of art: "Allan Kaprow made the statement that the moon landing was probably the most significant piece of art 'cos it had everything—it was soft sculpture, it was video presentation, it was kinetic, it was culturally relevant, and everyone saw it. It fulfilled all the criteria of what is supposedly significant. And it had the biggest budget!"[28]

Smithson, meanwhile, created *Partially Buried Woodshed*, which was exactly that. His most recent series of works included pouring various substances into land masses—including *Asphalt Rundown* in Rome, *Concrete Pour* in Chicago, and *Glue Pour* in Vancouver—while photographing the processes. As the cold January weather prevented him from pouring a truckload of mud down a Kent hill, he hastily conceived a new project. Finding an old, unused farm woodshed on the edge of the university campus, he simply piled mounds of dirt on it using a backhoe until its roof beam gave way.

This unusual project created problems for the university and highlighted some of the conflicts between school administrators, the unorthodox artists taking part in the festival, and the conservative town of Kent. According to Subotnick, the execution of the project was scheduled for 6:00am to shield it from the local townspeople. "The administration was very nervous that seeing a building get buried on the campus would just be one of these things of: oh, these smart ass intellectuals, what are they doing burying buildings?" he recalled. "The buzz was that they did it early so that there would be no townspeople there, very little information about it as possible and that they would then, when we left—we were leaving that day—that they would simply unbury the building and it would be over."

Before leaving Kent, and without informing anyone of his intentions, Smithson had the piece insured for $10,000 and transferred its ownership to the university, effectively ensuring that it had to stand as it was. "So they couldn't unbury it," Subotnick said. "The tension just grew: it was like you could just feel it, it was just horrible." Smithson intended for the piece to be allowed to decay naturally. It was to stand as a monument of 'entropy made visible,' a concept that would later be echoed in one of Devo's earliest slogans: 'The important sound of things falling apart.'

Although the *Woodshed*'s significance would take on a new dimension in the coming months, many saw the relevance of it at the time. "It's about the breaking down of the system," *Akron Beacon Journal* art critic Dorothy Shinn later wrote. "About things falling apart. About the center not holding. About things that we took for granted as being solid and permanent being ephemeral and falling away right before our eyes. Smithson and other artists, people who are sensitive to events around them, must have felt that. And the idea of something cracking, a system cracking, breaking apart probably seemed very appropriate for the time."[29]

It wasn't just Smithson's project that contributed to the general feeling of unease. Kent State also had a Black Studies Program, which began as the Institute for African American Affairs the previous year, and whose members, as Subotnick recalled, "had sort of sealed themselves off from the white community and the college. The reason I remember it so well is that Allan [Kaprow] and I were invited in to talk to classes. It was like going into a parallel world … you were on the same campus but you were no longer on campus as soon as you entered the doorway to the classroom and closed it. You were in a whole different space." He was surprised even to have been granted admittance. "It was set off so strongly that it felt unusual that we were invited in. I would have to say that my workshop, and probably Allan's too, were fairly successful in the fact that we sort of bridged the gap between the political situation that was going on."

Subotnick had already become embroiled in his own political controversy when he and his colleagues tried to hire radical neo-Marxist philosopher Herbert Marcuse for the faculty of CalArts. The school's owners, Walt and Roy O. Disney, responded by trying to shut down the school before it had even opened. "The context is that for Allan and I to feel the way we did when we went to Kent State was striking because we thought we were already in a politically charged situation," Subotnick recalled. "We felt like we were in a battle zone. It must be like what Libya or Syria feels like to some reporters going in there. It was at any moment something was going to explode, it really felt that way."

Mark's younger brother, Bob, was nearing the end of his senior year of high school, but on Friday May 1 1970 he was playing hooky and spending the day hanging out at the SDS headquarters at Kent State. The previous night, at 9:00pm, President Nixon had appeared on all three TV networks to announce that he was launching incursions into formerly neutral Cambodia to attack the Viet Cong who had taken refuge there. This escalation of the already unpopular Vietnam War was intended to capture "the headquarters of the entire communist military operation" in South Vietnam.[30] "It is not our power but our will and character that is being tested tonight," he continued. "The time has come for action." Perhaps predictably, a protest was organized, not by the banned SDS but instead a small group of history graduate students with the provocative moniker World Historians Opposed to Racism and Exploitation (or WHORE), as well as a group of younger faculty members and graduate students from the more soberly named New University Conference. They held a peaceful rally during which they ceremoniously buried a copy of the United States Constitution near the campus landmark Victory Bell, claiming it had been "murdered" when Nixon invaded Cambodia without either a declaration of war or consultation with Congress. An ominous sign fixed to a nearby tree asked: "Why is the ROTC building still standing?"

As the day turned to night and the weekend alcohol began to flow, however, a crowd began to cluster around the downtown bars on North Water Street and soon clashed with police. Within an hour the crowd had lit bonfires, vandalized local stores, and blocked traffic. Among them that night was Mothersbaugh's former bandmate, Chrissie Hynde, then an 18-year-old art student at Kent State. "We took these big garbage cans from the side of the road, wheeled them into the middle of the street and set them on fire," she recalled. "It was an awesome sight." When a lone car tried to travel down the street, she added, "we just jumped on his car and kicked all the windows out to punish the driver for having the gall to interfere with our protest."[31]

The SDS-affiliated Casale would later dismiss these events as "spring-break-type violence ... students with raging hormones mixed with some political ideas."[32] Nonetheless, Kent Mayor Leroy Satrom declared a state of emergency at 12:30am and ordered the bars to close—which only had the adverse effect of increasing the crowds gathered in the street. Eventually, combined city and county police forces used teargas to herd the crowd back toward the university. They had expected Kent State to take over at that point, unaware that the university's Police Chief, Donald L. Schwartzmiller, had instead instructed his forces to guard campus buildings. A standoff developed between police who would not cross the campus border and protesters who were afraid to venture beyond it. By the time the standoff ended, 15 people had been arrested.

The following day, in an effort to quell further unrest, Mayor Satrom banned the sale of alcohol, firearms, and gasoline (unless pumped directly into the tank of a car). He also instituted a curfew from 8:00pm to 6:00am, subsequently amending it to 1:00am to 6:00am for those at the university (perhaps sensing the futility of an 8:00pm curfew for a campus full of restless college kids). Not everybody was aware of the different curfew times, however, and far from averting further violence the measure seemed to have precisely the opposite effect. By the end of the evening, around 1,000 students—who would most likely have otherwise been downtown on a Saturday night—had gathered around the ROTC building, which had long been a source of irritation among anti-war activists. As a mob mentality took hold the wooden structure was bombarded with a combination of rocks, garbage cans, and railroad flares.

Bob Mothersbaugh had returned to campus that day and found himself in the middle of the melee. He participated in the burning of an American flag, which may or may not have been the ultimate cause of the building's demise. Hynde was there too and recalled: "Though we were angry, the whole scene was kind of a gas too … it was awesome to see the hated ROTC building going up in flames. It was definitely a night to remember."[33] Bob Lewis, meanwhile, had attended professor Dick Myers's Kent film festival that night. "The first showing got out about 9:30 or so," he recalled. "When we came out of the auditorium we could see the light from the burning ROTC building. It was pretty much gone by that time."[34] It was at this point that Mayor Satrom called for the National Guard. Guardsmen were redirected from the Rubber Bowl stadium in Akron, where they had been stationed three days earlier to monitor a truckers' strike, and promptly dispersed the protestors with teargas. No one was apprehended for the ROTC fire, although FBI agents later visited the Mothersbaugh household and presented Bob's mother, Mary, with photographs of her son holding a flaming American flag over the building.

There were accusations from both sides that outside agitators had been sent to the university to instigate and fuel conflicts. It was most likely these individuals that Ohio Governor Jim Rhodes had in mind when he delivered a speech the following morning in which he pounded the table and described the protestors as "worse than the Brownshirts, and the Communist element, and also the Night Riders, and the vigilantes. They're the worst type of people that we harbor in America. ... They are not going to take over campus, and the campus now is going to be part of the county and the state of Ohio. There's no sanctuary for these people to burn buildings down," he added, perhaps referring to the standoff at the gates of the university on Friday night. Having effectively declared martial law after taking control of the campus through the National Guard, the Governor also banned all demonstrations. Nevertheless, a group of students assembled on the Commons that evening, until an immediate curfew was declared around 9:00pm. Teargas was once again used to disperse the crowd and 51 people were arrested, mostly for curfew violations. Bob Lewis later recalled that his roommate, Bob Webb, had been arrested at gunpoint after taking his telescope ("he was an amateur astronomer") out onto the back porch to observe the proceedings from a distance.[35]

Classes resumed on Monday May 4—even after a reported bomb threat—but most were still focused on the weekend's events. Word soon spread that the National Guard had arrived at Kent State. Jerry Casale was in a drawing class that morning when it was announced that classes would be cut short. Around 10:30am, an impromptu meeting was called at the student union (commonly referred to as the Hub). Aspiring musician Chris Butler and his friend Jeffrey Miller witnessed members of the university's radical political factions debate what sort of action, if any, should be undertaken that morning. Butler was a transplanted Clevelander majoring in Sociology while Miller was originally from Long Island and had recently transferred from Michigan State University. The assembled group had collectively decided against taking any decisive action. "If there ever was going to be a conspiracy to cause trouble," Butler recalled, "that would have been it, and those were the people who would have done it."[36] A previously announced noon rally was still scheduled to take place on the Commons, although the National Guard had been given orders to put a stop to it.

Bob Lewis and some friends had just finished breakfast at the Commuter's Cafeteria and were on their way out onto the Commons, where a few students had been making brief speeches. "There's these walkways on campus that are just overarched on both sides with 80, 90-year-old lilac bushes," he later recalled. "May 4 was this beautiful, beautiful sunny day, and you could smell the lilacs."[37]

Just before noon, however, approximately 116 National Guard troops arrived on the scene and were ordered by Ohio National Guard General Robert Canterbury to "lock and load" their M1 Garand rifles—an order that is only given when troops expect to have a reasonable chance of firing their weapons. Chris Butler characterized the mood on campus as "extremely irate" due to the events of the previous night. As the students were ordered to disperse they responded with increasing anger and chants of "pigs off campus" and "sieg heil." By now around 2,000 students were either participating in or observing the confrontation, some of them stood on steps or balconies of nearby buildings or up on the slopes of the surrounding hills.

The gasmasked National Guard formed a line, having affixed

bayonets to their rifles, and fired teargas into the crowd, although this proved ineffective due to the heavy wind that day. They then marched up Blanket Hill, pushing students past Taylor Hall and effectively clearing the Commons before attempting to push the crowd down the other side of the hill, across an access road, and past a football practice field. A small group of students followed the soldiers and continued to taunt them and pelt them with rocks from a nearby construction site. The Guard would periodically launch canisters of teargas, which were often hurled back at them. When they reached the football field the Guardsmen kneeled down and aimed their rifles at the group of students—among them Casale, Butler, and Miller— now gathered in an adjacent parking lot. There are conflicting reports as to whether a warning shot was fired at this point; according to Butler, many of the assembled students laughed at this point, finding the whole situation "extremely ridiculous."[38]

After ten minutes in formation the Guardsmen headed back up Blanket Hill, with students continuing to pelt them with rocks all the while. Bob Lewis had been behind the troops but now found himself being pushed back up the hill. As Casale later described it, the whole thing looked "like party games. It's kind of almost laughable."[39]

Chrissie Hynde had just arrived on campus around this time and had been told that a "peaceful demonstration" was to take place, but the sight of troops armed with rifles gave her a "very bad vibe." It was then that she heard what she thought were fireworks.

Casale was watching the troops when, from the crest of Blanket Hill at 12:24pm, a number of the Guard stopped, turned, kneeled down, and opened fire on the students. He turned to run when the hail of bullets began and immediately saw a student, Allison Krause, lying face down in a pool of blood. A single bullet had entered and exited her left arm and lodged in her chest. She had been standing approximately 20 feet behind Casale when she was shot, the pair of them more than 300 feet from the National Guard.

Butler had been carrying a small bucket of water, which he was using to soak bandanas in order to filter the tear gas. When it had run dry he went into nearby Prentice Hall to refill it from a water fountain. He would later estimate that he had been separated from Miller for about 30 to 45 seconds before the shots were fired. As he walked back to the parking lot, Butler heard gunfire and ducked behind a car, which moments later had its windows shot out, covering him in broken glass. He and the rest of the students were soon marched off campus, and it wasn't until he watched the evening news that he discovered that Miller was one of the four killed that day. A single bullet had entered his open mouth and exited the base of his skull, killing him instantly.

Casale sat down shaking when the 13 seconds of shooting stopped and the bullhorns ordered everybody to "stay where you are." Moments earlier, he had seen a girl he would later learn was 14-year-old runaway Mary Ann Vecchio screaming and gesturing in the crowd. Only later, after seeing John Filo's Pulitzer Prize-winning photographs of the scene, did he realize that Vecchio had been standing over Jeffrey Miller's dead body. Casale had befriended both Miller and Krause as underclassmen the previous summer while he was working as a counselor.

Mark Mothersbaugh was off campus setting up his new art studio at the Davey Warehouse, an art facility on Water Street, when the shooting took place. "I was decorating [the studio] when there were police cars going down the street with megaphones going: The school is shut down. The city is shut down. Please go to your homes."[40] After staying put for what seemed like hours, the students were eventually marched off campus single file. To add insult to injury, hostile locals had been deputized and were patrolling the streets with guns; newspaper reports that night erroneously stated that students had killed Guardsmen. Casale was forced to walk the four miles to his Water Street apartment in fear of his life.

Altogether, four students were killed and nine were injured, with one permanently paralyzed from the chest down. Sandra Scheuer, a

20-year-old honors student, was shot in the throat while walking between classes, and William Schroeder, a 19-year-old ROTC applicant, was shot in the back while laying down in an attempt to avoid the gunfire.

Prior to the shooting, Allison Krause had been distributing flowers, which she reportedly said were "better than bullets." She had probably been inspired by a photograph taken by Bernie Boston and published in the *Washington Star* of another protestor, mop-topped and turtlenecked George Harris, placing carnations in the barrels of soldiers' rifles outside the Pentagon on October 12 1967. Two years earlier, beat poet Allen Ginsberg had written a 12-point plan for diffusing tensions with police (or what he described as "patriotic" Hell's Angels), the first of which noted: "Masses of flowers ... can be used to set up barricades, to present to Hell's Angels, police, politicians, and press and spectators whenever needed or at parade's end."[41] (Fellow Beat writer William S. Burroughs, whose influence would overtake Ginsberg's during the following decade, disagreed. "Giving flowers to cops just isn't going to work," he later remarked. "The only way I like to see cops given flowers is in a flower pot from a high window."[42])

On June 10 1970, Allison Krause's father, Arthur Krause, filed a $6-million suit in federal court against Governor James A. Rhodes and two Ohio National Guard commanders. The suit stated the three men had "intentionally and maliciously disregarded the lives and safety of students, spectators, and passersby, including Allison Krause." Krause also filed a $2-million suit in Portage County Court of Common Pleas against the state of Ohio.

The Kent State campus was closed immediately after the shootings and would remain so for the next 40 days until seniors were invited back on June 13 for their commencement ceremony. Jerry Casale was

not invited back due to his membership in the SDS. He graduated in absentia.

At some point during the school's closure, the words "MAY 4 KENT 70" were anonymously painted in bold white letters on the lintel of Smithson's *Partially Buried Woodshed*, making it something of an unofficial memorial to the events of that day. Far from being viewed as a debasement, the graffiti became an integral part of the piece's meaning, keeping it relevant in ways that it otherwise would not have been. "Had it not been for those few strokes of white paint," critic Dorothy Shinn remarked, "one wonders if the *Woodshed* might not have been left to rot in relative quiet." Smithson's wife, artist and filmmaker Nancy Holt, told Shinn: "Obviously the students, or whoever did that graffiti—it's an example of graffiti that enhances— the students obviously recognized the parallel. Piling the earth until the central beam cracked, as though the whole government, the whole country were cracking. Really, we had a revolution then. It was the end of one society and the beginning of the next."[43]

Casale has pinpointed May 4 1970 on numerous occasions as the date that Devo was born. "All I can tell you is that it completely and utterly changed my life," he said in 2003. "I was a white hippie boy and then I saw exit wounds from M1 rifles out of the backs of two people I knew."[44] The experience led directly to a new way of thinking. "I would not have started the idea of Devo," he said, "unless this had happened."[45] Devo the band was still a few years away, but the first seeds of Devo as a concept had just been sown.

Casale's change in perspective was also reflected in his outward appearance. "When David Crosby sang that song with Crosby Stills Nash & Young about how he almost cut his hair ... well I did," he said.[46] "I cut my hair, got rid of my flared pants and velour shirts, and went to this pimp store in Cleveland, where I bought straight-legged pants, high, black shoes, and a long leather jacket, like you'd see the Black Panthers wearing."[47]

Although the ideas were germinating, the newly radicalized

Casale was generally underemployed and spending his evenings after work jamming with a loose group of friends, many of whom lived in the same apartment complex, including Peter Gregg and Bob Lewis. Much has been made about the Devo aesthetic formulating during the three months that Kent State was closed after the shooting, but musically speaking it looks like Casale was really just continuing to do what he had been doing for the past few years.

The apartment complex where Casale and his friends congregated was serendipitously located above Dayho Electronics, a repair shop that also housed the owner's makeshift recording studio ('dayho' being Vietnam-era slang for anyone who worked a dayshift). The adjoining business, Guido's Pizza Shop, also proved convenient for fueling late night gatherings. Sometime during 1971–72, the three friends convinced Dayho's owner to record some of their songs on his Teac four-track. With Jerry on bass, Peter Gregg on guitar, and Bob Lewis on slide guitar, they recorded a number of tracks they had been kicking around for some time, including 'I Need A Chick,' 'I Been Refused,' 'The Rope Song,' and 'Auto Modown.' (These recordings have never been issued, but a number of these tracks have subsequently appeared in rerecorded form on Rykodisc's two-volume set of *Hardcore Devo*. And while pre-fame doodles such as these should not be exposed to the same level of scrutiny as later Devo successes, it does beg the question as to why songs with so little redeeming value would be rerecorded once again for Casale's 2006 album as Jihad Jerry & The Evildoers, *Mine Is Not A Holy War*.)

These songs bear no trace of the anger Casale experienced after the shootings but are instead, for the most part, juvenile odes to sexual frustration set to rudimentary blues riffs. 'I Need A Chick' is based around an insistent bassline, which the guitar mimics before wandering off into twangy embellishments. But while the lyrical theme is familiar, the words themselves ("I need a chick / To suck my dick / I need a dog / To lick my hog") are blunt and lacking in humor in a way that Devo's would never be. 'I Been Refused' fares only marginally better due to the non-sexual non sequiturs peppered throughout the song as Jerry makes reference to his real-life arrest while working in an adult bookstore ("Judge said / You're the porno king / Go to jail for a while") before describing taking pictures of his sister's genitalia.

On 'The Rope Song,' Casale has finally found "a girl with a pretty face" but is seemingly keeping her against her will, having "tied a rope around her waist." There's an echo of Nabakov's *Lolita* as the narrator convinces himself that the girl is enjoying her captivity. He then ends by asking: "What do I want to do?"—a means either of disingenuously obscuring his real intentions or simply admitting that he is too naïve to know. 'Auto Modown' wisely shifts the subject away from sex to another rock standard: senseless violence. The narrator coldly recounts the scene in nearby Youngstown, Ohio, of a runaway car that has plowed into a crowd of pedestrians. Casale plays a funky bassline against clipped fuzz-guitar while intoning a lyric about "bodies in the street" and "bodies with no feet." In an early example of how much of Devo's work would be informed by the media, the song was inspired by a front-page story in the November 2 1971 edition of the *Youngstown Vindicator*, published under the headline 'Car Hops Curb Downtown, 3 Die.' "Purses, shopping bags, shattered glass, a woman's wig, and shoes were strewn amid the bodies lying on the sidewalk," the article ran. "One woman's leg was reported ripped off by the careening car."[48] The band did take liberties with at least one detail, however, since the car involved was not a "'55 Dodge" but a '61 Lincoln.

While these songs do undeniably bear a strong blues influence, it is not the effortlessly loose version of the blues that so many of Casale and Lewis's generation had come to admire and seek to emulate. This particular interpretation of the blues is much more tightly wound and almost claustrophobic in its rigidness, and as such bears more resemblance to Captain Beefheart's avant-garde stylings than anything else at the time. According to *Simpsons* creator Matt

Groening, who would later cast Devo in the 100th episode of his subsequent series, *Futurama*: "Beefheart fans were the people who had even been rejected by the hippies, the people who were too weird for the hippies"—a neat summary of Casale and his friends.[49] While Beefheart was interested in taking the sound and instrumentation of classic blues—electric guitar, bass, drums, harmonica, and occasional horns—and merging it with free jazz-inspired structures, Casale and his friends replaced those unconventional arrangements with lockstep, almost robotic grooves while still basing the riffs around recognizable blues patterns. They also seem to have been equally inspired by Beefheart's frequently nonsensical lyrics, which a *Rolling Stone* critic once praised for their "ability to juxtapose delightful humor with frightening insights"—another line that could be perfectly well applied to Devo in the future.[50]

The members of Devo would subsequently come to ascribe significance to the months after the Kent State shootings, suggesting that this was when they first assembled and formulated their songs as well as the concept of the band. This may be the result of foggy memories, or simply a desire to provide an abridged history to journalists, but by most accounts it seems that Jerry Casale and Mark Mothersbaugh had yet to formally meet, let alone work on any music together. What this period did provide, however, was plenty of idle time for Casale and Lewis to work on ideas prompted by a number of factors, including the shootings, which would of course have still been fresh in their minds.

Another formative moment was the arrival at Kent State of guest lecturer Eric Mottram, on loan from King's College London. Mottram was a British poet and early champion of American Beat writers including Allen Ginsberg and William S. Burroughs, about whom he would later write two books. Mottram's own work would make extensive use of techniques such as found poetry, collage, and the cut-up technique. The last of these was popularized by Burroughs and his friend Brion Gysin and then adopted by David Bowie on songs like 'Moonage Daydream' ("I'm an alligator / I'm a mama-papa coming for you"). Ostensibly a poet, Mottram had a broad array of interests, including the early work of Karl Marx (especially the *Economic & Philosophical Manuscripts*, in which Marx argues that the conditions of modern industrial societies result in the estrangement or alienation of wage-workers from their own lives); Charles Darwin (particularly *On The Origin Of Species*, which famously announced the concepts of natural selection and evolutionary biology); and mid-period Sigmund Freud (including such works as *The Psychopathology Of Everyday Life*, which examines deviations from the stereotypes of everyday behavior, *Three Essays On The Theory Of Sexuality*, which includes an essay entitled 'The Sexual Aberrations,' and *The Joke And Its Relation To The Unconscious*, which holds that humor allows the expression of thoughts that society usually suppresses or forbids). Casale and Lewis would then search their own surroundings for inspirations that might provide the same meaning. They would soon find them in unlikely places, including anonymous rubber factory workers, the idea of evolution moving in reverse, pornography, and the couching of these disparate ideas as a semi-serious joke.

Meanwhile, the Kent State shootings incited a wave of protests—both non-violent and violent—on college campuses nationwide as well as a coordinated student strike. During the remainder of May 1970, more than 450 college campuses and high schools were shut down, and more than four million students took part in protests. Campus ROTC buildings were often a favorite (and easy) target of protesters, just as at Kent State, and 30 of these buildings were burned in the subsequent protests. Two students at Jackson State College in Mississippi were shot and killed and another 12 wounded in the early morning hours of May 15.

Prior to that, on May 8, 11 students at the University of New Mexico suffered bayonet wounds after the New Mexico National Guard advanced on protestors outside a Student Union building, even though, it was reported, the police were not provoked and "the

50

protestors offered no resistance."[51] No officers were ever arrested. That same day, approximately 1,000 college and high school students gathered at the steps of Federal Hall in Lower Manhattan to hold a memorial for the four students killed at Kent State. Initially, around 200 union construction workers (eventually rising to 400) were called for a counter-rally to show their support for President Nixon. The construction workers attacked the protesters and attempted to raise the flags outside City Hall, which were flying at half-mast. More than 70 people were injured but only six arrests were made following what has become known as the Hard Hat Riot.

On May 9, five days after the shooting at Kent State, more than 100,000 protestors descended on Washington DC. Nixon's chief speechwriter at the time, Ray Price, would later describe the capital as "an armed camp. The mobs were smashing windows, slashing tires, dragging parked cars into intersections, even throwing bedsprings off overpasses into the traffic down below. This was the, quote, student protest. That's not student protest—that's civil war."[52] In an echo of de Gaulle's retreat in the face of French protests two years earlier, Nixon was whisked away to Camp David for two days and the army was called to a neighboring building of the White House. The deluded Nixon eventually convinced himself that the student groups were being manipulated by foreign Communist influences, even though none of the information gathered supported this position.

When David Crosby showed his bandmate Neil Young the May 18 edition of *Time* magazine containing John Filo's photo of Mary Ann Vecchio crying and kneeling over the dead body of Jeffrey Miller, Young immediately composed the song 'Ohio,' with its famous refrain "Four dead in O-hi-o." CSNY promptly recorded the song and rush-released it as a single in June, whereupon it eventually rose to number 14 on the *Billboard* Hot 100. 'Ohio' was not so well received by Casale and his friends at Kent State, however. "At the time we just thought rich hippies were making money off of something horrible and political that they didn't get," he recalled. "I know there were big, screaming arguments in SDS meetings about Young being a tool of the military industrial complex. I just said, well, it wasn't a very good song."[53] (Casale later put aside these feelings in 2002 when Devo contributed a version of the song to the aptly named compilation album *When Pigs Fly: Songs You Never Thought You'd Hear*.)

"The choices at that point were either to join the Weather Underground and start trying to assassinate some of these evil people—because that was *their* modus operandi: killing anybody who tried to make a difference in this society or give people hope—or just have a creative whacked-out Dada art response," Casale later recalled.[54] Lewis also considered violent tactics. "My impression was, if you wanna blow something up, hey, I'll drive, but please—no more meetings!"[55] They wisely chose to forgo the violence in favor of art. "Post-Kent State I wanted to retaliate and do something," Casale recalled. "One choice was to have gone militant and joined the Weather Underground people and that would have ended up in jail and death. I knew them and they were scary, crazy people and I didn't see it winning out in the end. I didn't want to go down that road so I took the creative approach; I started working on my art projects, which were polarizing and creative, and eventually that became Devo."[56]

If Casale and Lewis had opted for violent resistance instead of an artistic statement it would not have been entirely without precedent. One of the earliest and best known of the German krautrock bands, Amon Düül II, had grown out of a politically active artists' commune formed in Munich in 1967 named Amon Düül. The German youth of the time faced dissatisfaction not only with the current political climate but also with the residue of World War II. "In those days there were bloody Nazis around all over the place," Amon Düül II founder and guitarist John Weinzierl recalled. "There was rebellion against them. We had these big revolutionary things in the 60s—all Munich was on the street fighting against police, against politics, against all of that. We didn't have guns or the tools to chase them away, but we could make music and we could draw audience. We could draw people with the same understanding, with the same desires."[57] A band was formed only as a means to generate income, but everyone who lived at the commune would take part in concerts regardless of musical ability or experience. When the ad hoc band was offered a recording contract they promptly split up, leading some of the more musically inclined among the group to form a new band, Amon Düül II.

Among those who followed Amon Düül II were Andreas Baader, a petty criminal and son of a German soldier who never returned from World War II, and his girlfriend Gudrun Ensslin, the daughter of a pastor who attended university on a scholarship and left her husband and son to be with Baader. In their first act of homegrown terrorism, Baader and Ensslin, along with two others, firebombed a department store in Frankfurt on April 2 1968, in protest against the public's indifference to the "genocide" in Vietnam. They were arrested two days later. They were sentenced to three years in jail but released on parole in June 1969, having served a little over a year, under an amnesty for political prisoners. After Baader's and Enselin's release from prison they surprised the members of Amon Düül II, who returned from a tour to find them and another associate, Ulrike Meinhof, at the commune. They were summarily kicked out. The decision to parole Baader and Enselin was reversed the following November and the two became fugitives before Baader was re-arrested in April 1970. Meinhof, a journalist, arranged an interview with the convicted Baader in a library outside the prison the following month as a ruse to help him escape and then became a fugitive herself. The Baader–Meinhof Gang embarked on a spree of bank robberies and bomb attacks in an "anti-imperialistic struggle" over the next two years, killing 34 people in the process. They were eventually caught and arrested in June 1972 and subsequently committed suicide in prison, but not before inspiring a second generation of what became known as the Red Army Faction.

In another of the former Axis powers, nine members of the

Japanese Red Army Faction (the youngest of whom was 16-years-old) hijacked Japan Airlines Flight 351 on March 31 1970, in what has become known as the Yodogo Hijacking. Armed with samurai swords and pipe bombs, the hijackers intended to fly to Cuba, not realizing that the plane only had enough fuel to make it to its original destination of Fukuoka, Japan. It was there that 23 of the 129 hostages (all women and children) were exchanged for the Japanese transport minister. The plane flew on to Seoul, South Korea, where the remaining hostages were released in exchange for permission to fly to Pyongyang in Communist North Korea, where the hijackers were given political asylum and hailed as heroes. They were personally welcomed by Premier Kim Il-sung and provided with chauffeured Mercedes-Benzes and Japanese wives who had been secretly brought into the country. As time went on, however, the hijackers' privileges disappeared and they found themselves living under strict rules imposed by the government. Four of the hijackers are still confirmed to be in North Korea—the others have either been convicted after returning to Japan or died in North Korea—and continue to petition for their return to Japan.

One of the hijackers remaining in North Korea is Moriaki Wakabayashi, the original bassist of the long-running avant-garde psychedelic band Les Rallizes Dénudés. The band billed themselves as 'The Radical Music Black Gypsy Band' and alienated all but their most devoted fans with a live show bent on extreme sensory assault through the use of hypnotically repetitive songs, deafening volume and feedback, and abuse of strobe lights and mirror balls (inviting easy comparison to The Velvet Underground). Wakabayashi was with the band when they had performed in April 1969 at the legendary Barricades-A-Go-Go festival in the basement of Kyoto's Doshisha University, at which they were all students. The festival had been organized by the university and sponsored by a local newspaper in an attempt to avoid the *gakuen funso* or campus disputes that affected 150 universities across Japan in 1968 and forced the closure of the

University of Tokyo for nearly a year. Rumor has it that Les Rallizes Dénudés singer Takashi Mizutani was also offered a role in the hijacking but declined to take part.

Back in Ohio, Mark Mothersbaugh was still an undergraduate art student at Kent State, playing keyboards in various shortlived musical endeavors. One of the longer running of these was a collaboration with a talented but unstable drummer named Mike Powell in a duo christened Flossy Bobbitt. The band combined Mark's progressive rock-inspired keyboard runs with Powell's extremely busy drumming. They left no recordings to posterity but Mark has alternately described them as a "kind of a trippy Soft Machine electronics band,"[58] or "an experimental prog-rock kind of band, or something— I don't know what you would call it."[59] They must have made an odd couple: Mothersbaugh was an introverted artist who obsessively collected his drawings and writings in numerous sketchbooks, and Powell was an intimidating figure with a penchant for guns and an undiscerning taste for drugs (which no doubt played a role in a later stint in an Arizona prison).

Flossy Bobbitt's performances—of which there were a surprising number in and around Akron in the early 70s—were by all accounts chaotic and often confrontational spectacles. Powell's frenetic drumming was often the focal point, while Mothersbaugh remained buttressed behind multiple keyboards. A couple of his friends, Ed Barger and Marty Reymann, who he had met through Powell, took an artistic as well as financial interest in him. They had previously bought Mark a Hammond B-3 organ, as well as a prohibitively expensive Mellotron, which usually only showed up in the hands of the most successful of bands (such as The Beatles or Led Zeppelin). Mark also played an electric clavinet, the Farfisa organ that he had insisted his father buy after seeing John Lennon playing a combo organ on *Ed Sullivan*, and a homemade kit from PAiA Electronics, an

Oklahoma-based company that provided a first foray for a number of those musicians willing and able enough to solder together their own electronic instruments. "I built a modular synth from a company that sends you pieces in the mail," Mothersbaugh later recalled. "That was the first synth I ever played."[60]

Like much of Devo's inception, the story of how Mark came to acquire his second synthesizer, a state of the art Minimoog, shortly after its release in 1970 can be ascribed, albeit indirectly, to the Vietnam War. Mark would later describe Barger and Reymann as a pair of "jock football players" who, on returning from the war and failing to find work, had decided instead to form a band—the only obstacle being that neither of them played an instrument. Mark was duly drafted in as keyboardist and songwriter, and after offering to buy him a new keyboard his new bandmates made the unusual decision to take him not to a local music store but to the Moog factory in Western New York. "I remember walking into this barn that had been converted into a warehouse," he recalled. "I remember seeing a rack that was about 30 feet high that had Minimoogs stacked up. It seemed so futuristic."[61] (It's likely that this visit was to the R.A. Moog Co facility in Trumansburg, New York, where the very first Minimoogs were made.)

If Mark's means were meager, his taste was impeccable. In their book *Analog Days*, authors Trevor Pinch and Frank Trocco declare the Minimoog "the first synthesizer ever to become a 'classic.'"[62] Designed as an easy-to-use and portable alternative to the monolithic and daunting modular synthesizers, the Minimoog was an instant success. It would go on to figure prominently in the sound of multiple genres of the 70s, including progressive rock, funk, jazz-fusion, pop, and disco. (Unlike his contemporary and friendly rival, Don Buchla, Bob Moog was happy to not only install keyboards on his synths but also to produce the stripped-down and portable model that they had been requesting.)

Despite investing large sums of money in Mark's new gear, Barger and Reymann never did form their band with him. But Mothersbaugh did gain a reputation as the only guy in Akron with a Moog.

Meanwhile, Casale and Lewis continued to chew on some of the ideas that Mottram had planted in their heads while maintaining their long-standing interest in the lowbrow detritus that was all too common then (as now). What was perhaps unique to their way of thinking was that they never gave precedence to one or the other— the two coexisted as equals in their minds. As much as the Western history of ideas of the past two centuries was fresh in their minds, they were also absorbing comic books and horror movies.

Sometimes these inspirations were obvious, as in the case of Casale's 'Can U Take It?,' which name-checks a famous cartoon sailor and contains the line "Popeye's big punch knocks Bluto cold." Others were less so. In March 1959, DC Comics' *Mystery In Space* #50 featured a story entitled 'Riddle Of Asteroid 8794,' subsequently reprinted in late 1970 in *Beyond The Unknown* #9. In the story, the "space disc jockey" Clark Hale plays a request for "a romantic song called … 'Space-Girl Blues!'" The lyrics describe a space-girl who is "as cold as ice! / She'll freeze you once and freeze you twice! / You'll shiver, shake, and then turn blue! / And then you've got the space-girl blues!"[63] The fictional song's catalog number, "Comet Recording No. 8,794," turns out to be a clue that the DJ has been kidnapped and taken to Asteroid #8,794, from which he is later rescued. Casale's song 'Space Girl Blues' (a version of which appears on *Hardcore Devo Vol 1: 1974–1977*) features a funky bassline, fuzzed-out guitar, and clipped riffs against an industrial rhythm and eerie synthesizer. It also contains the lines "Space girls are as cold as ice / They'll kiss you once and kiss you twice / You'll shiver and shake and then turn blue / Next you got the space girl blues." (Of course, the song is also given the proper Devo treatment with lines like "Sado-maso is the rule.")

In *Wonder Woman* #9, from the summer of 1944, Wonder Woman saves a child from Giganta, "the biggest gorilla in captivity," in the story 'Evolution Goes Haywire.' Rather than put the gorilla to sleep, Professor Zool intervenes by imploring: "Wait—I have a wonderful idea! I'll subject Giganta to my electronic evolutionizer—it will transform the ape into a human being!" Zool succeeds in turning the gorilla into a "beautiful girl of Amazonian proportions" with flowing red hair. The transformed Giganta then attacks Wonder Woman, screaming "Grr-rr-arr-ggh! Igga-wogga wu!" (ape-speak for "I hate thee—thou interfering she!").

In the ensuing scuffle, the evolutionizer becomes damaged and Zool exclaims: "My evolutionizer—it's reversed! It's devolving us— it'll change us into apes!" Trying to avert this outcome, Wonder Woman throws the machine out of the window before realizing that the machine has been halted on the way to turning everybody into apes and stopped at "cave people." The machine, now outside and still sputtering, has also changed the environment for miles around, taking everything back by 60 million years. The zoo animals have taken on the form of their "ancestors," with elephants becoming mastodons and a crocodile becoming a Tyrannosaurus Rex.

This confused mélange of misunderstood evolutionary theory and ill-researched biological history was the brainchild of William Moulton Marston, a psychologist, lawyer, and inventor of the first functional lie detector polygraph, who wrote this entertaining piece of fluff under the pseudonym Charles Moulton while moonlighting from his day job. The storyline is suddenly picked up again four years later, in *Wonder Woman* #28, when Giganta appears during a demonstration of the machine—now equipped with a lever to switch between "EVOLUTION" and "DEVOLUTION"—in which Professor Zool inexplicably reverses the evolution of a monkey to a tree fox and then a crocodile. Giganta and her accomplice (the Atlantean Queen Clea) appear and toss the Professor and his audience into the machine in an attempt to lure their nemesis, Wonder Woman. Zool and the college girls start to devolve into apes, and when Wonder Woman appears and attempts to turn them back to human form by throwing the switch in the opposite direction, she finds that the evolution current doesn't work. The subjects have become "gorillas except for their heads!"

A reprint of *Wonder Woman* #28 fell into Bob Lewis's hands in late 1971, and he in turn showed it to Jerry Casale. Mark Mothersbaugh too had fond memories of the comic. "He'd push the lever forward, and there was like this, um, vacuum capsule," he later recalled. "And inside that there'd be a guy that was in there. And when he pushed it forward, the guy's head would blow up like a light bulb, and his hair would fall out, and he'd look like a progeria kid. And he'd pull it backward, and then his brow would drop, and he'd get covered with hair, and he'd be like a caveman."[64]

The members of Devo would also have remembered *Island Of Lost Souls*, a 1933 film that aired on *Shock Theater*, a late night television show from Cleveland in which the host, Ghoulardi, would present B-grade science fiction and horror films interspersed with his own irreverent commentary. *Island Of Lost Souls* was an adaptation of H.G. Wells's novel *The Island Of Dr Moreau*, in which a baby-faced Charles Laughton plays the titular doctor, whose island is shrouded in mystery. After the shipwrecked Edward Parker is rescued by a freighter delivering a cargo of assorted animals to Moreau's island, he gets into a fight with the ship's captain over the treatment of a servant. As punishment, Parker is then unwillingly left on the island in the care of the reluctant Moreau. He finds Moreau rules over his island of "strange looking natives" with an expertly handled bullwhip. As an experiment, Moreau introduces Parker to Lota, whom he describes as "a pure Polynesian, the only woman on the entire island." Soon he stumbles onto what Lota calls the House of Pain ("Somebody's being tortured!"), where Moreau is performing excruciating surgery—a form of live dissection—on one of the natives. Attempting to escape, Parker and Lota run into a group of grotesque "natives" on their dash through the jungle. Moreau suddenly appears and tames the crowd with cracks of his whip and quizzes them on the arbitrary laws he has established for them. After repeating each decree, the hirsute Sayer of the Law (played by Bela Lugosi with a distinct and inexplicable Hungarian accent) asks the rest of the motley assemblage: "Are we not men?"

Moreau finally comes clean and explains that his experiments with hastening the evolution of plants proved so successful that he soon attempted to do the same with "more complex organisms." All animal life, he theorizes, "is tending toward the human form," and he has been attempting to speed this evolution through "plastic surgery, blood transfusions, gland extracts, and ray baths." Later, after kissing Lota, Parker notices her claws and realizes that she too is one of Moreau's experiments. Moreau had claimed Lota as "my most nearly perfect creation," but he despairs when he discovers that some of her animal traits are reappearing and she is in fact devolving. When Moreau orders one of the natives to kill a sailor who has come to rescue Parker, they see that the law "not to spill blood" no longer applies and take Moreau to the House of Pain.

Upon seeing the film, Mark Mothersbaugh saw more than a little of his native northeast Ohio in Moreau's island. "At one point," he later noted, "they were walking in a line around a fire in the woods at night while the doctor's working in the House of Pain, and they were casting shadows on the side of the House of Pain, and I saw these shadows of these sub-human creatures just slouching past the wall, and I was like: holy crap, I know all those people, they live here in Akron with me."[65] Casale too saw the parallel. "We pretty much lived in fear of illegitimate authority and weird stupid people," he said. "I mean we really felt we were surrounded by moronic mean people. In my mind when I would look at certain people I would see exactly what you see in the *Island Of Lost Souls*."[66]

"Devolution was a combination of a *Wonder Woman* comic book and the movie *Island Of Lost Souls*," Casale quipped in an interview with Jon Savage for *Sounds* in 1978. "That was various things I'd been thinking about devolution: going ahead to go back, things falling

60

apart, entropy. It grabbed every piece of information and gave it some kind of cohesive presence—it was a package."[67] It almost seemed like he was joking.

On July 23 1971, US District Court Judge James C. Connell dismissed a $4-million lawsuit against the state of Ohio filed by Louis Schroeder in connection with the death of his son, William. The judge maintained the position that he had established with three previous suits filed by the parents of slain students: that the state has sovereign immunity and cannot be sued without its consent.

CHAPTER 2
1972-73

Man is least himself when he talks in his own person.
Give him a mask, and he will tell you the truth.
OSCAR WILDE

In the spring of 1972, Jerry Casale and Bob Lewis relocated to Southern California. Their friend Gary Jackett—a regular from the Commuter's Cafeteria at Kent State who would soon make contributions to Devo's first video and album—had recently taken a job at a free paper called the *Los Angeles Staff* as an artist, and had promised his friends he could get them work writing for the paper. By the time they arrived, Jackett had quit, having not been paid (and having subsequently been threatened while looking down the barrel of an increasingly erratic editor's gun), but Casale and Lewis got the job anyway. They were given carte blanche to write whatever they wanted over four pages of the rapidly floundering magazine.

Casale, Lewis, and their girlfriends lived with Jackett in a duplex just a few blocks from the ocean in San Clemente. They would make the trip to Los Angeles about once a week to work on the magazine but spent the rest of their time whiling away hours on the beach, playing Frisbee, or jamming in their garage. It was around this time that news began to emerge of a break-in at the Watergate building. The growing scandal would eventually implicate President Nixon, whom Lewis already believed to have authorized the shootings at Kent State. "I'm convinced that the shootings at the top of the hill were not accidental or coincidental, that there was an order to fire," he later recalled. "That it was orchestrated, and—I'd go a little farther—I think that the clearance to fire if necessary came from higher up than any of the National Guard that were there at the time, including the General. I think it had come from at least [Governor Jim] Rhodes, and maybe from Nixon."[1]

Casale and Lewis also spent a lot of time having intense discussions about the finer points of the theories they began formulating in Ohio—ideas that would first see the light of day on July 14 1972 in the form of two essays published in the *Los Angeles Staff*.

Lewis's contribution was 'Readers vs. Breeders,' a florid 1,500-word rant against technology. "We find a continuing schism between the perfection of man's machines," he writes, "those stalwart servants which will enable us to achieve the Utopia and the 'perfection' of those who are supposedly benefiting from their services: humanity." He wastes no time in quoting French philosopher Jacques Ellul's most famous work, *The Technological Society* (1954), which argues that man is forced to adapt to the needs of technology. (Ellul was also a favorite of Theodore Kaczynski, aka The Unabomber, and a copy of the same book was found in his cabin when he was finally apprehended.) "It often seems that in the pursuit of technological paradise, the demands of this particular evolutionary route continually force us to eliminate, deny, or ignore that which makes us whole, and rather to become machines, and imperfect ones at that," Lewis continues.[2] He also quotes anarchist and ecologist Murray Bookchin's writings under the pseudonym Lewis Herber, in which Bookchin suggests that it's possible to have it both ways—to move backward toward primitivism while simultaneously utilizing technology: "What we seek then, is that transcendent state most fully engendered by Fred Flintstone—technologically sophisticated cave-man." Lewis then cites some vague ideas from G. Spencer-Brown's *Laws Of Form*, a work of mathematics and philosophy that caused a sensation on its release in 1969—especially after being reviewed in the hippie bible *The Whole Earth Catalog*—to somehow show that such "devolution" is possible. Lewis then characterizes "Readers" and "Breeders" as "those who should know but don't, and those who don't know but should." Readers, he writes, have given up part of "their human identities for the chance of immortality, even if they must live as machines." By contrast, the Breeders' only shot at immortality is by having children. "They are unthinking slaves of the organic processes they do not understand, and live only to reproduce themselves, and thus perpetuate the cycles of corruption and exploitation at the hands of their masters." (In a sense, he seems to be predicting the growing chasm, hastened by the emergence of technology, between the 'haves' and the 'have-nots.')

By the second half of his essay, Lewis has taken to referring to these concepts as "Devo." He suggests that these concepts should remind the Readers "of the belch, fart, and belly laugh" and "inject some notion of the transcendent into the bleak existence" of the Breeders. (Casale would later adapt Lewis's Readers and Breeders into what he would call "high devo" and "low devo" before abandoning that distinction altogether.) All in all, it's a hodgepodge of ideas that race toward a conclusion that's very different from the philosophy that Devo the band would adopt. Shrouded in obscure concepts and esoteric references, the essay at its heart was not very different from what the rest of Lewis's generation was thinking at the time. (Ted Kaczynski arrived at a unique solution in an essay of his own from 1971: "stop scientific progress by withdrawing all major sources of research funds." When that didn't come to pass, he resorted to sending mail bombs to professors and executives.)

Casale's contribution to the *Staff*, 'Polymer Love,' was much less didactic, veering instead into the surreal and scatological. It begins with a defense of plastic, echoing Andy Warhol's claim that "everything's plastic, but I love plastic ... I want to be plastic." Casale reminds us of the common negative connotation associated with plastic but praises it for being "nearly unlimited in its capability to be transmuted in form and function."[3] He goes on to claim that "some health-food die-hards and hippies and professors who feel the same way about the French fry and the doughnut ... [they] fear the hot grease and the sticky frosting." This is followed by a detailed examination of the genital grooming habits of Barbie and Ken before Casale returns to the unlikely pairing of fries and doughnuts, in which he finds "the disturbing remnants of decay." By examining the positive/negative dichotomy surrounding these various man-made creations, Casale consistently—and perhaps counterintuitively— champions their positive aspects in ways that many had not yet considered. He is also aware of the flipside of this argument, however, and stresses that as we become more enamored of technology and what it can do for us we will have to find new ways to balance the equation. We will eventually get nostalgic for these organic processes, he says: "New taboos must be created by the cybernetic pioneers of creative evolution, hence Barbie and Ken titillated by the possibility of 'having a baby.'" He goes on to predict a time when "amplifiers [will] look like trees, and houses look like caves." Never one to miss an opportunity to offend, he goes on to suggest that Ken will buy Barbie "Essence of Woman spray that smells just like real cunt; she will apply plastic smegma to his cock from a tube in preparation for human-beast love (a simulation of the way the 'live ones' used to do it)."

Casale's themes of contrarianism, everyday objects imbued with deeper significance, and disturbingly frank sexual discourse would recur repeatedly throughout Devo's career. Unfortunately, he would never again have the freedom from scrutiny that his ideas found in the obscure, failing *Los Angeles Staff*. These essays are also notable for being the first time that the word "Devo" appeared in print. Lewis refers to the followers of the concept—effectively just the two of them at this point—by various appellations, including "de-evolutionaries," "devolutionaries," and "Devo-tees." In at least one respect, though, he does accurately describe a future characteristic of the band: "These Devoists may be called childish, smutty, or even foolish, but they are unashamed." Casale, meanwhile, ends his essay by concluding: "To explore is divine, but to ignore is Devo."

Mark Mothersbaugh, meanwhile, was back in Akron doing some writing of his own. Like many visual artists he kept a number of sketchbooks, but Mothersbaugh also incorporated found images alongside his own drawings, including pictures cut out from catalogs, medical texts, and newspapers, often altered and juxtaposed with and accompanied by his rambling text. Many of these pages were eventually collected and released later in the decade, although much of the material appears to date back to the early 70s. Upon its release, it was given the provocative title *My Struggle* and self-published as a small 4½" x 5½" book with a red leatherette cover. The packaging was a sly homage to *Quotations From Chairman Mao Tse-Tung* (commonly referred to in the West as *The Little Red Book*), which collects writings and speeches from—as well as photographs of—the leader of the Chinese Communist Party. All citizens were expected to own a copy, and it was commonly issued in a compact package that could be taken anywhere and easily referred to at any time. It is supposedly one of the bestselling books ever published, and it also became popular with some of the more politically radical Western hippies of the time. In a 1971 article entitled 'Why We Study Mao,' Magdalene Sinclair, Minister of Education for the White Panther Party, writes: "They told us that if we wanted to call ourselves revolutionaries and call ourselves the WPP [White Panther Party] we would have to study and learn the language of revolution. That made sense to us and we finally started opening up our little Red Books (which up until that time we had just carried around with us as a fad) and started relating to its content."[4] It was also most likely *The Little Red Book* that John Lennon was referring to in the lyrics of The Beatles' 'Revolution,' a song not entirely sympathetic to the radical left ("But if you go carrying pictures of Chairman Mao / You ain't gonna make it with anyone anyhow"). Some copies of *My Struggle* even had the title and author's name embossed in gold on the front cover, or a prayer ribbon bookmark, adding further to the similarities with Mao's book.

The title, of course, comes from the English translation of Adolf

Hitler's *Mein Kampf,* the book he wrote while in prison in 1925 charged with high treason for unsuccessfully trying to incite a revolution two years earlier. Hitler's book combined elements of autobiography with political ideology, and Mothersbaugh's could be said to do the same. *My Struggle* contains just under 300 pages of crudely cut-out images and typewritten text in two alternating fonts pasted by hand in an occasionally lopsided fashion. Within its 24 chapters the narrator successively (if not explicitly) addresses various unnamed persons, as well as the reader directly, producing a disorienting rambling monologue. He often breaks into singsong, rhyming verse, sometimes parodying popular songs, and frequently veers into Lewis Carroll-inspired nonsense, such as: "As sea monkeys dance upon Chevy Nova Scotia Sepula Sip a Nickle Nipponese cheese Cortina black sole, in the superb fly roustabout bloody water closet." He recounts various seemingly random experiences, including wrestling a "deer woman," snapping the neck of his girlfriend's sick cat before shooting the girl in the head with a rifle, watching television for 36 hours without moving, driving a car through a guardrail and into a river while receiving oral sex, and being visited by the "independent poop stain investigator" and subsequently eating his girlfriend's panties rather than have a stranger handle them. Very rarely will a small glimmer of actual humanity creep into the discourse—and when it does it is, of course, immediately followed by more juvenile shock tactics.

"It's all just kind of lonely, when you find that those you once knew, have closed the door to new things, and simply did away with life," Mothersbaugh writes. "That those you thought had something, that made you just a little understanding, for they had in commen [sic] the desire to fight those that stick it up your ass. So many people you once knew, now walk around like slumpers, their butt is filled with pig-thoughts and their minds have rotted out. They've lost the ability to complete thoughts—know only how to exist, and make a habit of squirting stink on children, who soon sub-come [sic]. Friends I once knew now scramble, to get a little higher, refusing to see the parody of their bending at the waist."

Frequently recurring topics include children, sex and sexual organs, bodily functions, human deformity, and various combinations of the above. (In at least two instances, penises have been drawn, graffiti-style, onto the pictures.) It is by turns amusing, frightening, and repulsive. It is also difficult to read very much of the book in one sitting, since so doing inevitably leads the reader to worry about Mothersbaugh's mental health, although that is something he anticipated: "Right about now you may be saying, that Mark ... oooh I think he's losing it, this time. Well go to hell. If you had any shit together of your own, you would be doing something instead of trying to write me off as another kook. You're an asshole, and you're full of shit. ... They never get it right ... misquoting, misusing information, just general distortion of what is real and what is meant to be. Wanna watch me jump off the high level bridge? Sorry. I ain't ever gonna do it. You will a long time before me."

Mothersbaugh has maintained his tradition of keeping sketchbooks. "I recently have been looking at some of the ones from the 70s," he said in 2005, "and I don't think the same way I did back then. You see the threads of thought when you don't edit what you're thinking and you're not trying to make something on purpose—it's kind of like you took a blood sample every day and broke it down and saw what was in your system at any particular time. Some of the old ones I really love, and some of them I think: I certainly was obsessed with women back then."[5]

What the book is also notable for is what it doesn't contain, despite the allusions to Hitler and Mao—namely any sort of political statement. Perhaps, as his future bandmate Bob Lewis has said, Mothersbaugh was never a politically inclined person. Indeed, in 2006 Lewis claimed: "I don't know that I have ever heard Mark make an overtly political statement."[6] The only time the subject is broached is in Jerry Casale's introduction, and even then it is only to dismiss the conventional forms of political action that the rest of his generation still adhered to. "The science fiction films of the 50s were merely paranoid projections of inner collapse," he writes. "Of course we know that *we* were the monsters and aliens from 'another' planet. Proles refuse to realize this. They continue to invade themselves, resorting to beer-drinking and hero-worship, folk songs and outmoded symbols of individual rebellion. Their fate is sealed. However, the so-called 'humanistic' approach, popular in the 60s, is just as sentimental, therefore just as degenerate."

It's difficult to pinpoint exactly how and when Jerry Casale and Mark Mothersbaugh first met, particularly as they have both provided different stories over the years. Recent interviews suggest that they began working together in the months that Kent State was shut down following the shooting on May 4 1970, but this seems a bit revisionist, introduced perhaps for the sake of establishing a simpler and more compelling narrative. Prior to that, a 1979 *Rolling Stone* article about Casale had stated that he and "fellow Kent State weirdo Mark Mothersbaugh" first hooked up in 1972.[7] The liner notes to the band's own 1988 CD reissue of their debut album agree, tracing the band's genesis to "the chance meeting of two art students … at Kent State University in 1972."[8]

Casale and Mothersbaugh's own recollections may be murky because it seems that they were most definitely aware of each other before they actually came into direct contact. This was perhaps inevitable: here were two people with unique visions in a small and fairly conservative environment. By the fall of 1972, Casale and Lewis had returned to Akron, and Casale had enrolled in the odd class at Kent. Mothersbaugh has indicated that he first became aware of Casale "in an English class, after class was over—two teachers were talking about this student that had written these offensive acid porn stories and was distributing them, and as soon as I heard that I was like: I gotta meet whoever that is." Casale has a reciprocal story: "I was trying to track down the guy who was ... going around campus with decals placing them on like trophy cases and places that you're not supposed to have things like that and they were really great like a man puking on the moon and a cow with extra udders ... I said I gotta meet this guy. I gotta find out who's doing this."[9]

The most common story about their first meeting revolves around one of Casale's infamous guerilla performances as Gorj. Casale had found a weathered leather ski mask with holes for the eyes and mouth and immediately christened it 'Gorj' upon seeing himself wearing it. He wasted no time in putting it to good use: he would put on the mask while wearing a butcher's jacket and an enema bag bandolier filled with milk. A friend would play the provocatively christened Poot Man, clad in a black wrestling suit and mask (easily obtainable due to the popularity of the Indiana-based World Wrestling Association), and would be led around on a leash in a squatting position. They would attend local gallery shows, where Gorj would ask for Poot Man's judgment on the pedantic landscapes and still life drawings. Poot Man would then be rewarded for recognizing the artists' lack of merit. As he later recalled, Casale would feed Poot Man milk "every time he gave the right answer ... he would wiggle—he couldn't talk, of course—he'd wiggle and hold his nose and push his butt at the painting and then we'd feed him as a reward and we would get kicked out and threatened and campus police would come after us so we were having fun at that time making people angry." Casale would later refer to these stunts as "performance art—although there was no word for performance art then."[10]

When Mothersbaugh witnessed Gorj making a mockery out of others' mindless art it was inevitable that he and Casale would become fast friends. "I saw him do the Poot Man thing, and I was like: Who's this guy?" he recalled. Confirming the proverb "the enemy of my enemy is my friend," he added: "Everybody hated Jerry, so I *knew* I was going to like him."[11] (Mothersbaugh would later pay tribute to

Gorj by name in *My Struggle*: "My doctor asked me to pee into a cup. I asked if he had ever met the famous Gorj. Negative, he assured me.")

Later the same year, Casale and the undergraduate Mothersbaugh both enrolled in an experimental art class along with an aspiring filmmaker named Chuck Statler, who would later play a role in the Devo story. For now, however, Casale had decided to put his own artistic visions on hold and instead return to his interest in straightforward electric blues by joining an established band named 15-60-75, commonly referred to as The Numbers Band and led by the dictatorial singer/guitarist Robert Kidney.

Kidney took the band's name from a seminal book about the blues, Paul Oliver's *Blues Fell This Morning: Meaning In The Blues*. In a chapter detailing the intricacies of the numbers racket (an illegal and often rigged lottery which took hold in many black, urban areas just after the onset of the Depression), Oliver explains the significance given to the three-number combinations that players of the lottery would submit to the organizers. The act of choosing the three numbers carried so much importance that many turned to 'dream books,' which provided a set of numbers corresponding to various "aspects of human experience, with objects natural and manmade," for help.[12] The sequence 7-6-9, for example, represented death; 15-60-75 could be found in the dream book under the entry 'Big Dick.'

Kent State alum Chris Butler, who would play bass in the band from 1975 to 1978, described Kidney as a "very charismatic-slash-scary individual obviously possessed with whatever blues feeling, healing feeling, the devil, whatever," adding that he was at "the top of the musical food chain in Kent if not in all of Northeastern Ohio as far as I'm concerned."[13] Perhaps unsurprisingly, Casale was setting his sights high.

The Numbers Band had formed in 1969, and by the early 70s were playing four nights a week to a growing fan base, having become the lynchpin of the local scene. Their rotating line-up, built around the core of Kidney and saxophonist Terry Hynde (older brother of Chrissie), used Chicago blues as their starting point but eventually incorporated elements of jazz and even leaned a bit to the experimental side—but wisely never far enough to alienate the bar patrons on Water Street in Kent. "I did not want to spend the rest of my life playing the blues," Kidney later recalled. "This was a music that I understand and could create and have operative for an audience and the music was relatively popular. However we weren't considered a blues band by blues bands, we were considered hacks."[14]

If that's how Kidney saw it, however, Casale felt constrained by what he saw as a traditional take on the blues. "You had to toe the line," he said in 2010. "That was church."[15] The band's debut album, *Jimmy Bell's Still In Town* (a live recording of a performance at the Agora Ballroom in Cleveland, where 15-60-75 opened for Bob Marley & The Wailers) was issued by Warner Bros in 1976. It was later reissued on CD by Hearpen Records, the label run by Pere Ubu's David Thomas, who called it "the only good album ever recorded by anyone." In a review of the reissue for *Mojo* magazine, critic Joe Cushley drew unsurprising comparisons with Santana and The Doors before finding similarities with the less likely Captain Beefheart and Talking Heads. "Kidney is a [Don] Van Vliet on the distaff side," he wrote, "or a less hung up David Byrne."

In the 80s, Kidney became involved with another band with a rotating line-up, Anton Fier's Golden Palominos. The Palominos would record a version of 'The Animal Speaks' (the leadoff track from *Jimmy Bell's Still In Town*) for their 1985 album *Visions Of Excess*, with John Lydon providing vocals. Here, the horn-driven, boogying original becomes a typical 80s rock song, with reverbed snare drum and screaming distorted guitars, while Lydon starts the song with a lone belch.

Casale's efforts to push 15-60-75 into the territory that Devo would eventually occupy were not received well by the authoritarian Kidney. One night, Casale surreptitiously brought a chimpanzee mask on stage and put it on midway through one of the band's most popular request songs, 'Who Do You Love?' (which usually clocked in around three times as long as the Bo Diddley original). About halfway through the song, clued in by the crowd's pointing and laughter that something unusual was taking place, Kidney glanced over at his bassist and saw the mask. "That was it," Casale later claimed. "After the set, he said: you're gone."[16]

According to Kidney, Casale's stunt was the culmination of a long brewing disagreement. "Gerald became extremely difficult to work with," he recalled. "He was very unhappy with the music and the band. The other band-members and I were fed up with his insistence on playing his bass at a deafening volume. When I asked him to turn it down, he told me to come over and turn it down myself. He told me I was a lot like Adolf Hitler. Then Gerald began suggesting that everyone wear masks onstage in order to shock the audience. I would never wear a mask on stage for any reason—I wasn't into gimmicks. I told him at the next band meeting that I thought he was an intelligent and creative person, and he should leave and form his own band."[17]

A few months later, Casale had the perfect opportunity to do just that. As the 1972–73 school year began, Lewis received a phone call from his old poetry professor, Robert Bertholf, asking for help moving a washer and a dryer. The appliances were for a visiting professor, Ed Dorn, whom Bertholf was helping move into a rented house. In an effort to quit smoking, Lewis had adopted the unusual tactic of substituting marijuana for tobacco. After explaining his situation to the visiting poet, Dorn offered Lewis a cigarette, and the two became friends.

Ed Dorn was a poet who had studied at the fabled Black Mountain College and had a particular fascination with the American West. His best-known work was a long poem in six parts entitled *Gunslinger*. *Book I* was published in 1968 and the final *Book IIII* in 1975. Far from being a traditional western genre exercise, as its name might imply, *Gunslinger* was in fact a rambling, free form, experimental work. "His West is not that of John Wayne or Gary Cooper," Marjorie Perloff writes in the introduction. "It is the plastic, gestural 'West' we encounter on TV, in comic strips, rock songs, drug argot, and pulp science fiction."[18] The story follows the exploits of the 2,000-year-old Gunslinger, his horse Claude (to whom every character responds with "Lévi-Strauss?" in reference to the famed anthropologist, and who can not only talk but also roll joints), a character named I (not the same as the first-person narrator), and a cabaret owner called Cocaine Lil, who are headed to Las Vegas to find Howard Hughes, whom they consider a robber baron planning on "hustling the future." They pick up a hitchhiker by the name of Kool Everything, who has a five-gallon can of LSD, which they pour into I to embalm him when they think he has died (he hasn't). *Gunslinger* draws freely on influences from high and low culture; according to the *Encyclopedia Of Beat Literature*, "Dorn is putting a mirror to the face of America and pointing out that the American individualism that we glamorize in our mythic portrayals of American outlaws comes from the same source that contributes to the soullessness of our capitalist society."[19] Or, as Dorn himself would put it: "Entrapment is this society's / Sole activity I whispered / and Only laughter / can blow it to rags."[20] Jerry Casale would later echo this sentiment. "The human condition is something so pathetic and obnoxious that the only shock reaction is laughter," he said in an early interview. "That's the way Devo has felt for a long time."[21]

When Bertholf and Dorn were tasked with curating the 1973 Kent State Creative Arts Festival, they arranged for Casale and Lewis to perform, unperturbed by the fact that they didn't yet have a band. "It was like something out of a *Little Rascals* show," Casale recalled. "You know: we can do it, we can put on a show. I've got an amplifier, you've got a hammer!"[22] He hurriedly assembled a group for the occasion, bringing together a mix of musicians he had and hadn't played with before, some chosen on artistic merit and others for pragmatic reasons. Casale took the opportunity to approach Mark Mothersbaugh, having recently seen Flossy Bobbitt perform. According to Lewis, it was a decision that Casale made on his own. "Mark was two or three years younger than us, so I didn't really know him," he said. "I certainly recognized him from school. I think he and Jerry may have had an art class together."[23]

As might be expected, Casale played bass and Lewis played guitar, but their old recording partner Peter Gregg was surprisingly absent (reportedly due to stage fright). The band's singer was Fred Weber, a friend and roommate of Lewis's who had previously sung with Joe Walsh's band The Measles while Walsh attended Kent State. (Walsh had left The Measles a year earlier and moved to Cleveland to join The James Gang; in late 1975, he would join the Eagles just in time for their multi-million-selling album *Hotel California*.) Casale enlisted drummer Rod Reisman, who had also performed with The Numbers Band, and invited his own younger brother, Bob, to play guitar. Bob Casale was the first of three younger siblings drafted into the band for a very simple reason. "There was no one we could talk into being in the band besides our family," Mark Mothersbaugh later recalled, "so we recruited our younger brothers."[24]

Casale and Lewis had been kicking around the idea of de-evolution for quite some time now and had both ended their *Los Angeles Staff* essays by referring to themselves as Devo, so it was only natural that their band would take the same name. The addition of 'Sextet' seems to have been more of an opportunistic ploy. "We thought if we call it Sextet Devo, we can trick 'em into thinking we're a jazz band and letting us play at this jazz festival."[25]

The band's debut performance took place at 7pm on April 18 1973 in the Ludwig Recital Hall, which the university describes as "an intimate facility where most student and faculty recitals are held." The ten or so songs the band played included 'Wiggle Worm,' which Casale and Lewis had been playing for a few years already. The rest were new originals, save for Mothersbaugh's solo opener 'Here Comes Peter Cottontail' and his instrumental rendition of the theme to *Mr Jingeling* (an inadvertently creepy low-budget special, broadcast every Christmas in Cleveland). Someone had the foresight to film at least part of the concert, and a grainy, black-and-white clip of 'Mr Jingeling' and 'Private Secretary' can still be found floating around online. Mothersbaugh has since described the clip as looking "like bank robbery movies, 'cos they were shot on half-inch reel-to-reel movie cameras, black-and-white, so it looks like we should be pulling out guns and robbing someone."[26] 'Mr Jingeling' highlights his skill as a keyboardist, although the organ sound might have been better suited to a shopping mall at Christmastime than a cutting-edge arts festival. 'Private Secretary' employs a primitive stomp overlaid with an anemic guitar riff, while Mothersbaugh interjects atonal squiggles from his synthesizer. It is clearly a collision of two worlds not yet coming close to meshing into a cohesive whole. The song itself has not yet mutated far enough from its blues-based inspiration, while Mothersbaugh's synth adds some tentative color but not much more.

Before getting as far as the music, however, the first thing to strike any viewer of the footage is Mothersbaugh's outfit of white robe and pants with chimpanzee mask (perhaps the same one that Casale had worn with The Numbers Band). Curiously, despite Casale's insistence on wearing a mask with his previous band, his face is uncovered here. He wears a long yellow coat and matching pants—possibly the same variety of lab coat that he would soon famously modify, but here it ends up looking more like the once-faddish Nehru jacket that had by now gone out of style. Bob Casale stands behind his brother dressed in light blue hospital scrubs (on loan from his job as a radiology technician) while Reisman is completely hidden from view and Lewis almost so. It's hard to tell whether the monochromatic color schemes they are wearing are part of the presentation or merely coincidental.

If Mothersbaugh represented one visual extreme onstage, Weber easily represented the other. He stands sideways to the audience and affects a rigid stance that would have been more appropriate to a crooner of his parents' generation than a rock singer of his own. He is wearing a blue turtleneck and jeans and retains some of his old high-school football-playing physique. He looks like he'd be more comfortable in a fraternity house—or anywhere else at all—than on a stage with Devo.

The camera operator also had the good sense to briefly film the audience during the performance, and their reactions are invaluable. The sparsely populated, 'intimate' crowd reveals a cross section of disinterested faces, giggles, and stupefied stares. "I think the people at the festival would have been a lot happier if we had been a baroque string trio or a heavy metal band," Casale later recalled. "They didn't know what to make of us"—which was presumably his goal. His description of the band's music is evocative if misleading. "Our sound then was like Chinese Computer Music."[27]

Mothersbaugh would later describe the performance in *My Struggle*. "I want people to be able to look at me and say there goes a responsible man, or there goes a respectable guy, or even both. Somehow, though, I always end up being the clown at the fishpond, or the monkey onstage. My band finally gets a chance to perform at the Creative Arts Festival at Kent State University—a real intellectually pretentious affair!!! Virtual orgasm for the I.Q. conscious Spud; and how do I walk out onstage? In a doctor's robe with a monkey mask on, standing at an organ playing 'Here comes Peter Cottontail, Hopping down the bunny trail, Hippity hoppity look at peter go; basket full of fun and toys … joy for all the girls and boys … hippity hoppity look at Peter go … there's a nurse for Uncle Johnny and a boat for sister Sue, there's a douche sack for my mommy and a box of bunny poo … etc etc etc,' and all the other guys just stood there in the wings for a full five minutes, while my face turned bright red under the mask! Not at all the way I wanted to see it!" (His account would subsequently prompt Bob Lewis to note: "Being a 'respectable person' was at the bottom of the list for bohemian artists of the 60s and 70s, but Mark's rebellion always seemed to be of a very personal nature."[28])

If the band was still finding its footing, Mothersbaugh too was about to discover a piece of music that would inspire his future musical direction. "I remember one particular synthesizer solo I heard, more than anything else, (which) really shocked me and inspired me," he recalled, "and that was a song by Roxy Music, called 'Editions Of You.'"[29] Eno famously played a British made EMS VCS3 with a joystick controller and no keyboard (although he most likely used an additional external keyboard), and his solo on this aggressively driving song was sandwiched between much more conventional instrumental breaks by Andy Mackay on saxophone and Phil Manzanera on guitar. As such, Eno's solo comes across as less of a musical performance and more of a sound effects track from a science fiction movie. For his 30-second turn in the spotlight he employs a favorite trick of analog synth players: namely turning a pitch knob with the left hand while simultaneously triggering sounds with the right, resulting in a sweeping, harmonically disorienting barrage that sounds not unlike a more frenzied precursor to Mothersbaugh's queasy lead on 'Mongoloid.'

Roxy Music's second album, *For Your Pleasure*, containing 'Editions Of You,' was released in late March 1973, one month prior to Devo's first performance. No one could have foreseen that within five years of that low-key debut, Eno would play a pivotal yet controversial role in Devo's rise to fame.

On December 4 1973, attorneys for parents of three students killed on May 4 1970 asked the U.S. Supreme Court to allow their clients to sue Ohio Governor James A. Rhodes and National Guardsmen as individuals. Their earlier suits against the entities of the state of Ohio and the National Guard had been dismissed under the doctrine of sovereign immunity.

CHAPTER 3
1974

The virtue of dress rehearsals is that they are a free show for a select group of artists and friends of the author, and where for one unique evening the audience is almost expurgated of idiots.
ALFRED JARRY

In 1925, Tennessee passed the Butler Act, the full title of which is 'An act prohibiting the teaching of the Evolution Theory in all the Universities, and all other public schools of Tennessee, which are supported in whole or in part by the public school funds of the State, and to provide penalties for the violations thereof.' It was not the first anti-evolution legislation in the United States. Laws had been enacted in Oklahoma and Florida two years earlier (Oklahoma's was repealed in 1925) and bills had been introduced in Kentucky in 1922 and Tennessee in 1923, but had failed to pass. The author of the Butler Act, John Washington Butler, was a farmer serving in the Tennessee House of Representatives who by his own admission knew nothing about evolution when he drafted the legislation. Section 1 of the act revealingly clarifies its aims and motivations: "Be it enacted by the General Assembly of the State of Tennessee, that it shall be unlawful for any teacher in any of the Universities, Normals [teachers' colleges], and all other public schools of the State which are supported in whole or in part by the public school funds of the State, to teach any theory that denies the story of the Divine Creation of man as taught in the Bible, and to teach instead that man has descended from a lower order of animals."

The Butler Act was introduced in the Tennessee House of

Representatives on January 21 1925 and was signed into law by the governor exactly two months later on March 21. On May 4, an article in the *Chattanooga Times* reported that the American Civil Liberties Union (ACLU) was willing to finance a test case challenging the law. The ACLU described the venture as "a friendly test case [that] can be arranged without costing a teacher his or her job." One person who read the article with interest was George Rappleyea, a New Yorker who had moved to Dayton, Tennessee, three years earlier. Rappleyea was working as Superintendent of the Cumberland Coal and Iron Company, which like much of Dayton's industries had fallen on hard times. He felt that challenging the law in Dayton and hosting the ensuing trial there would be economically beneficial for the area. It was common knowledge that the law was not being enforced, and Rappleyea reasoned that if he won the trial the law would be overturned, while if he lost the existing law would simply be enforced. He did not have much to lose. He arranged a meeting the next day with a group of influential members of the community and they set about finding a teacher to plead guilty to breaking the law. After the regular high school science teacher declined, a 24-year-old football coach and substitute teacher, John T. Scopes, agreed to the plan. The imposing William Jennings Bryan, three-time Democratic presidential nominee and former United States Secretary of State, came out of retirement to act as counsel for the prosecution, while Clarence Darrow, the most famous trial attorney in America, headed the defense. (One of the attorneys on Bryan's team was a local man named Sue K. Hicks who may well have been the inspiration for the Johnny Cash song 'A Boy Named Sue,' written by children's author and songwriter Shel Silverstein, who is known to have attended a conference in Tennessee at which Hicks spoke.)

The trial turned into a spectacle that finally gave Darrow his long-awaited opportunity to confront Bryan when he took the unorthodox move of calling Bryan to the stand to testify as an expert on the Bible. The judge eventually halted their heated argument and struck the testimony from the record but not before it was broadcast to the country on national radio—a first for a trial in the USA. After eight days of trial, Scopes was finally found guilty and given the most lenient sentence possible, a $100 fine (equivalent to around $1,280 when adjusted for inflation today). Bryan died in Dayton five days after the trail ended and some have attributed his death to Darrow's intense questioning. Two years later, the case was revived by the Tennessee Supreme Court, which upheld the constitutionality of the Butler Act but overturned Scopes's conviction on a technicality (the judge had set the fine instead of the jury). The Butler Act would not be officially repealed until 1967.

The trial inspired a deluge of monkey-themed souvenirs, dolls, and other ephemera, but the most popular medium for those who misinterpreted Darwin's theory and believed it claimed that man descended from apes was song. These included 'Evolutin Riddle: Dedicated To The Evoluted Monkeys,' 'Monk's No Kin To Me (Evolution Foxtrot Song),' 'The John T. Scopes Trial (That Old Religion's Better After All),' 'Darwin's Monkey Trot,' and 'I Hope The Monkey's Win.' Their lyrical content ranged from the earnestness of 'Bryan's Last Fight' ("When the good folks had their troubles / Down in Dayton far away / Mr Bryan went to help them / And he worked both night and day") to the humor of 'There Ain't No Bugs (On Me)' ("There ain't no bugs on me / There may be bugs on some of you mugs / But there ain't no bugs on me"), later recorded by Jerry Garcia and David Grisman for a children's album. Mark Mothersbaugh even played a version of 'Evolution Mama' recorded by Turk Murphy when he appeared as a guest on *The Dr Demento Show* on October 19 1980.

It was from this milieu of early-20s anti-evolutionary fervor that *Jocko-Homo Heavenbound* emerged. The pamphlet's author, Bertram Henry Shadduck, had in his own words been a "wild" youth until a sermon changed his life and he became first a Salvation Army soldier and then a Methodist pastor with a PhD in philosophy. Shadduck was

81

well into his career as a pastor in churches in Ohio and West Virginia before he felt compelled to add 'author' to his résumé after he happened to see a sculpture by Carl Akeley entitled *The Chrysalis* in New York City's West Side Unitarian Church in 1924. Akeley was a noted sculptor and taxidermist who advanced the field to such an extent that he was considered the father of modern taxidermy. He had become fascinated with gorillas and made several expeditions to Africa to study them, including one on which he was accompanied by accomplished game-hunter Theodore Roosevelt just weeks after the end of his presidency. *The Chrysalis* is a statue of a naked 'modern' man gracefully emerging from the discarded skin of a gorilla. It had been rejected by New York's National Academy of Design before the Reverend Charles Francis Potter approached Akeley and asked to display the statue in his church. Potter was as supportive of evolutionary theory as Shadduck was opposed to it, and the fact that this blasphemous sculpture was housed within a church irked Shadduck further. He responded by writing *Jocko-Homo Heavenbound* (literally 'ape-man heaven-bound'), a 32-page screed which featured a pen-and-ink drawing of *The Chrysalis* with an additional winged angel, index finger pointed upward, emerging alongside the man. "Since Satan imitates sacred things," Shadduck writes, "[*The Chrysalis*] might better be called 'The Modernist Madonna.'" He goes on to refer to "Christian evolutionists" and their "mongrel theology" before noting: "I remember that I have met the old 'gal' before. I regret that I know of no way to heave a brick at the old squaw and seem perfectly polite to the enamored bystanders."[1]

Shadduck's primary argument is not that species don't change over time, but that a useful appendage could not possibly develop from nothing. He has no problem with once-useful appendages being shed, however. "The boasted law of evolution is that organs not used tend to wither and disappear. Before it was useful, it was nuisance. The consummate folly of it is, that our ancestors lost their tails *because they did not use them* and the rattler developed a rattle box on one end and a deadly contraption on the other *before he could use them.*" This leads him to the conclusion that this is "NOT EVOLUTION, it is the *opposite. It is going the wrong way.*" To illustrate this point, Shadduck includes a drawing of an ape chewing on a bone. Behind the ape is a stairway, with the bottom step labeled "MIGHT MAKES RIGHT" and the rest progressing through such colorful vices as "COCK FIGHTING" and "ORGIES" up to the top step, "WORLD WAR." (Curiously enough, the penultimate step is marked "TAX, USURY"; Devo would later joke that the last one said "punk rock."[2]) A horned, winged devil stands in front of the stairs, pointing to the top, his bare chest emblazoned with the word "D-EVOLUTION."

Finally, Shadduck presents the 12 "trick rules" which "the evolutionists have made their rules so that they will work three speeds ahead and *reverse.*" The polar opposites in each rule are meant to show how Darwinism was contradictory and self-serving. Devo took four of them to make up their Devolutionary Oath:

1. Wear gaudy colors or avoid display (Shadduck's tenth rule)
2. Lay a million eggs or give birth to one (Shadduck's fourth rule)
3. The fittest shall survive yet the unfit may live (Shadduck's second rule)
4. Be like your ancestors or be different (Shadduck's first rule)
5. We must repeat!

Quite why Devo chose to ignore such gems as "Grow big or stay little; either will help you survive or not," "Fight your neighbors or unite with them; one way or the other will help," and "Polygamy will help survival, unless you prefer to mate in pairs" remains a mystery.

Jocko-Homo Heavenbound was such a success that it would eventually go into ten printings and sell 93,000 copies. Shadduck would go on to write numerous other booklets—making him something of a Jack Chick of his day—with such titles as *Puddle To Paradise, The Toadstool Among The Tombs, Alibi, Lullaby, By-By, The Gee-*

Haw Of The Modern Jehu, and *Rastus Augustus Explains Evolution,* in which Rastus Augustus, "a pompous old colored man," listens in on a Biology course, renounces his belief in evolution, and stops working at his church. In a chapter entitled 'A PHILOSOPHY OF BUNGHOLES,' Rastus declares: "I is an evolutionary, I is." Politically correct Shadduck was not. With the onset of the Depression in 1929, he stopped producing pamphlets; the anti-evolution legislation movement would lay dormant for 45 years.

The tradition of propagandizing religious pamphlets remained alive and well, however—especially in the American heartland. Mark Mothersbaugh would find himself collecting these pamphlets, old and new, among many other pop culture artifacts that caught his eye, and would turn to them for inspiration. "I was sitting in this shitty apartment in Akron, Ohio, a $65-a-month apartment, and I had quack religious pamphlets that I'd been collecting," he later recalled. "I always invited Jehovah's Witnesses in because they had great gravitas, and they were always attacking evolution. So they were the ones who got me thinking about all this great stuff—you know, things that I could use for pro-de-evolution. I could just use all their information, so I would invite those people in and they'd stay around, and they'd walk around and look at all the masks I had on the walls, and I could hear them saying: he has one room. He doesn't have a bed. What is this? Is this a real apartment, or what is this? Hell?"[3]

Jocko-Homo Heavenbound would of course inspire one of Devo's signature songs after the band stumbled upon a copy of the pamphlet shortly after their performance at the 1973 Kent State Creative Arts Festival.

After that initial performance, Devo would lay dormant for a full year. It wasn't until the following year's Creative Arts Festival that they reemerged—and as a very different beast. Robert Bertholf was once again in charge of assembling the festival line-up. Ed Dorn, having finished his year as a visiting professor, was a featured poet for the festival and served as an unofficial curator.

In addition to Devo, Dorn also invited Holbrook Teter and Michael Myers to participate, having met them following a reading at a book fair in San Francisco in 1971, shortly after Teter and Myers had started their Zephyrus Image poetry press, and collaborated with them on two issues of *Bean News* in 1972. Teter was a typesetter who was involved in social justice movements while Myers was an unpredictable artist more interested in drinking, drugs, and skateboarding (and reportedly the inspiration for Dr Flamboyant in Dorn's *Gunslinger*). The two men began working together in 1970 after Teter saw one of Myers' linocuts of a hippie Jesus standing in front of a stack of car radiators holding a crucifix wrench. They quickly developed a distinctive style, which according to poet Kyle Schlesinger "combined first-edition poetry with original linoleum cuts and 'found images' reproduced from discarded cuts bought wholesale from old newspapers and job shops. Their collaboration yielded a striking visual sensibility with a tasteful randomness—at times reminiscent of the Dadaists and Futurists."[4]

At Kent State, Teter and Myers produced a series of broadsides featuring poetry by the festival participants. The broadside for Dorn's piece 'Green Poems' features his fragmented texts, each set at a different angle in its own metal type, superimposed over an unrelated found zinc block print of Hitler smiling while shaking hands with a giant. The poetry is similarly nonsensical: "Flam on the horizon / Driving an avocado w/ a white vinyl Landau ... Eye Props / when you snooz / you lose / (C. P. Frag) ... in this Land a man's wealth / is reckoned by the size / of his Garbage."[5]

Devo were also the recipients of a broadside produced for the festival entitled 'The Waltz.' The accompanying poem, which instructs the reader to "count 1-2-3 as you read" and is surrounded by Myers's art deco-inspired linocut, is shockingly blunt. "A Valium prayer to the God of Depression / Headaches, confusion, my muscles won't work /

I'm tired of doctors, I'm tired of nurses / I'm tired of assholes who think I'm a jerk." Although the poem is credited to 'Devo' rather than any individual—apparently the first such instance—it contains an emotional directness never again broached in their later work. "The years, the pain / the tears remain," the 'chorus' reads. "Once you get on it / you never go back / Oh Yeah." (Around the same time, Zephyrus Image also published a pamphlet entitled *Semi-Hard*, the cover of which featured an image of a boy stuffing more of a hotdog into his mouth than would seem wise. Devo would subsequently issue a similar promotional shot showing them stuffing themselves with hot dogs at Tail O' The Pup in West Hollywood.)

Having shortened their name to Devo, the band performed in the 150-capacity Governance Chambers—an odd choice of venue and a step down from the 264-capacity Ludwig Recital Hall, where they had played a year earlier. Unlike the Ludwig, which had rows of seats on a slope facing the stage, the Governance Chambers had a long conference table in the middle of the room with a raised pulpit-like rostrum at one end and rows of gradually raised seats and long, shared desks on the other three sides.

Describing his sartorial presentation for the show, Mothersbaugh would later recall: "When Devo first played, the first job I was a chimpanzee in doctor's clothes: the second job I was a mad doctor with this plastic brain cap on!"[6] Not until their next show would he find the alter ego that would become a permanent part of Devo lore. Singer Fred Weber, who had looked so uncomfortable during the band's first show, did not return for the second, leaving Casale to handle vocal duties. Also out was their drummer, Rod Reisman, whom Mothersbaugh suggested they replace with his youngest brother, Jim; Jim brought with him the middle Mothersbaugh brother, Bob, with whom he had played in a band named Jitters. Jitters played largely straightforward blues and blues-rock covers and originals, but Jim had also been experimenting with a homemade electronic drum kit. "I thought, this is a great idea! I'll start working with some jazz musicians and see if I can play with them using this equipment," he recalled in 1985. "Well, as soon as they heard the high-pitched electronic sounds, they said, that's nice, but can't you get some regular drum sounds? That's when Mark and Jerry said they were doing an art project at Kent State University—this concept of Devo. I asked if I could use my electronic drums, and they said, you can do whatever you want. They gave me a free, open ticket to experiment and toy and develop sounds."[7]

To create his kit, Jim had taken Remo practice pads and attached Barcus-Berry contact microphones—with chewing gum, no less. The practice pads consisted of drumheads without any wooden shells, and were meant to help players practice in relative quiet; the contact mics were designed to be attached to an acoustic guitar or any other acoustic instrument to pick up the surface vibrations of the instrument itself (as opposed to picking up vibrations of sound waves, as a standard mic would). Once Jim had the output from the drum mics he was able to process them in any way he wanted. He arranged the four pads on top of a custom made metal 'V' and played them standing up. (Before alighting on the idea of using minimal practice pads, he had attached contact mics to a full acoustic drum kit and ran the signal through an array of available effects available at the time including wah-wah, fuzz, and delay units.)

"It was really crude and it was really scary-sounding," Mark Mothersbaugh recalled. "I don't think I've ever heard anything since that was quite like what his drum kit sounded like back in those days." Not only was the sound unusual, it was often unpredictable. "Sometimes he'd be in the middle of a song and all these explosions would go off. It sounded like an ammo dump had just got lit."[8] In 1977, long after abandoning the idea, the band would boast of how "the closest thing to them now is the new stuff Bowie's doing on his *Low* album, and the new *Lust For Life* album by Iggy Pop."[9] (Those particular sounds were, in fact, the result of producer Tony Visconti's prohibitively expensive Eventide Harmonizer.)

Mark has also claimed that Jim's drum kit was "one of the first electronic drum sets ever in use on the planet."[10] He may just be right. An ocean away, Kraftwerk had been building their own "drumpad," which made its debut on the German arts television show *aspekte* in October 1973. Its inventor, the long-haired and mustached drummer Wolfgang Flür, can be seen providing a rudimentary rhythm backing to Ralf Hütter's electric piano and Florian Schneider's flute. (Flür claims to have conceived of and created the instrument alone, but would learn years later that Hütter and Schneider had copyrighted the design in the United States in 1977 without his knowledge, listing Hütter as the designer.)

The American public would have to wait until mid 1975, when Kraftwerk appeared on the *Midnight Special* TV show during their first American tour, to see the drumpad in action. Flür and Karl Bartos stood above flat panels containing round metal disks playing a drumpad each using thin metal sticks with wires attached to the bottoms. The first of these kits took two years to be built using a rhythm box repurposed from an electric organ. The drums formed part of an exposed circuit—when the metal stick came into contact with the metal disk it would close the circuit and a sound would be triggered. The design was similar to the Stylophone, which Kraftwerk surprisingly would not get around to using until 1981's 'Pocket Calculator.' (OMD's Andy McCluskey would later describe the drumpad as looking like "electronic tea trays with wired up knitting needles."[11])

The two bands' approaches to constructing electronic drums were as different as the sounds they produced. Devo probably wouldn't have heard Kraftwerk until after the release of their breakthrough album, *Autobahn*, in late 1974, by which time Jim Mothersbaugh had already built his own kit, but the parallel illustrates the lengths one had to go to in order to acquire electronic instruments in the early-to-mid 70s. It wasn't until 1976 that Pollard Industries (founded by Beach Boys/Grass Roots drummer Joe Pollard) released the first commercially available electronic drum, the Syndrum. The Syndrum looked deceptively like an acoustic drum until you noticed the handful of knobs for 'tune' and 'sweep' on the side of its truncated shell. There was also a hefty control panel containing an imposing number of sliders, switches, and knobs, as well as a rocker pedal that needed to be added to the existing acoustic kit. The Synare was released the following year by Star Instruments and operated on a similar concept, except its drums looked more like black flying saucers than conventional acoustic drums. The Syndrum would find its way onto such cutting-edge records as Donna Summer's 'MacArthur Park' and LPs by Linda Ronstadt, Barbra Streisand, and Rod Stewart, while the Synare features on Anita Ward's disco classic 'Ring My Bell.' (Alan Myers can be seen playing two of them in the 1980 video for 'Whip It.')

Most of these recordings simply used the instruments for occasional emphasis and accent. It wasn't until 1981 and the introduction of the iconic hexagonal Simmons SDS-V—"the world's first fully electronic drum set"—that the traditional could be replaced entirely. The SDS-V was quickly put to use by Spandau Ballet, Duran Duran, and Talk Talk, among others, but back in the mid 70s, in order to acquire electronic instruments, one had to either have the means and motivation to build them or a wealthy patron (often an academic institution) to donate them. Thankfully, Devo had both.

Among the bands that had to build their own were Silver Apples, a New York duo formed in 1967. Singer Simeon Coxe III built his own primitive and highly idiosyncratic synthesizer, the Simeon, which according to the liner notes to the band's 1968 debut consisted of "nine audio oscillators and 86 manual controls enabling Simeon to express his musical ideas. The lead and rhythm oscillators are played with the hands, elbows and knees and the bass oscillators are played with the feet."[12] Simeon also outfitted the rig with a system of telegraph keys and pedals to control tonality and chord changes. The band's other member, Dan Taylor, played a large yet conventional drum kit in a propulsive, repetitive style.

Another early proponent of electric sounds in rock music were The United States Of America, formed at the same time but on the opposite coast, in Los Angeles, by Joseph Byrd. Byrd was well versed in the contemporary avant-garde and had been studying as well as teaching at UCLA, where he met Tom Oberheim, who would go on to manufacture a range of synthesizers and drum machines in the 70s and 80s. Oberheim designed a ring modulator effect for the band as well as other electronic devices, while another instrument builder, Richard Durrett, provided "the DURRETT Electronic Music Synthesizer"—built at Byrd's request because the only other alterative, the Moog, cost more than $20,000 at the time. The United States Of America's music was more closely aligned with the psychedelic rock of the time than that of Silver Apples, but the band only made one album, partly, as Byrd later put it, because of a clash of "too many personalities; every rehearsal became group therapy."[13]

San Francisco's Fifty Foot Hose would likewise have fitted squarely within the psychedelic music scene except that bassist and founder Cork Marcheschi also played a homemade 'synthesizer' of almost Rube Goldberg-like complexity comprised of everything from a "tube-type Theremin" to a "wonderful plastic speaker from a World War II Navy boat."[14]

These bands were far from the vanguard of commerciality—debut albums by Silver Apples and The United States Of America reached numbers 193 and 181 respectively on the *Billboard* 200. Those who built their own electronic instruments in the late 60s and early 70s were consciously heading down a rocky road, opening themselves up not only to assured technical problems but also to indifferent or even hostile reactions from audiences. Like ham radio operators or early adopters of computers, they were a dedicated minority who enjoyed being on the forefront of an emerging technology despite the ensuing difficulties. By all accounts, it would have been much easier to simply plug a guitar into an amplifier.

Within the space of a decade, however, this equation would be flipped. While Devo would undoubtedly benefit from these same technological advances of the late 70s and early 80s, they also had one foot planted firmly in the previous age of the intrepid tinkerer/inventor, which would set them apart from their eventual new-wave contemporaries.

On April 17 1974, a week before Devo's second performance at the Kent State Creative Arts Festival, the Supreme Court ruled that parents of three students killed by National Guardsmen at Kent State could sue Ohio officials and officers of the guard.

With Mark Mothersbaugh now fully ensconced the band quickly resumed recording in the way that Casale, Lewis, and Gregg had done years earlier. Many of Casale's compositions were re-recorded, including 'Auto Modown,' 'I Been Refused,' 'I Need A Chick' (co-written with Gregg), and 'The Rope Song' (co-written with Lewis) from the Dayho sessions, plus 'Can U Take It?,' 'Space Girl Blues,' and others. Mothersbaugh would add his Minimoog to the arrangements, and while the synthesizer undoubtedly added a new dimension to the tracks it was obviously an afterthought, tacked on long after the songs were originally conceived. "We called the Moog a poison gas vapor," Casale recalled. "It was allowed to come in and swirl around and interject rude and random things that didn't fit a rock'n'roll lexicon. We were hoping for that."[15]

While the songs still clearly bore the influence of Captain Beefheart, the addition of electronics took the music in a direction that the Captain's had only hinted at. The only Beefheart compositions to feature electronic instruments were 'Autumn's Child' and the aptly titled 'Electricity' (both 1967), on which the sound of a Theremin weaves around the otherwise fairly conventional blues-based instrumentation. It was played by Dr Samuel Hoffman, whose playing features on the soundtrack to films such as *The Day The Earth Stood Still* (1951) and *Billy The Kid Versus Dracula* (1966), and whose solo recordings *Music Out Of The Moon* (1947) and *Perfume Set To Music* (1948) suggest that he shared Devo's view of electronic sounds as vapor.

Mothersbaugh also brought with him some original compositions that made evident his shared love of appropriation. 'Mechanical Man' was somewhat inspired by Charles Manson's song of the same name (released in 1970 on an album titled *Lie: The Love & Terror Cult*). "There probably wouldn't have been a song called 'Mechanical Man' if he hadn't done it first," he later confessed. "But that said, it was just kind of a touch-point … we were always kind of obsessed with the darker side of pop culture, you know."[16] Another song was directly inspired by the sort of textbook that was, in fact, nothing more than an excuse to present pictures of scantily clad native women. *The Secret Museum Of Mankind* (published in 1935 but lifted directly and without attribution from J.A. Hammerton's *Peoples Of All Nations* from 1922), advertised in magazines such as *Keen*, was a mail-order-only affair that boasted "the world's greatest collection of strange & secret photographs, containing everything from female beauty round the world to the most mysterious cults and customs." Pictured inside is a topless Ethiopian girl alongside the caption "BUTTERED BEAUTY OF THE NEGROID NORTH, This girl of Tigré has thickly oiled and buttered her hair and arranged it in wave-like plaits pinned to the front braid. At night she sleeps with her neck on a wooden rest." Mothersbaugh's song 'Buttered Beauties' contains the lines "Buttered beauty of the negroid north / Come spread your tallow on me / Oiled wonder of a midnight forest / Toss down your glossy web." 'Fraulein' blatantly lifts the riff from Raymond Scott's 'Powerhouse' (1937), popularized by the Carl Stalling recording used in numerous Warner Bros cartoons, and 'U Got Me Bugged' was inspired by 'You Got Me Bugged' by The Buggs, as featured on their 1964 album *The Beetle Beat*—the first album Mark ever bought, mistakenly thinking it was by The Beatles. The cover boasted "the original Liverpool sound" and claimed the album had been "recorded in England"; in fact, The Buggs were from Omaha, Nebraska, and had made their album at Kay Bank Studios in Minneapolis, Minnesota. "I got it home and I didn't recognize any Beatles songs," he recalled. "One track pissed me off so much it eventually inspired the nasty Devo song 'U Got Me Bugged.'"[17]

Musically, as well as lyrically, Devo were interested in pushing the boundaries of what was acceptable within the confines of a rock song. Jerry Casale would later explain the sonic component of these informal recording sessions by noting how "everybody had a whacked-out sound. There were no normal sounds on any of the instruments. They had all been tweaked. What you hear on the *Hardcore Devo* CD [on which many of these recordings would finally see release] is how we would sit around in a living room in 1974 or '75. Mark would have a Minimoog on a table and an ARP Odyssey [synth], I would have a Gibson bass and a tiny amp, Jim Mothersbaugh would have his electronic drums, and Bob Mothersbaugh would have a guitar coming through a little Champ [amplifier]."[18]

In addition to guitar, bass, and synthesizer they were also finding inspiration in other less orthodox sounds. "In the early days, when Jerry and I wrote songs together, we used washing machines for a rhythm track," Mark recalled. "I remember he wrote lyrics to a song while we were in a car once to the sound of his windshield wipers. He was singing 'Weave to the left bob to the right / Or you'll be a flat tire on the freeway of life'"—lyrics and a rhythm that would eventually become 'A Plan For U.' "We were looking for sounds that were outside of the clichés of rock'n'roll."[19]

If Devo discovered one of their first major inspirations shortly after their debut performance, they would become aware of the next shortly after their second concert. *The Beginning Was The End* was published in 1971 by Oscar Kiss Maerth, its cover bearing the phrase "Man came into being through cannibalism—intelligence can be eaten!" Not much is known about Maerth (and the world is probably a better place as a result). He was apparently born in 1914 in what was then Hungary and claimed to have lived in South America, Australia, and Asia. He said he had written the book in a Chinese Buddhist monastery before moving to Lake Como, Italy, which has long served as a playground for the rich and famous. He may have been a Nazi or Nazi sympathizer who escaped through the ratlines to South America, or he may have been imprisoned in a concentration camp by the Nazis during the war. He may have made millions from a shoe manufacturing business, or he may have been a penniless ex-Catholic priest. (When his daughter was kidnapped in 1982 under questionable circumstances and released under equally dubious conditions, Maerth claimed that he was not rich, even though his opulent surroundings suggested otherwise.) A video interview from the time of the book's publication shows him lounging at home in a white robe, gardening, doing yoga, and playing with what appears to be a pet monkey. If he hadn't existed, Devo would have had to make him up (which I'm reasonably certain they didn't do).

Maerth's book is an odious piece of pseudoscience, and a far cry from Betram Shadduck's evolution denials of nearly 50 years earlier. Maerth sets his stall out early, explaining on the first page that man "fancied himself the center of the world as he imagined it, and by God's will its appointed master." A couple thousand years of scientific advances had shown man was in fact not the center of the universe, and his ego had taken a bruising, the final straw coming 150 years ago, when he discovered he was the product of evolution rather than divine creation. Thus man had "placed himself at the apex of an imaginary self-constructed pyramid, and he has had to climb down from it step by step in the course of the last two thousand years. He stands at present at the lowest step, but he must now retreat even further from there."[20]

Worse still, for Maerth, is having to confront the fact that evolution is the result of "a chain of criminal acts contrary to the laws of nature." It's here that he makes the outlandish claim that our ancestors began eating the brains of their peers, and that so doing somehow led to an increase in the size of the eater's brain but also led to an increase of pressure on the skull (which remained the same size), resulting in madness. "Man has become the lunatic genius of the universe whose diseased mind with its absurd objectives is necessarily and inevitably becoming his doom," he writes. Eating brains, he adds, caused early man to lose his body hair, tail, innate extra-sensory perception, and "the capacity to reach understanding with his fellow man through thought transference." Of course, there is a conspiracy on the part of researchers who know all of this but won't reveal it. "Because all this is inconsistent with natural development, which they want to prove at all costs, they keep quiet about it."

Just as suddenly as our ancestors had begun eating brains, Maerth continues, they stopped "about 50,000 years ago"—except Bigfoot, who had decided to get out of the brain-eating racket much earlier, and whose devolution was consequently halted. "There were ever more numerous cases of a brain disease similar to epilepsy and of extreme madness, and with no room for doubt man was able to trace these back to the pressure on his over-large brain. He recognized that this was a consequence of cannibalism, and for this reason saw himself compelled to give up eating brain." (Just as humans collectively realized that eating meat was causing an epidemic of heart disease all around the world and unanimously decided to eliminate it from our diets all at once. Oh, wait …)

After explaining what a bad thing all of this is, Maerth then describes his own feelings of "warmth" and "vitality" after he himself eats "fresh ape brain." And as if all of that wasn't enough, he goes on to say that Africans have smaller brains than Europeans, who have smaller brains than the Chinese, and—just in case you're not yet offended—that women are not as smart as men, since eating brains was an activity in which only men partook. "If someone wanted to commit the error of giving woman man's intelligence, then woman would have to begin eating brain and continue doing so for several tens of thousands of years." He cites no references to back up his claims, providing no index and no bibliography, but he does present eight pages of side-by-side photographs showing "startling resemblances between types of ape and different human races." These are simply black-and-white photographs of mainly African and Arab individuals alongside different types of apes to which there are some vague facial similarities (or not). If Maerth had simply hinted at being a racist up to this point, here he seems to confirm it in no uncertain terms.

Devo's relationship with this kind of work has always been tricky. Despite maintaining a straight face when speaking of their admiration for the book they have also called it "very nice quack stuff."[21] They have often maintained that they were simply "reporters … we just ingest information and feed it back out to people. Provide it." (One astute early interviewer, Martin Perlich, countered this by noting: "If culture is shit and you're taking a picture of culture then you have beautifully photographed shit."[22])

Of all of the inspirations for Devo's worldview, *The Beginning Was The End* is the only one that was contemporary, having been published in Germany in 1971 and translated into English in 1974. Although it would take them years to obtain an actual copy of the book, they were certain just on learning of its reputation that they would like it—and of course they were entirely right. Having discovered it, they spoke of the book in reverent and secretive tones. "Should we tell him about the book?" Casale asked Mothersbaugh during the course of a 1978 interview with *New Times*. "I think so," Mark replied.[23]

Until this point, Devo had been dealing largely in outmoded kitsch—hastily written superhero comic books, Golden Age Hollywood horror films, and fringe religious pamphlets. That *The*

Beginning Was The End's content is so radical as well as confused is at least in part a testament to the time in which it was written. By 1971, the hippie dream was in a shambles, and over the course of the decade it would become even more so. The communes of the 60s were becoming the cults of the 70s. Former hippie guru and aspiring folk singer Charles Manson had orchestrated the Tate/LaBianca murders in 1969, while Reverend Jim Jones, founder of the Peoples Temple in California, would lead over 900 members in a mass suicide in Jonestown, Guyana, in 1978. This turmoil was not limited to fringe elements, however. The morality of the country as a whole seemed to have come undone. President John F. Kennedy's assassination in 1963 set off a wave of conspiracy theories following the publication of the Warren Commission. By the early 70s, the market was flooded with books detailing various alternative theories about Kennedy's death, and today the number of books written about the assassination runs to the thousands. The Watergate scandal destroyed what little remaining faith there was in the office of the president. As a result, a political outsider and Georgia peanut farmer was elected with high hopes only to leave office four years later a disappointment.

With *The Beginning Was The End*, Devo now had a modern confirmation of their quickly formulating theory of de-evolution and a deep well of inspiration from which to draw. Years later, in the early 2000s, they would try, unsuccessfully, to republish the book with their own introduction. That scheme may not have come to fruition, but by then they had succeeded in using the American cover of the book in the artwork for their 1989 live album *Now It Can Be Told: DEVO At The Palace 12/9/88.*

The rest of the year saw Devo make tentative steps toward playing live outside of the auspices of Kent State University. Despite Casale's ill-received stage antics a couple of years earlier, Devo scored a slot opening for The Numbers Band at Kent hotspot the Kove. Casale had stepped up his visual presentation by debuting an item of clothing that would soon become part of early Devo lore, and to which Mark Mothersbaugh would later allude in *My Struggle* when, beneath three illustrations depicting a magician's preparations for an illusion, he captioned the second panel "painting tampons for the tampon coat." As the name suggests, Casale's coat was a white lab coat with hundreds of tampons dipped in various shades of paint hanging from it—a demented variation on the then-popular fringed suede jacket. Along with Jim Mothersbaugh's electronic drums, it served as a visual statement of intent before the band had even played a note.

During the fall, Devo also played a benefit for Shelly's Book Bar at JB's Down Under to celebrate the launch of a new literary magazine, *Shelly's*. The magazine was the product of Tuesday night meetings at the store (where the assembled poets would "proclaim, contest, and disseminate") and was released in comb-bound editions running to nearly 100 pages. Casale, Mothersbaugh, and Lewis all made contributions to the inaugural *Shelly's*, as well as many subsequent issues, often alongside pieces by Eric Mottram and Ed Dorn. The third issue reprinted Jerry's 'Polymer Love' and Bob's 'Readers vs. Breeders,' billed as "two Devolutionary propaganda tracts [from the] now defunct *LA Staff*," as well as two pages of text and art by Mark that would later appear in *My Struggle*. The same issue also included a poem by Ed Dorn entitled 'The Contract,' which detailed a "Middle West" whose "spiritual genius is so apt / To prepare itself to leave / This overpowering condition (to avoid implosion) / And to migrate to the neutralized / And individuating conditions of the coasts."

At this point, the band's line-up was still relatively fluid. Bob Casale most likely wasn't present at the Kove, while Peter Gregg appeared to have temporarily overcome his stage fright enough to show up onstage at JB's, although his nerves prevented him from actually playing anything. The *Shelly's* benefit, however, was the last show that Bob Lewis would play with Devo.

The year 1974 would prove to be pivotal in other ways as well, not least on August 4, when a common plea heard from students across the country—one that only intensified after the Kent State shootings—was finally answered. In one of the rare autobiographical passages in *My Struggle*, Mark Mothersbaugh writes: "I am sitting here in my efficiency apartment still staring at the TV mounted on the bookshelves in the corner of the room ... There is no feeling in my arms or my legs ... They could weigh as much as dump trucks, or be as light as balloons ... As of five minutes ago, the president of the United States, the leader of our nation, has resigned from his post."

Around the same time, another of Mark's sketchbooks would cost Jerry Casale his shortlived teaching job. During his only semester teaching art, Casale had encouraged his students to keep journals and sketchbooks. Upon examining his students' lackluster efforts he decided to bring in a number of sketchbooks his friends had created in order to provide his students with some much needed inspiration. One of these sketchbooks was Mark Mothersbaugh's. Realizing that his friend's art could tend toward the scatological, Casale wisely marked the pages he deemed acceptable for an undergraduate audience. During a break in the two-and-a-half-hour class, however, one of the female students took it upon herself to peruse the rest of Mothersbaugh's sketchbook in the otherwise empty classroom. She was shocked by what she found. "I wasn't stupid," Casale later explained. "I knew what the limits of showing imagery in school were, so I didn't show the X-rated stuff—things like Mark's self-portrait of himself as a butcher-doctor, where he'd take illustrations out of medical books and alter them, putting himself in as the doctor but holding two halves of a baby coming out of a woman, because he'd had to saw the baby up to save the woman."[24] Casale was promptly summoned to the dean's office and, despite protesting that he had taken every effort to shield his students from the offensive material, he was let go.

That summer, Casale had also experienced a musical epiphany

that would only strengthen his resolve to pursue music as his medium of choice. "I saw the *Diamond Dogs* tour by David Bowie in 1974," he later recalled, "and realized that maybe I could do something creative about the way I felt."[25] The *Diamond Dogs* tour was also one of the most elaborate of Bowie's career, and his most expensive to date. The stage set was a warped (and bleeding) German Expressionist-inspired cityscape featuring skyscrapers, catwalks, streetlamps, a giant hand, and a cherry picker to lift the singer over the audience. For the second half of the tour, however, Bowie would ditch the overt theatricality for the more spartan Philly Dogs set.

On November 8 1974, US District Court Judge Frank J. Battisti dismissed charges against eight former Guardsmen in Cleveland, ruling that US prosecutors had failed to prove charges that guardsmen willfully intended to deprive the four students killed and nine wounded of their civil rights, and suggesting they should have been tried instead by state officials.

CHAPTER 4
1975

To keep up even a worthwhile tradition means vitiating the idea behind
it which must necessarily be in a constant state of evolution: it is
mad to try to express new feelings in a "mummified" form.
ALFRED JARRY

By the time of Devo's next high-profile gig, and their first of 1975, on April 4, they were back at Kent State. This time it was due to the patronage of another of Jerry Casale's former professors, experimental filmmaker Richard Myers. Casale had been a student of Myers's as an undergraduate and had contributed to his films *Confrontation At Kent State* (1970), a documentary filmed the week after the shootings of May 4, and *Deathstyles* (1971), a "relentless visual and aural montage of anger against the America of the early 1970s ... encompassing the racial strife, anti-Vietnam War demonstrations, conservative response, new sexual freedoms, and growing media and advertising overload of the time." Myers also assembled *Allison* (1971), "a short, simple film about Allison Krause, one of the four students murdered at Kent State in May 1970 by the Ohio National Guard" from existing footage in which Krause was unwittingly filmed.

Myers had begun weekly film screenings on campus called Tuesday Cinema shortly after his arrival at the university in the mid 60s. (He would also host the Ann Arbor Film Festival Tour, in which submitted films would travel to and be screened at over 30 locations throughout the world, when it stopped in Kent.) "We started off with the films of the 30s," he later explained, "experiments by the French surrealists and then little by little we started adding schlock because we weren't getting that big of a crowd for just experimental films ... little by little we started showing the kind of cult films that we recognize as cult films today—*Pink Flamingos* was one of the first of that type that I think we showed."[1]

It was prior to the screening of John Waters's film—one of the most depraved in a catalog built on depravity—that Devo performed. The pairing was inspired and Devo rose to the occasion. *Pink Flamingos* (1972) proudly pushed the envelope on the amount of deviant acts that could be squeezed into a film and portrayed in graphic detail. A sampling of the deeds that gleefully made the cut included cannibalism, mother-son fellatio, castration, something that can only be called the "chicken fuck," and an infamous final scene of the 300-pound transvestite, Divine, eating fresh dog feces. While many regarded Waters's films as nothing more than degenerate filth, Casale defended them as "heavily influenced by Greek theater and Shakespearean tragedies—there are a lot of classical references in both *Pink Flamingos* and [its follow up] *Female Trouble*—they are really like morality plays, passion plays or Greek tragedy more than Elizabethan—but they are very packed with allusions both to classical drama and Hollywood movies—they are really incredible, classical in structure."[2] Devo seemed to have found a kindred spirit who was also equally attracted to the high and the low.

The poster for the event billed Devo as "The De-evolution Band," asking "How LOW can you go!" and listing the members as "Boogie Boy, China Man, Jungle Jim, & The Clown." Seemingly taking a page from the Kiss playbook, they had assumed characters for the performance. Gerry was China Man, so named for the "un-PC glasses that had plastic oriental eyes inside the black frame" he wore beneath fake V-shaped eyebrows. (Mark Mothersbaugh can be seen wearing the same glasses on the cover of the 1982 LP *Oh, No! It's Devo*.) Mark debuted a mask of a blond haired, fresh-faced infant, whom he dubbed Boogie Boy, "the infant as old as the mountains but is yet unborn."[3] (His name would later morph into 'Booji Boy' after the band ran out of the letter 'g' while captioning an early film with dry transfer letters, but would retain the pronunciation 'boogie' rather than 'bougie.') Mark would remain in character for the length of the performance. "It's one of the only times that I was Booji Boy all night," he later noted. "Leaving the mask on that long just suffocates you to wear it for more than a couple songs. It was a full head mask that closed off underneath—at least the original version did."[4] We can only surmise that Jim Mothersbaugh had become Jungle Jim due to the fact that his homemade electronic drum kit, which sat on a base of bent and welded "chrome muffler tubing," had the appearance of a jungle gym.[5] The reasoning behind new recruit Bob Mothersbaugh's moniker was anyone's guess. "I don't remember who gave me the nickname Clown," he later admitted, "and I still can't imagine why they did."[6]

Bob Mothersbaugh had been sitting in with the nebulous band from time to time and his superiority as a guitarist over Bob Lewis eventually led to one Bob replacing another. This was an arrangement that Lewis seemed to be more than happy with. "I became more of a manager than a player because we decided someone had to do it," he recalled. "I liked that other [managerial] stuff better anyway."[7] Bob Mothersbaugh's introduction to music seems to have largely come from his older brother. "I remember we used to go down to the basement where all the dirty clothes were piled up," he said. "We had a little 45rpm record player and we'd lay on the pile of clothes and he'd make me listen to The Kinks."[8]

The same British Invasion bands that had inspired his bandmates had made a similarly large impression on Bob. "I'm just old enough that I listened to The Kinks and The Rolling Stones when they were happening," he later recalled, but he seemed to have followed the nascent guitar-god worship of Beck, Clapton, and Hendrix in a way that the others didn't. Oddly enough, however, Bob's first guitar wasn't a guitar at all but a Coral Sitar, an electric instrument invented to allow guitar players to easily emulate the sitar sounds on records like The Beatles' 'Norwegian Wood' and The Rolling Stones' 'Paint It Black.' It was an electric guitar with an additional course of sympathetic strings, which would vibrate as the guitar's body vibrated but were not intended to be struck by the player, and a plastic 'buzz' bridge. Bob Mothersbaugh eventually lost interest in the exotic sound and sawed off the sympathetic strings with a jigsaw. "The guitar was put in the barn and I kind of forgot about it," he later recalled.[9] Despite this initial foray into a faddish but shortlived vogue, however, Bob soon honed his chops on a proper guitar. Casale later described him as "a very, very good rock'n'roll guitar player, schooled in the tradition of everything from Keith Richards to Ariel Bender [of Mott The Hoople] and Captain Beefheart."[10] If Devo began as art students tentatively trying their hands at music, Bob Mothersbaugh would bring a much-needed dose of rock respectability to their sound.

For the time being, however, the *Pink Flamingos* warm up act was received with bewilderment if not outright hostility, as friend and sometime collaborator Gary 'General' Jackett recalled. "When Devo came on, of course … people didn't really get it. … All I remember were people saying what's this? or this isn't music. … In the early days there was nothing musical about what they were trying to do." Jackett saw the logic of the pairing but most audience members were more receptive to the envelope-pushing antics on film. "In a sense it was just like *Pink Flamingos* in that the intent was to assault the viewer," Jackett noted.[11]

The film was shown twice that night and Devo played before each showing. "It wasn't a full house, I can tell you that," Mark Mothersbaugh recalled. "We had about ten diehard fans in those days, and there would be the unsuspecting 30 or 40 people who accidently would wander in and slowly filter out before the set was over." According to Jackett, "it was a pretty good crowd—pretty raucous."

Later that month, Devo would return to play their third Kent State Creative Arts Festival.

On May 28 1975, the first trial related to the Kent State Shootings began, just over five years after the event. It was the first time all of the gathered evidence was considered in depth, with the wounded students and parents of the slain seeking a total of $46 million in damages from Governor James A. Rhodes, former Kent president Robert I. White, and 27 former and current Guardsmen.

On August 27 1975, after hearing three months of highly conflicting reports about the events of May 4 1970—complicated by controversial rulings about whether or not certain evidence was admissible—the federal court jury in Cleveland exonerated Ohio Governor James Rhodes and the 28 other defendants from any financial or personal responsibility in connection with the shootings. The jury's decision found that the plaintiffs had not been denied their civil rights, nor had they been victims of the "willful or wanton misconduct, or of the negligence of some or all of the defendants."

Five months later, Devo had their first gig outside of Akron/Kent and away from anything that could be considered a sympathetic audience. Rodger Bohn was the owner of Cleveland's Smiling Dog Saloon, whose concerts were broadcast weekly on local radio station WMMS every Saturday at midnight. WMMS was the region's premier album-oriented rock station, playing a steady diet of blue-collar rock for a primarily down-and-out populace. The station's iconic cartoon buzzard mascot had nothing to do with native bird populations but was rather a symbolic choice. Program director John Gorman summed up the reasoning behind it when he suggested the city was dying, and "what better mascot you could have than something that represents something that's dying, and that was the buzzard."[12] While the station regularly came up with new slogans to explain their call letters—including 'We're (your) Modern Music Station' or 'Where Music Means Something'—many listeners preferred the unofficial catchphrase 'Weed Makes Me Smile.' While WMMS rigidly adhered to its AOR format, Bohn's booking policy for the Smiling Dog was much more adventurous. His stock in trade was jazz but he wasn't averse to augmenting it with anything from "rock and reggae to comedy." Bohn decided to throw a private Halloween bash to show WMMS his appreciation and rented the WHK Auditorium to be the venue. The auditorium had opened in 1913 and served successively as an opera house, a vaudeville/burlesque venue, and a movie theater before falling into disrepair and neglect. Cleveland's homegrown *CLE* magazine put it even more bluntly: "There is no escaping the fact that the place was a PIT!"[13]

Bohn's headliner for the evening was Sun Ra, the avant-jazz legend and famed eccentric whose Arkestra (at that time dubbed the Intergalactic Myth-Science Arkestra) could number over 30 and include not only musicians but singers, dancers, acrobats, and, on occasion, fire-eaters, sometimes accompanied by film projections and light shows. Sun Ra also claimed that he came from Saturn and routinely dressed himself and his band in sparkling floor-length robes, amulets, and Egyptian inspired headdresses or glittering beanies (actually spandex tank tops), sometimes even incorporating flashing lights and propellers. His 'space shades,' immortalized on the April 19 1969 cover of *Rolling Stone*, consisted of large opaque lenses with thin vertical slits, to which Jerry's China Man glasses bore more than a passing (yet presumably coincidental) resemblance. He spoke in Zen-like riddles, espousing a philosophy that ultimately served to confuse more than enlighten. He deliberately obscured his extensive background in early jazz in favor of an outsized mythology with ostensibly no earthly musical antecedents that made Devo's later claim of being "the band who fell to Earth" even more applicable to the Arkestra.

Behind Sun Ra's surreal visual presentation lay a stunning musical skill on piano, which he also applied to synthesizers, having been given a prototype of the Minimoog Model B by Bob Moog himself. In an effort to transcend the electronic instruments' limitations, Sun Ra often modified them by hand to produce truly unique sounds. Moog employee Jon Weiss checked in on the synth during a live performance, and later reported: "I don't know what he had done to it, but he made sounds like you had never heard in your life: I mean just total inharmonic distortion all over the place, oscillators weren't oscillating any more, nothing was working but it was fabulous."[14] The band's performances were closer to ceremonies or 'happenings' than concerts, and the music often incorporated a disorienting mélange of polyrhythms played on multiple percussion instruments (some homemade), freeform improvisations, and lengthy solos. For all his outré experimentation, however, he was also fond of quoting from his favorite Disney songs or 'Somewhere Over The Rainbow,' which led his *New York Times* obituary to remark: "His ability to remake popular culture—by turning pop songs into electronic kitsch, for example— was completely modern."[15] With one foot planted firmly in the past (vintage blues and swing as well as ancient Egyptian mythology) and one in the distant future (newly available electronic sounds and far flung space travel) he singlehandedly created his own genre.

Devo had been hand-picked by Bohn to open for Sun Ra, most likely as a result of Mark's friend, sometime patron, and Devo soundman Ed Barger being a Smiling Dog employee, given that their reputation had still not spread beyond a handful of acquaintances. The Halloween bash was a private party for WMMS and Smiling Dog employees as well as Bohn's friends and filled only a fraction of the 1,500-capacity auditorium. The fact that the auditorium was in the same building as WMMS might also have had something to do with why it was chosen for the gig. The host provided his guests with an oversize vat of Tequila Sunrise and personally greeted each of them with a hit from a tank of nitrous oxide—commonly referred to as laughing gas because of its capacity to induce "euphoria and/or slight hallucinations"—an inspired choice for a party where many guests came in costume.

Devo had settled on the first of their matching costumes that night of blue coveralls or 'janitor outfits' that made them look, as

Mark later put it, "like a clean-up crew."[16] They were actually firemen's work suits that the band found in a uniform shop—something blue-collar Akron had an abundance of—which the band paired with clear plastic masks, found in a novelty shop, that gave them permanent grins. "They did give us a uniform look, which we were trying for," Mark recalled. "We wanted to be like five pieces of a machine rather than five individuals."[17]

Despite sporting identical suits, Devo also appeared as their theatrical alter egos, suggesting that they were caught between two very different approaches to presentation they had yet to resolve. Would they adopt an almost anonymous, Kraftwerk-like 'music worker' stance, or would they become the thinking man's Kiss with their wildly individual personalities and caricatured images?

There seems to be no agreement between those responsible for the booking and the band themselves on any of what followed except for the fact that the set ended in physical confrontation and verbal abuse. (As Cleveland writer Charlotte Pressler put it: "If they had been beer-can collectors, it would have been a good gig."[18]) According to Gorman, Bohn regarded Devo as "really weird but good—a perfect fit" to open for Sun Ra. "They came out and did a bizarre set like nothing we'd seen before. The crowd loved them."[19] Jerry Casale, however, felt that they had been hired "as a practical joke,"[20] while Mark Mothersbaugh remembered the audience "getting really pissed off at us and the music we were playing."[21] The band felt that the hostility directed toward them was entirely the result of the music they played, including one signature song that received its debut that night, 'Jocko Homo.' "It was in 7/4 time," Mark recalled, "and those people just didn't go for it, because it wasn't the kind of song that went along with the natural flow of your body. When we got to the end of it, when it gets into 4/4 time, they thought we were going to let them off the hook—until they realized we were going to chant 'Are we not men? We are Devo!' for about 20 minutes—or however long it took for them to get really angry."[22] Gorman, however, has claimed that it was simply the band's refusal to stop when their allotted time was up that provoked such venom, rather than the sounds they were producing. "The crowd loved them—until they wouldn't stop playing and kept repeating their set over and over," he recalled. "Sun Ra was becoming impatient. Devo's unending performance was preventing him from taking the stage, and he wouldn't play if he didn't go on at a certain set time. The crowd, which first supported Devo, shouted for them to get off the stage, demanding Sun Ra. They refused."[23] As the costumed audience stormed the stage, a truly surrealistic milieu ensued. "All of a sudden, drunk mummies were shaking their fists at us," Mothersbaugh recalled. "Draculas were shouting obscenities at us."[24]

Thankfully, the set was captured for posterity, and five of the seven songs were released in 1992 on Rykodisc's *Live: The Mongoloid Years*. After 'Bamboo Bimbo,' the second song of the set, Casale asks: "We cleared the place out didn't we?" He then offers his explanation for the exodus: "You guys just can't take it." Later, during the call and response of Mark's impassioned 'Jocko Homo,' a voice can be heard calling the band "a bunch of assholes!" Without missing a beat, the band's ragged chant changes from "Are we not men?" to "Is he not a man?" The anonymous voice responds by inviting "everybody in favor of getting these assholes off the stage" to stand up, suggesting that the crowd is filtering back in.

Although it might have felt like 20 minutes, the song actually lasted just over six, after which Devo close their set with one of their most offensive songs, 'I Need A Chick.' "It just goes on and on and on," Casale says. "You never get off." He's not taking about leaving the stage, however, but about what happens when you have a "three speed vibrator" and "you do it yourself." Cheers are heard when it looks like the band are about to play their final note. "Get this fucking band off," somebody interjects. "What the fuck's going on? ... There's another band waiting to go on. Everbody's been throwing [unintelligible] past these people and all kinds of shit."

"Why don't you get out of here?" the band replies. "I'm telling you to get out of here." Finally, as the musicians are forcibly unplugged, the track ends with somebody saying: "Let's do it right now, motherfucker." Despite the air of confrontation, however, the recording showcases a confident and competent band.

Whether Devo were intentionally seeking to enhance their reputation by engineering their involvement in a confrontation or not is debatable. They may have just been overzealous in their preparation for an expected rejection based on their overall presentation. "When you're that ostracized and disenfranchised in your peer group and in your local culture, you turn unfriendly back," they later explained. "I know we didn't appear to be friendly, but it was self-defense. It was part of our manifesto to separate ourselves out—we were more like aliens making satirical comments on the culture. We took pleasure in being lightning rods for hostility and freaking people out."[25]

As Gorman tells it, Sun Ra never did perform that night, although he did honor his agreement to play his scheduled show at the Smiling Dog the following evening. However, Devo would later insist that, after they had driven the entire audience away, the Arkestra did indeed take the stage—but they were the only people left to witness it. According to Jerry Casale, "only the band and a half-dozen friends from Akron" were present for Sun Ra's "incredible" performance, which supposedly began with a 30-minute song entitled '25 Years To The 21st Century.'[26]

On April 9 1919, the eighth and final Dada soirée took place in Zurich, Switzerland. It was staged at the Saal zur Kaufleuten—the Dadaists having lost their spiritual home when the Cabaret Voltaire closed nearly three years earlier—and was the first since the end of World War I. It was typical of the events staged by the artists' collective in that it encompassed the realms of theater, music, dance, poetry, painting, and performance art. Writer Walter Serner directed a program heavy on spoken word pieces, while Hans Arp and Hans Richter painted a backdrop of "huge black abstracts" that looked like "gigantic cucumbers."

The first of the three planned segments began with a stern and humorless lecture about abstract art by Swedish artist and filmmaker Viking Eggeling, which, as Richter put it, "only disturbed the audience insofar as they wanted to be disturbed but weren't." After that, Rudolf Laban and Suzanne Perrottet danced to compositions by Arnold Schönberg and Erik Satie; Käthe Wulff read poetry by Richard Huelsenbeck and Wassily Kandisky. It wasn't until Tristan Tzara's 'Poème Simultané' that things began to get heated. It called for 20 people to vocalize on top of each other, and according to Richter, "all hell broke loose … this was what the audience, and especially its younger members, had been waiting for. Shouts, whistles, chanting in unison, laughter … all of which mingled more or less anti-harmoniously with the bellowing of the 20 on the platform."[27]

The Dadaists most likely welcomed this as part of the work, having declared the simultaneous poem "a powerful illustration of the fact that an organic work of art has a will of its own."[28] After an intermission, which provided a cooling-off period for the increasingly emboldened spectators, the second segment began with Richter reading his 'Gegen, Ohne, Für Dada' ('Against, Without, For Dada') before resident composer Hans Heusser performed his "tunes or anti-tunes" on piano and Arp his concrete poetry 'Cloud Pump,' prompting a smattering of heated interjections. Then, after more of Perrottet's dancing, Walter Serner solemnly took to the stage in traditional wedding garb carrying a limbless and headless dressmaker's dummy. He then brought out a bouquet of roses, holding them ceremoniously where the mannequin's head should have been, before placing a chair on the center of the stage, facing the audience. Straddling the chair with his back to the crowd, he began to read from his 1918 Dada manifesto *Letze Lockerung*, which translates either to 'Last Loosening' or 'Final Dissolution.'

111

Serner was a late convert to Dada. Born in Bohemia, he earned a law degree in Germany but fled to Switzerland after the outbreak of war and began publishing the avant-garde journal *Sirius*. It was here that he first began to criticize Dada, which he felt lacked rational understanding and offered no clear alternatives to the things it set out to destroy. When he eventually had a change of heart, he became one of the most radical voices of the group, expressing a "profound nihilism that ... annihilated the ground of aesthetic judgment and creation, dismantling convention with irony and obscenity."[29] In *Letze Lockerung*, he asks: "What did the first brain to find itself on this planet do? Presumably it was astonished at being here and hadn't a clue what to make of itself and the filthy vehicle beneath its feet. In the meantime people have come to terms with their brains by regarding them as so unimportant as to be not even worth ignoring."[30]

As Serner read from his pointed invective, the audience became increasingly agitated, hurling insults and then trash at the writer. Serner continued to read until he was chased offstage by a mob swinging pieces of the balustrade torn from the floor. Worked into a frenzy, they smashed the mannequin and chair and stomped on the flowers. "At last!" Richter later noted. "This was just what the audience had been waiting for."[31] Serner had set the bait, and the audience willingly took it.

While the riot was still raging, Hans Richter and some of the other artists went searching for Tzara, Dada's de facto leader, whom they worried may have been hurt during the melee. They finally found him not in the hall but in a restaurant, calmly counting the receipts for the night—the most the Dadaists had earned to that point. Amazingly, the performance continued after the audience members returned to their senses and the third segment ran without incident. There was a performance of the ballet *Noir Kakadu* choreographed by Sophie Taeuber with dancers from the Laban school, and Serner even returned to read more of his work—without incident, this time—

before Tzara closed proceedings with his 'Proclamation Sans Pretension.'

Eight days later, a derisive review entitled 'Eine skandalöse Soirée' appeared in the *Berliner Börsen–Courier*, attributed to an M. Ch., who recommended the Dadaists "confine their manifestos to their numerous magazines ... and not burden the public with them." M. Ch. was, in fact, a pseudonym for none other than Walter Serner.

The parallels were not lost on Gerald Casale, who has since stated that there was "a Dada sensibility on purpose" during the early days of Devo.[32] The similarities do not end with each group inciting a sole riot. The initial catalyst for Dada was the outbreak of World War I, which played out in many of the artists' backyards. Although this unnecessary and costly military action spurred the movement, the attendant loss of faith in political leadership was only the first institution to come under attack. In his 'Lecture on Dada' in 1922, Tristan Tzara looked back on the movement's inception as it was winding down:

"The beginnings of Dada were not the beginnings of an art, but of a disgust. Disgust with the magnificence of philosophers who for 3000 years have been explaining everything to us (what for?), disgust with the pretensions of these artists-God's-representatives-on-earth, disgust with passion and with real pathological wickedness where it was not worth the bother; disgust with a false form of domination and restriction en masse, that accentuates rather than appeases man's instinct of domination, disgust with all the catalogued categories, with the false prophets who are nothing but a front for the interests of money, pride, disease, disgust with the lieutenants of a mercantile art made to order according to a few infantile laws, disgust with the divorce of good and evil, the beautiful and the ugly (for why is it more estimable to be red rather than green, to the left rather than the right, to be large or small?). Disgust finally with the Jesuitical dialectic which can explain everything and fill people's minds with oblique and obtuse ideas without any physiological basis or ethnic roots, all this by means of blinding artifice and ignoble charlatans' promises."[33]

Rather than earnestly rail against the absurdity that they saw around them, the Dadaists chose to embody that absurdity in their work, reflecting it back like a mirror held up to society with a vengeance. The superficial similarities to Devo abound. The Dadaists were obsessed with masks, fashioning them from paper, burlap, board, and twine, while Devo preferred to get theirs from cheap novelty shops. Hugo Ball's famous 'cubist costume,' which he donned at the Cabaret Voltaire to read his nonsense poem 'Elefantenkarawane' ('Elephant Caravan'), included a hat that could have passed for an elongated energy dome, along with the sort of childlike attempt at a shiny robot's shell that would have been perfect for a Devo stage show (except that it most likely would not have been conducive to performance).

The Dadaists—in particular Kurt Schwitters, Hannah Höch, and Raoul Hausmann—embraced the collage techniques recently pioneered by Cubists such as Pablo Picasso and Georges Braque but abandoned all trace of the figurative (guitars and fruit bowls) in favor of abstraction, creating dense, overlapping montages of worthless ephemera such as train tickets, candy wrappers, calendars, newspapers, and maps. Devo would also flirt with collage, but in an aural sense. They would blatantly incorporate the lyrics of a popular fast food restaurant's jingle, and their cover of an iconic 60s classic wouldn't really be a cover at all but an entirely new piece of music with the lyrics to a Rolling Stones song sung over top of it.

"Devo, rather than just showing pictures of itself, just takes snapshots, cut-ups, a piece, a segment, an environment, pulls it out of context," Casale later would note. "Probably a lot like the Dadaists did."[34] They both saw their philosophies as representing universal truths not restricted by any manmade distinctions. Even Tzara's quip to Man Ray and Marcel Duchamp that "Dada belongs to everybody" would be echoed in Booji Boy's proclamation that "we're all Devo."

The Dadaists prided themselves in their overarching contempt for nearly every institution, and this ire seems to have found its way to their audience as well. These lofty goals aside, they also took a gleeful pride in their simple ability to agitate. "Nothing is more delightful than to confuse and upset people," Tzara wrote.[35]

Without specifically name checking them, Mark Mothersbaugh may have also been alluding to the Dada artists when he claimed, whether facetiously or not, that the band had taken "our cues from the Viet Cong and the subversives during World War I and World War II in Europe, as opposed to from the hippies and the punks."[36] They learned early on that "individuality and rebellion were obsolete" and "thought the punks never learned from the failure of the hippies. Rebellion always gets co-opted into another marketing device."[37]

About half a century earlier, one of Dada's leading lights may have foreseen this very situation. "We had a dim premonition," Hans Richter recalled, "that power-mad gangsters would one day use art itself as a way of deadening men's minds."[38]

PART 2
THE BEGINNING WAS THE END (1976–78)

CHAPTER 5
1976

A designer is an emerging synthesis of artist, inventor, mechanic, objective economist and evolutionary strategist.
R. BUCKMINSTER FULLER

By 1976, Devo were beginning to feel that they had exhausted their options. They had fewer than ten shows under their belts, a dearth of venues in which to showcase their music, and had received less than welcoming receptions in those where they had appeared. They had also been sending demos to anyone they thought might listen, but to no avail. One night at around 3:00am, sitting in an all-night diner with his old college friend Chuck Statler, Jerry Casale revealed that they were seriously considering calling it quits. "Not so fast," Statler replied. "Before you split up, let's do a film."[1]

Devo had clearly been interested in documenting their work from the beginning. Part of their 1973 Kent State Creative Arts Festival performance had been captured on grainy black-and-white Portapak video, and most of the audio from the WMMS Halloween show had been recorded as well, suggesting that the band approached their work with an artist's interest in preserving and curating. "From the beginning, on purpose, Devo was a multi-media idea," Casale later noted.[2] It seems only natural, then, that they would be interested in expanding into film. They had already ticked visual art, writing, performance art, and music off the list, and would later claim that their decision to go into music was based entirely on economy. "The equipment was just inexpensive. We couldn't be filmmakers because we couldn't afford the equipment."[3]

Cost aside, Devo would probably have ventured into the medium sooner, had any of them actually known how to make a film. Statler did. He was an Akron native who had stayed close to home to attend Kent State, where he began (but ultimately dropped out of) a BFA in film studies. He met Jerry and Mark in an experimental sculpture class at the university. Since the class was largely self-directed, Statler's work consisted mainly of "boxes with motors in them that just kind of vibrated," while Casale's project was titled *The American Dream* and recreated a summer barbeque indoors, complete with working grill, hot dogs, radio, and artificial grass.[4]

Although Statler appreciated what Devo were doing musically, what was more important was that they shared a common aesthetic. "We had grown up together ... and had a mutual appreciation for everything from John Waters and Russ Meyer to Luis Buñuel," he later recalled.[5] It was appropriate that their taste in film would reach back nearly 50 years from the contemporary 'Pope of Trash' and the 'King of the Nudies' to Buñuel's pioneering surrealism. Soon, in the age of MTV, bands would find themselves paired arbitrarily with a director; Statler and Devo, by contrast, had a shared history.

"One thing about the Devo films and my relationship to Devo is that I'm familiar with the music and I've heard it for years, and there's a whole understanding there, there's the aesthetic similarities and stuff because we came from the same place," Statler continued. Mothersbaugh, for his part, has always been more than willing to give Statler credit for his contributions. "Chuck's role in Devo should not be underrated," he said in 2010. "He was the only one of us who took film classes and actually knew how to put a film together, which obviously was huge for us."[6]

Unlike most music videos, the project was not conceived of as a promotional tool to get exposure for the band. Devo barely even existed at this point—Jim Mothersbaugh had left the band but agreed to return for the film—but saw no contradiction in creating a film for a nonexistent band. In fact, they hoped the film would serve as a substitute for a traditional band. "Devo would be like The Three Stooges," Casale explained. "You'd watch these film shorts that were music-driven with stories. We were going to put out one a year—we didn't even want a record deal."[7] The band realized that people had "always made films to music. Duke Ellington did it. The Beatles did it. It was just that we were already thinking of it as the only way it would be presented."[8]

The means that they would use to achieve this end was the newly developing technology of home video, specifically the Laserdisc format. "I still remember the day Chuck came over, and he had a *Popular Science* magazine with this married couple on the front, all smiley," Mothersbaugh recalled. "They're holding up what looks like an LP. It said: Laserdiscs: Everybody will have them for Christmas."[9] (The article in question was probably the one headlined 'Here at last: VideoDisc players' in the February 1977 issue of the magazine. It claimed that both the RCA SelectaVision and Philips/MCA VideoDisc systems would be on the market by Christmas 1977, but neither arrived. Laserdiscs appeared in one test market, Atlanta, on December 15 1978, and then in Seattle the following February, but only became available nationwide at the end of 1980.)

The band saw far-reaching implications in the announcement of this new media format. It was more than just another medium in which to express themselves; it was nothing less than the arrival of Andy Warhol's brand of multimedia pop art aesthetic in the staid world of rock music. While Warhol made his name in painting, silk screening, and sculpture, he also directed numerous films in wide-ranging genres, 'wrote' several books, and even 'produced' *The Velvet Underground & Nico*, although his role entailed little more than paying for the studio time. His ability to encompass these disparate fields was undoubtedly a factor in his pervasive influence on art and culture in the later 20th century, and it was precisely this straddling of mediums that Devo were aiming to exploit. "This is totally going to change who's making pop art," they reasoned. "It's not going to be some guy sitting over there with a band in a bar, and it's not going to be somebody that's sitting on a hill painting a landscape, it's going to be somebody that works in the pop media of our time. They're going to be doing stuff that goes on television and it's going to be music and pictures together. And that's what we wanted to be. We wanted to be in the new art form."[10]

Once the band had the means, the only remaining obstacle was the prohibitive cost. Statler had been working on commercials for an advertising agency, and fortunately had access to the company's film and editing facilities. The band would only be required to pay for the cost of the film stock. The project would be shot on 16mm film (cheaper than the motion picture grade 35mm, yet a significant step up from the hobbyist 8mm or Super-8). Mothersbaugh had started a small gallery and store the previous year called Unit Services, in which he sold his prints, including many made with rubber stamps, and silkscreened T-shirts. The shop was located in Quaker Square, a little mall in downtown Akron housed in the disused silos of Quaker Oats. Much of the money the shop earned went directly toward paying for the film. The ten-minute movie took four months to complete and required the band to raise $3,000 in funding. It was a homegrown effort in every possible way: supporters lent money, local organizations generously provided locations, and a number of friends and family members made appearances.

The film was titled *In The Beginning Was The End: The Truth About De-Evolution*, a nod to one of the band's key inspirations—Oscar Kiss Maerth's book—while one of the two songs featured was 'Jocko Homo,' inspired by B.H. Shadduck's pamphlet *Jocko-Homo Heavenbound*. The film begins with the band, clad in their coveralls and hardhats, finishing a day's work at the rubber plant (actually a display in Goodyear's World Of Rubber museum, located across the street from the company's headquarters in Akron). Booji Boy—the only remaining character of the five that the band had conceived of the previous year—is the last of the workers to leave, and the only one not wearing a clear plastic mask. They pile into Mark's battered 1967 Chevy Biscayne, take a short drive, and enter a nondescript building, instruments in hand, to perform Johnny Rivers's 1966 song 'Secret Agent Man,' with Bob Mothersbaugh on lead vocals. (The version in the film had been recorded two years earlier in 1974.) The set is now the lower level of JB's in Kent, with the band performing on a small stage with low, dropped ceiling tiles. The back of the stage is lined with huge letters spelling 'D-E-V-O,' fashioned from what look like crudely cut panels of riveted steel, which were actually constructed by Gary Jackett years earlier during the summer Mark and Jerry spent with him in California. The performance is intercut with visual non-sequiturs: men in monkey masks and satin boxer shorts spanking a woman in a bathrobe, and a china doll mask with Ping-Pong paddles emblazoned with the faces of Richard Nixon and Mao Tse-Tung; Chinaman fondling a coat hanger in the shape of a woman's spread legs, complete with red panties; a leather-jacketed Jackett animatedly playing two thrift-store guitars bolted together and plugged into a space heater instead of an amp; Mark wearing a pink and purple balloon-sleeved and butterfly-collared shirt with quilted mustard-colored pants and a mask with a pompadour, slowly gyrating with his redheaded girlfriend Marina, who is dressed in a powder-blue waitress's uniform; and a shaggy-haired man in a monkey mask, wraparound sunglasses, and a fur collar, eating a popsicle. The song ends with Mark in a John F. Kennedy mask and coveralls, waving goodbye to the camera.

Booji Boy is then seen in orange coveralls (more prisoner uniform than factory worker's) rushing past a two-story building with an expansive mural painted on the side. It features the words 'SHINE ON AMERICA' radiating from the Statue of Liberty's torch, as well as a somewhat arbitrary choice of portraits of Benjamin Franklin, Abraham Lincoln, and Chief Joseph. Right above the Indian chief's head are the U.S. Apollo and Soviet Soyuz spacecraft, which happened to dock while the mural was being painted. Booji Boy bounds up the stairs at the back of the building and into the stately office of General Boy, who is sitting alone at the head of a lengthy table wearing a decorated Army uniform, a grey comb-over, and large sideburns. The first character not portrayed by a member of the band, General Boy was in fact played by Mark's father, an amiable salesman who agreed to take on the role after a lawyer friend of the band backed out over concerns that the film would color his reputation. "At first he didn't get the idea," Mark recalled, "but once he saw himself on screen, he totally got the acting bug."[11] The building Booji Boy is seen entering may have been the one that housed Mothersbaugh senior's Great Falls Employment Agency; the set for General Boy's office was none other than the 'President's Room' of a local McDonald's.

Booji Boy dutifully delivers the papers that Chinaman gave him to General Boy. Then, over a simple and repetitive synthesizer figure, General Boy declares: "In the past, this information has been suppressed, but now it can be told. Every man, woman, and mutant on this planet shall know the truth about De-evolution." "Oh Dad," Booji Boy replies. "We're all Devo." A snippet of the band's 'Mechanical Man' plays as the letters 'D-E-V-O' are spelled out in neon ("we were originally going to spell out the name with ketchup and mustard bottles," Statler recalled, "but the neon looked nicer").[12] Mothersbaugh is then seen in white lab coat, tropical shirt, large maroon bowtie, orange dishwashing gloves, and swimming goggles as he sings 'Jocko Homo' to a table of four professionals in surgeons' caps, masks, and 3D glasses. He animatedly gesticulates with his gloved hands, his call of "Are we not men?" answered by a trio of talking heads in wraparound sunglasses and bank robber-style masks: "We are Devo!" During the song's bridge, Mark does a strange backward-leaning, side-to-side dance, which according to the band is the 'poot' that the teachers and critics of the lyrics perform. (Asked years later to describe the poot using no more than three phrases, Bob Lewis replied: "Uh, squatting, loping rondo."[13])

For the second half of the song, the rhythm shifts to a pounding, insistent, almost tribal beat, and we see that Mothersbaugh is, in fact, addressing an entire lecture hall—actually the same Governance Chambers of Kent State that was the setting of the band's 1974 Creative Arts Festival appearance—full of students wearing the same caps, masks, and 3D glasses, pounding the tables and pumping their fists. Atop a conference table in the middle of the room are three writhing, pupa-like figures with their arms and legs constrained in yellow plastic bags, whom Mark would describe as being "like maggots, paramecium, foetal things... . That's the nature of research or birth or discovery. It's pretty disgusting."[14] The end credits run over an electronic version of The Beatles' 'Because' (achieved by running the original song through a ring modulator) and distorted close-up images from television screens, before the tenets of the Devolutionary Oath are flashed onscreen. (When the film was released on video, the unauthorized Beatles song was replaced with random electronic noise.) Finally, an unidentified man unmasks a seated, duct-taped Booji Boy and puts a knife to his chest.

If 'Jocko Homo' was the band's litmus test—a manifesto as much as it was a mere song—then *In The Beginning Was The End* was an "indoctrination to de-evolution. It is self-referential. In other words, it doesn't depend on anything outside of itself to exist. It's logical within itself."[15] It certainly isn't logical to anything outside of itself. Jerry would later describe the overall mood as "a combination of Fritz Lang's *Metropolis* and Ronald McDonald. We teeter between a kind of beehive collective mechanistic thing and Walt Disney."[16] The film's skewed worldview and deadpan nonsensicality predated and helped set the tone for the most significant development in popular music of the next decade.

The modern music video (as differentiated from the audiovisual documentation of live performance) can be traced back to the mid-

60s and The Beatles. A quick and low-budget attempt to capitalize on the band's surprise success, *A Hard Day's Night* (1964) makes sure its thin plotline doesn't detract from showcasing the band's effortless charisma. It may have just become another in a long line of movie vehicles for the current musical fad had it not been for Richard Lester's deft direction. Lester used numerous cutting-edge techniques, including shaky hand-held cameras and frantic cutting, then in vogue via the French new wave. Lester had previously directed comedian Peter Sellers in *The Mouse On The Moon* and the short *The Running, Jumping, And Standing Still Film* (just as Beatles producer George Martin had produced Sellers's album *Songs For Swingin' Sellers*), and his instinct for capturing comedic timing helped translate the band's lighthearted absurdity to celluloid. More importantly, for the medium that he inadvertently helped to create, his song segments stand on their own when removed from the whole of the film. 'Can't Buy Me Love' consists of not much more than the band running and jumping through a field, while a helicopter captures the action from above, but it still manages to convey their endearing giddiness.

The Beatles would eventually make standalone promotional clips, and 'Paperback Writer' and 'Rain' (both 1966) are more serious efforts, with the band playing their instruments in a sculpture garden, doing their best to suppress their smiles. They were both shot by *Ready Steady Go!* director Michael Lindsay-Hogg and stood in for live appearances on *The Ed Sullivan Show* that year. Lindsay-Hogg would also direct the following year's 'Penny Lane' and 'Strawberry Fields Forever,' by which time the Beatles aesthetic had taken some inspiration from surrealist art. In the former, the band are seen riding horses into a field to find an elaborate table setting, and are served by waiters in powdered wigs and brocade coats; in the latter, they play a strange, decrepit upright piano connected to a tree by additional courses of strings (standing in for the song's signature Mellotron). The surrealist influence suited The Beatles and other psychedelic bands of the era (many of whom were former art school students) well as it provided a context for delivering quasi-meaningful—or meaningless—imagery without qualification.

The equal and opposite reaction to this seemingly aimless yet amiable goofing around came from a relative stranger to such concepts: Bob Dylan. His 'Subterranean Homesick Blues' clip from 1967 shows him standing, unsmiling, in a New York City alley, holding a stack of oversize cards on which snippets of the song's lyrics are handwritten (often intentionally misspelled or presented as puns). Instead of lip-synching to the song, Dylan nonchalantly reveals and then tosses the cards in time to the music. It was an iconic piece of film—one that has since been mimicked countless times—but what many did not realize was that it was part of a full-length film, D.A. Pennebaker's fly-on-the-wall documentary about Dylan's 1965 UK tour, *Dont Look Back*. As Devo and others were soon to find out, innovative song segments that formed part of theatrical releases—or were stand-ins for an in-demand band unable to fulfill grueling touring schedules—were not the same as music videos, which made no money on their own.

Flying in the face of this conventional wisdom was Captain Beefheart, who directed a mock-commercial for one of his least commercial albums, 1970's *Lick My Decals Off, Baby*. The 90-second black-and-white spot wasn't exactly a music video, as the audio of 'Woe-Is-Uh-Me-Bop' stops every time Beefheart's disembodied hand flicks a cigarette against a wall. Between this repeated motif, an announcer introduces each of the Magic Band members by their assumed names, until the solitary figure of Beefheart appears on a spot-lit stage and, with our full attention, performs what he called his "hand and toe investment" (simply extending his right foot forward on his heel and pointing his outstretched right hand downward). In silence, and clad in black hoods and white gloves, the band-members cross the screen holding kitchen utensils, including an eggbeater and flour-sifter. Finally, Beefheart spills a bowl of batter on the centerline of a street with his foot. The clip ends with a zoom out of the album cover, with the announcer trying to find the appropriate tone for the words "New on Reprise, it's *Lick My Decals Off, Baby*." Not only are the visual non-sequiturs jarring, but so is the fact that nearly a quarter of the entire sequence is completely silent.

The commercial aired on public access television in Beefheart's home of Los Angeles but was rejected by the city's KTTV (despite having been scheduled to air during such programs as Sunday night's *Creature Features*, LA's equivalent to Ghoulardi's *Shock Theater*). Charles Young, the channel's station manager, was quick to defend his decision. "I just don't like it," he said. "I think it's crude and don't want it on my air." When pressed for a specific reason, Young declared the album's title to be "obscene."[17] After KTTV parent company Metromedia refused to air the ad on any of its stations nationwide, Warner/Reprise Records approached the National Association of Broadcasters (NAB) to lobby on its behalf. The NAB sided with Metromedia, however, and cited the General Program Standards section of the NAB's Code Authority (which, until the mid 80s, had to approve each and every television commercial before it aired): "Program materials should enlarge the horizons of the viewer, provide him with wholesome entertainment, afford helpful stimulation, and remind him of the responsibilities which the citizen has toward his society."[18] Warner/Reprise tried to salvage the situation by organizing a party for representatives of radio and press to view the banned commercial on the eve of Beefheart's tour, but the clip remained largely unseen at the time of its release.

By the mid 70s, there were at best a handful of bands—each working in relative obscurity—that were also inclined toward filmmaking. Devo aside, the most notable was The Residents. Although they have never revealed their identities, it is commonly accepted that they originally hailed from Shreveport, Louisiana, before they set out for San Francisco sometime in the late 60s. The story also claims that they were only 20 miles shy of completing their 2,000-mile journey when their car broke down in San Mateo,

California, where they decided to stay and move in above a car body shop. It was here—fittingly, just outside but looking in at a major music hub—that they began obsessively recording themselves on some of the first available consumer four-track and eight-track machines. The totality of this unreleased material is more than many bands ever produced in their entire careers, with the (supposed) titles of these albums including *Rusty Coathangers For The Doctor*, *The Ballad Of Stuffed Trigger*, and *Baby Sex* (the cover of which would surely get the band arrested today). Throughout this period they never played live, never considered themselves a proper band, and did not even have a name to attach to their work. In fact, band 'spokesman' Hardy Fox was reluctant to even characterize them as musicians, describing them instead as "a group of people who work together based on shared ideas rather than their craft with a musical instrument."[19] Even their self-proclaimed influences were nearly interchangeable with Devo's. The band's other vocal 'spokesman,' Homer Flynn, later revealed: "Captain Beefheart was an early influence. It was obvious to them that he was taking John Coltrane and Howlin' Wolf and twisting them around in a wonderfully unique and interesting way."[20]

They also drew inspiration from film music. "The last hero was Ennio Morricone, the Italian soundtrack guy. We still dig up some of his old things like *When Women Wore Tails*" (presumably meaning either *When Women Had Tails* or *When Women Lost Their Tails*).[21] It was more common, however, for inspiration to come from the realm of visual art. "They don't pay much attention to other people that are working in music," Flynn said. "They like television and movies a lot. They seem to take more ... escapist pleasure of visual artists. They like comic books, too."[22]

The biggest influence on The Residents appears to be the entire period in which their formation occurred. "It all seems to go back to the psychedelic era to some extent," Flynn explained, "which was very influential on The Residents." By the time the group began releasing their material, however, the climate had changed. "They felt things were progressing and changing, and all of a sudden it stopped. The Residents wanted to continue that feel of progress and change."[23] It was only when they sent a demo to Warner Bros Records—home of Captain Beefheart—that they found a name. The tape was sent back addressed to 'The Residents,' since no band name had been listed. These early recordings exhibit a healthy disrespect for copyrights (*Baby Sex*'s 'We Stole This Riff' lifts its jazzy chords directly from Tim Buckley's 'Down By The Borderline,' and even includes the lyrics "We stole this riff / From Tim Buckley") and a puerile view of sex ('Stuffed Genital' and 'Every Day I Masturbate On A Merican Fag,' both of which are on what came to be known as *The Warner Bros Album*). Sometimes both traits would be exhibited in the same song: 'Wholelottadick' is a rewrite of Led Zeppelin's 'Whole Lotta Love.'

In 1972, The Residents finally made it to San Francisco and began work on a feature film, to be entitled *Vileness Fats*. The plot revolved around Arf and Omega Berry, Siamese twin wrestlers hired to protect the village of Vileness Flats from a gang of marauding midgets, while also taking in plane crashes, volcanoes, memory loss, and an immortal Indian princess by the name of Weescoosa, who "spends eternity rescuing short people from life-threatening situations."[24] The aim, it seems, was to create both "The Underground Movie of All Time" and "Modern Home Entertainment."[25] The ambitious film was shot entirely on a makeshift soundstage constructed in The Residents' apartment in San Francisco's Mission District. The sets owed a large debt to German Expressionism and were constructed out of cardboard with a distinct lack of right angles, and since the working space was limited they made the pragmatic decision to have many of the characters be midgets (their stout costumes, designed for actors to crouch and waddle around in, only increasing the film's surrealistic quality).

After four years of shooting on evenings and weekends around their day jobs, and having accumulated fourteen hours of footage, The Residents abandoned the project. When they eventually released

30 minutes of footage as *Whatever Happened To Vileness Fats?* in 1984, they claimed that its failure "came not from its own inherent conflict, but, ironically, from that quality most admired by its creators— naïveté."[26] That naïveté was practical as well as artistic. Always early adopters of new technology, the band had sensed that video would be the next important medium, and as such had shot *Vileness Fats* on half-inch black-and-white tape—rendered obsolete in the mid 70s first by Betamax and then by VHS.

Before work on the film was halted, The Residents began issuing music on their own Ralph Records. Their interest in re-appropriating popular culture was evident from the start. Their 1974 debut album was titled *Meet The Residents*, its cover parodying that of *Meet The Beatles!* The follow-up, *Third Reich 'n Roll* (1976) features a cover image of Dick Clark dressed as Adolf Hitler, while the musical content consists of two sidelong pastiches of songs from the 60s, including 'Land Of A Thousand Dances' and 'In-A-Gadda-Da-Vida,' that Fox would later describe as "a terrorist attack on 60s rock."[27]

The Residents would quickly outgrow this phase, with Fox later declaring parody "uninteresting and boring."[28] Several thousand miles away in Ohio, Jerry Casale came to the same conclusion. "I remember being a teen listening to [The Mothers of Invention's] *Freak Out!*" he recalled. "I just liked it—I liked what was coming in. But as time went on I guess I thought Zappa was parody, and I really don't like parody beyond a point 'cos it doesn't do anything but breed itself, and it's actually too easy. I guess what I liked was surrealism, and a kind of nonlinear kind of absurdity."[29]

The Residents' output continued at a staggering pace as their albums grew ever more conceptual, culminating in *Eskimo* (1979), an elongated tone poem of life at the North Pole. Icy synths mix with ritualistic drums and eerie chanting, topped with sounds of water and wind. The album's glacial pace and sparseness of sound stand in stark contrast to the band's previous work. Written accounts of Eskimo life are included in the liner notes and were intended to be read while listening (preferably with headphones). Just how much of this ethnomusicography was based on actual research was never clear—which, of course, made it fit in perfectly with the Residents' overall aesthetic (various pop-culture phrases are hidden in the Eskimo chants, including "Coca-Cola Adds Life.")

The Residents subscribed to the Theory of Obscurity, credited to the—possibly fictional—Bavarian composer N. Senada. According to the band's 'representative,' Jay Clem, the main premise was that "the artist is doing what he's doing for himself primarily and with a minimum amount of input and/or feedback from the outside." This process led the band to record songs as if they would never be released. Some eventually were, as in the case of *Not Available*, recorded in 1974 but not released until 1978, by which time the band had supposedly forgotten about its existence.

Eskimo is "respectfully dedicated to N. Senada, who started the whole thing."[30] The album's artwork marked the debut of the band's iconic tuxedos and top hats with giant eyeball masks, in which they are elegantly posed among stylized icebergs and northern lights. Until then they had used a number of different matching costumes, including Ku Klux Klan-like outfits made out of newspaper, full-body mummy bandages, and HAZMAT suits, never revealing their faces or identities. "This is sort of an extension of the Theory of Obscurity put into practical use," Clem told a TV news reporter. "They have the idea that by remaining anonymous they remain less subjected to immediate feedback from other people who might influence what they do."

Although they had abandoned the *Vileness Fats* project, The Residents continued to indulge their interest in video. They produced a promo clip for the 'Land Of 1,000 Dances' segment from *Third Reich 'n Roll*, which has them in costumes made entirely out of newspaper that (inadvertently) resemble KKK robes animatedly bouncing around in a room covered in newspaper while playing newspaper covered percussion instruments (shot in black-and-white of course). The song degenerates into a cacophony of free jazz horns and machine gun fire as a tinfoil-covered gunman enters and mows down the players.

By late 1976, Devo had resumed playing live after taking nearly a year off to shoot their film and revamp their line-up. Jim Mothersbaugh had left the band, taking the unpredictability of his electronic drums with him. The decision wasn't entirely one of practicality, but also a conscious effort to gain some traction in more conventional rock circles. "I got so involved with the electronics then that we felt it was necessary to go back and have some real-sounding drums for the first albums," he said. "We wanted to fit, to some degree, in the rock'n'roll vein."[31] Just as another former member, Bob Lewis, continued to work with the band in a managerial capacity, Jim would maintain his ties with the others and provide technical support for the remainder of the decade. He would continue to work with the band behind the scenes, and toured with them until 1979, when he accepted a position as the chief technician at the American office of the electronic instrument company Roland.

In accordance with Devo's twisted logic, Jim's job was not always to fix things. In addition to customizing most of the band's gear, some of their synthesizers had been unintentionally modified. As long as their broken equipment produced useful sounds, Jim was in charge of making it stay that way. "He'd be like: don't let the ARP ever get fixed, because that's the only way I can get that one sound for 'Pink Pussycat,'" Mark recalled. As it was, "when you touched the keyboard, it would play two notes at the same time, which would go 'brr!' in opposite directions."[32]

Jim's replacement was Alan Myers, an experienced and knowledgeable drummer who had logged time indulging his passion for avant-garde jazz but who was practical enough to take on other gigs, too, including playing in a rock covers band with Bob Mothersbaugh. His timing was impeccable, and he was clearly comfortable with odd meters. He earned the nickname 'The Human Metronome' due to his uncanny ability to keep perfect pace in any time signature. Jerry Casale attributes this intense concentration to Myers's habit of routinely disappearing into the bathroom to do Tai Chi before each performance. Myers's only problem was he was just a little too proficient—or, as Mark put it, "too musical." Devo solved this problem by placing limitations on him. Initially, the new recruit was prohibited from using any cymbals at all, and his tom-toms would be draped with towels, rendering them useless. They even went as far as taping one of his hands behind his back to simplify his playing style. "We were taking it down to basics," Mark recalled, "especially with the drums. We wanted it to be very simple. We wanted to be the Lego-toy version of a rock band."[33]

Myers's arrival coincided with the return of Bob Casale. The younger Casale had the distinction of playing Devo's first two shows, at the 1973 and 1974 Kent State Creative Arts Festivals, but he soon chose married life over a life of music when he wed his high school girlfriend at the age of 21. Bob Casale (henceforth known as Bob #2) would play not only rhythm guitar but also the occasional synthesizer part, so that the band could "let Mark loose for the rapidly increasing bouts of crowd confrontation," as Jerry put it.[34] Bob Mothersbaugh (now dubbed Bob #1) remained on lead guitar, and for the first time since Devo's debut performance, the balance of Casales to Mothersbaughs was equal.

The addition of Myers and Bob #2 also conveniently offset any claims of Devo being an art school band (which, as the journalist Mary Harron would subsequently note, in an article about the British band Gang Of Four, was "not a correct thing to be").[35] At the time this five-piece version of Devo assembled, however, Bob Casale "was a lab technician by profession," Bob Mothersbaugh "delivers meat," and Alan Myers "puts up aluminum siding."[36]

Myers wasn't the only member in the unusual position—at least in rock-music terms—of having his abilities outpace his musical aims.

Mark, too, was a "schooled musician," as Jerry put it. "He was almost too full of clichés, if he didn't watch it, because he could play everything."[37] This once-tentative art project was in danger of turning into a formidable band—albeit of the wrong kind. So, before they settled into any bad habits, they decided some self-imposed restrictions were in order.

"We had rules," Jerry explained. "You weren't allowed to make a chord change unless you absolutely had to. We didn't want to follow 'song structure' and make a change because it was the traditional time to make a change. The drums had to sound like a caveman with one club could do the part. Nobody was allowed to play power chords. The whole idea was absolute minimalism, play the least notes you can get away with and try to never play at the same time as someone else. All the parts had to fit in between each other and be polyrhythmic." The band also realized that none of this would have been possible without the proper foundation. "It's all these parts that are offbeat to the next guy, but all over, a drum beat that keeps it normal."[38]

If this strict set of rules sounds more like something from an art manifesto, there's a good reason for that. Jerry and Mark had already formulated a guiding theory and liberally applied it to other mediums. "We said: what would this art that we'd been doing that we called de-evolution ... what would happen if there was music and there was Devo music—what would that be like?" Jerry recalled.[39] Having a discourse about the music that you were playing would be anathema to many, but to Devo it was an integral part of their process. "A lot of bands [are] distrustful of that, and they feel like the only way for what they really feel to come out is to be nonverbal about it," Mark noted, citing the example of the Ramones. "They were one of the best bands ever in the world, and I know that they would definitely back down from any kind of claims of any intellectual overtones to what they were doing. Yet they were one of the smartest bands ever. With Devo, we did talk about things ... . We were trying to figure out what we thought was going on."[40]

It was also around this time that Devo serendipitously discovered their trademark yellow suits. From the outset, Mark recalled, they had sought out "the most anti-rock'n'roll outfits" they could find. At the time, Jerry was working as a graphic designer for a janitorial supply company, while Mark was living in and acting as a maintenance man for an apartment building that his entrepreneurial father owned. Coincidentally, they both had their reasons to peruse janitorial supply catalogues. And it was in one of these catalogues that they stumbled across the hazardous waste cleanup outfits. "They were these two-piece, plastic-coated paper outfits," Mark recalled, "and we adopted them as our own. We figured that kind of described our jobs in life: we didn't think of ourselves as musicians, certainly not as rock'n'rollers, we thought of ourselves as musical reporters, reporting the good news in devolution."[41] The suits were designed to keep hazardous material away from the body, and had unintended consequences when wearing them playing live. "They don't breathe at all," Jerry recalled. "It is like a piece of Swiss cheese melting on a burger. When we were doing like 50-city tours in those, we would be so trim at the end of the tour. It was like kind of a weight-loss program."[42]

If Devo were making conscious efforts to more toward a slightly more conventional rock sound, they were not willing to do the same with their look. As General Boy explains in *The Men Who Make The Music*: "Artists and performers are usually good-looking guys and gals who couldn't hold a real job. Entertainment is sometimes the excuse by which these people perpetuate their selfish hoax. I ask all of you to help join Devo's efforts to correct this situation from the inside out."[43] This simple act of rejecting the prevailing image of the rock star as a symbol of individuality and virility—then arguably at the height of its popularity—was itself revolutionary. And it spoke volumes before the band had even played a note.

It was around this time that, in a seminal article for *New York Magazine*, Tom Wolfe coined the phrase "The 'Me' Decade" as he described how the hippie idealism of the 60s had given way to the flaccid, dopey new-ageism of the 70s. Having already abandoned their hippie ideals as ineffective and wrongheaded, Devo now watched them dilute further as they spread deeper into the national consciousness. By the time these ideals had fully permeated American society, it was no longer about changing the world but changing oneself. An irate sense of social injustice had devolved into self-absorbed navel-gazing.

"They plunged straight toward what has become the alchemical dream of the Me Decade," Wolfe writes. "The old alchemical dream was changing base metals into gold. The new alchemical dream is: changing one's personality—remaking, remodeling, elevating, and polishing one's very *self* ... and observing, studying, and doting on it. (Me!)" Wolfe also noted how this pursuit had recently extended further down the socioeconomic ladder than was usual. "This had always been an aristocratic luxury, confined throughout most of history to the life of the courts, since only the very wealthiest classes had the free time and the surplus income to dwell upon this sweetest and vainest of pastimes. It smacked so much of vanity, in fact, that the noble folk involved in it always took care to call it quite something else. By the mid 1960s, this service, this luxury, had become available for one and all, i.e. the middle classes. Lemon Session Central was the Esalen Institute, a lodge perched on a cliff over-looking the Pacific in Big Sur, California. Esalen's specialty was lube jobs for the personality."[44]

Wolfe traced this phenomenon back to the wartime spending of the 40s, which coincided with the Baby Boom, and alongside which came visions of how the working class could be transformed, beginning with housing. German modernism had arrived in America when the Bauhaus architects Walter Gropius and Ludwig Miës van der Rohe fled Nazi Germany in the 30s. Their austere style maintained

135

that form and function were one and the same, and they stressed utility over ornamentation. Gropius ultimately believed in a 'total art' that would encompass not only painting and sculpture but also architecture. "There is no essential difference between the artist and the craftsman," he writes in *Bauhaus Manifesto And Program.* "The artist is an exalted craftsman." This no-nonsense approach to architecture was then disseminated through Ivy League adherents, who tried to apply it in America. "I can remember what brave plans visionary architects at Yale and Harvard still had for *the common man* in the early 1950s," Wolfe continues. "They had brought the utopian socialist dream forward into the 20th century. They had things figured out for the workingman down to truly minute details such as lamp switches. ... All Yale and Harvard architects worshipped Bauhaus principles and had the Bauhaus vision of Worker Housing. ... It would be cleansed of all doilies, knickknacks, mantelpieces, headboards, and radiator covers. Radiator coils would be left bare as honest, abstract sculptural objects." But the American working classes were not interested. "Somehow the workers, incurable slobs that they were, avoided Worker Housing, better known as 'the projects,' as if it had a smell. They were heading out instead to the suburbs—the *suburbs!*"

Devo seemed to be swimming against the tide once again as they embraced the rejected visions of Bauhaus austerity. "We wanted to look like parts of a machine onstage," Mark recalled. "We were more influenced by agit-prop from Germany and Europe in the late 20s and 30s and Bauhaus, geometric shapes and the Italian Futurists and the Russian Suprematists. We were interested in pure art. And the yellow suits always felt to us like we were art."[45] While reclaiming their working-class roots, Devo also aimed their criticism at the same suburban refugees Wolfe wrote about. In the song 'Smart Patrol,' which was first performed live in 1975, they sing: "We're the smart patrol / Nowhere to go / Suburban robots that monitor reality / Common stock / We work around the clock / We shove the poles in the holes." The song had originally been called 'Smart Proletarian,' with which they reclaimed a term Wolfe felt had become passé in the 'Me' Decade (until they found it was too hard to sing and went with 'patrol' instead). "In America," Wolfe writes, "truck drivers, mechanics, factory workers, policemen, firemen, and garbage-men make so much money—$15,000 to $20,000 (or more) per year is not uncommon— that the word *proletarian* can no longer be used in this country with a straight face. So one now says *lower middle class*. One can't even call workingmen *blue collar* any longer. They all have on collars like Joe Namath's or Johnny Bench's or Walt Frazier's."[46]

Devo were not unaware of Wolfe's indictment. "They call us fascists because we represent something scary to them," Mark told *Rolling Stone*. "It's like all these 'Me Generation' people, whose politics are: I want to take as many drugs and consume as much energy and own two condos and big recreational vehicles and take up as much space for myself as I can. They don't want to be concerned about how they relate to other people on the planet and their responsibilities to other people on the planet. Those kinds of people are upset by Devo politics. Because if there's a politic behind what we do, it's people being aware of their responsibility to other people."[47]

The band would take this ethos one step further by referring to themselves first as the verboten proletariat and then as something rather more common and mundane. "We'd look at pictures of John Kennedy's family and all these clans with dynasties, and we'd go, well, these are asparagus people and we're more potato people," Mark recalled. "The asparagus is tall and beautiful and dignified, and potatoes were kind of dirty and asymmetric. They're rough and they grew underground, but they had eyes all around, so they saw everything that was going on." This peculiar terminology would serve either to heighten the mystique surrounding the band or make them seem exclusionist, depending on one's point of view. "We came up with our own vocabulary, and 'spud' was one of the words. 'Spud' was kind of like 'comrade'—it was interchangeable with comrade, but it could also be used pejoratively ... 'that's a good spud,' or ... 'that stupid spud.'"[48]

One of the first rock clubs that Devo would play, in their transformation from art project to proper band, was the Crypt, a basement bar located a few blocks from the Goodyear plant on the far edge of downtown Akron. It had previously been a run-of-the-mill blue-collar watering hole, until in the fall of 1976, a couple of enterprising local musicians, Ward Welch and Elmer Brandt, approached the owner about booking live music a couple of nights a week. Akron, like most cities in the mid-70s, had a distinct lack of venues to showcase original music, and even a rundown rubber-worker bar with a small stage would be better than nothing.

To Welch and Brandt's surprise, the bar's owner was more interested in retiring to Florida than continuing to have anything more to do with the bar, and the musicians took over the lease. By now, the duo had reinvented themselves as Rod Bent and Buzz Clic, singer and guitarist in a hard-rock covers band named King Cobra, and had already made the acquaintance of Mark Mothersbaugh, who happened to live next door to Welch. Mark was soon doing live sound for King Cobra, and while manning the desk he would also bring along his Minimoog and set it up at the back of the venue. When King Cobra played The Tubes' 'White Punks On Dope,' Mark would contribute the synthesizer parts.

Welch had previously invited Devo to play a pre-Crypt gig with King Cobra, but despite their friendship it was not a well-matched bill. "They put the playpen together where Booji Boy would sit with the baby mask," he recalled. "They did the whole shtick there, and the clientele in this bar was completely shocked. They were like: what the hell is this? They were screaming out [for] 'Freebird' and 'Stairway To Heaven,' and they weren't too impressed."[49]

The Crypt, on the other hand, became somewhere to seek out

challenging music, rather than somewhere for it to be thrust upon unsuspecting audiences. Devo played there regularly in late 1976 and early 1977, during which time the venue became something of a second home. Devo's nascent fan base didn't exactly fit the mold of the rowdy rock fan, however, with Robert Christgau of *The Village Voice* noting that the band's "arty crowd ... used to bring their own orange juice and stay all night."[50]

The Crypt was somewhere Devo could freely experiment with visual concepts as well as musical ideas—often with unexpected results. "Somebody in the band found these giant safety pins, like the kind girls wore on their plaid skirts," Bob Mothersbaugh recalled of one particular show. "We thought we could use 'em with towels and look like we were wearing diapers onstage. We went out and played two songs and the novelty wore off, and we had to stand up there with these stupid diapers on for another hour and a half in front of all 30 of our friends."[51]

Word of similar goings-on eight hours away in New York had probably filtered down to Akron, even if the music itself hadn't. "I'm sort of correcting people all the time," Welch later explained. "They don't realize no one ever heard the Ramones on the radio. They were more in the news than on the radio."[52] Instead, what King Cobra took from their New York peers was the idea of making a scene. "We had four bands," Welch recalled (the others being The Dead Boys, The Bizarros, and Devo). "We figured: OK we got enough to do an original CBGB's kind of thing here."[53]

The Dead Boys hailed from Cleveland, but were regularly enticed down to Akron by King Cobra before their permanent relocation to New York. They tried to pick up where Iggy & The Stooges had left off, with singer Stiv Bators—who later claimed to have been the fan who handed Iggy a jar of peanut butter, which Iggy proceeded to smear all over himself, at a concert in Cincinnati in 1970—even copping the Stooge's move of slashing himself up onstage. Some saw this as a cheap ploy, notably Lester Bangs, who compared the singer's behavior to that of "every male jerk in any fledgling band circa 1973 who smeared makeup all over his face, [thinking] it'll make them stars." (He did however concede that lead guitarist Cheetah Chrome "is at least as thuggish as Sid Vicious.")[54]

The first time Devo and The Dead Boys played together (with the Cleveland band headlining and King Cobra also on the bill) was rather uneventful. "Ward had told us to catch Devo, because he thought they were pretty good, very different," Chrome later recalled. "He told us they showed films and used props, and were a bunch of [former] Kent State students with a pretty good following." The guitarist was unmoved by this first exposure to the band, however. "They weren't using synthesizers, and [they] were a lot sloppier than they would be later. The little following immediately started dancing by sort of hopping, like bunny rabbits. Not pogoing—hopping. It looked strange, and a little cultish. We stayed and watched their set, and I had to admit that I just didn't get it. But these people loved them."[55]

It was the bands' second show together, on New Year's Eve 1976, that would become part of Devo mythology. In the liner notes to *Devo Live: The Mongoloid Years*, which contains four tracks recorded at the Crypt that month, Jerry Casale writes: "Our new precision-machine rock sound polarizes the audience into Pros & Cons. The crowd at the Crypt proves no exception. Dead Boys fans start altercations with Devo fans. We manage to keep grinning and picking, having just started to thrive on such hostility." About the only thing the varying accounts of the evening agree on is the song Devo were playing when the fracas ensued. "As we build toward the now-infamous finale of 'Jocko Homo,' things get ugly. Dead Boys guitarist Cheetah Chrome demonstrates the meaning of our maxim 'if the spud fits, wear it' by starting a fight when Mark approaches him during the 'Are we not men?' call and response. More Dead Boys join the action for two-minutes of classic unadulterated punk chaos."[56]

Welch corroborated Casale's version of the story, describing how, during Mothersbaugh's repeated "Are we not men?" refrain, Chrome asked: "Are you calling me a monkey?" Casale then responded in kind. "Jerry sort of put down his bass and came over to assist Mark," Welch recalled, "and then all the Dead Boys came over, and it was like a hockey rink for about five minutes there. And then we had to break them all up. It was pretty funny," he said, adding: "I think it was all theatrics."[57]

For his part, Chrome claimed that the incident was spurred not by a recognition of his place in Devo's theory of de-evolution but by cheap Thunderbird wine and a dare from a friend. It all started innocently enough, with Chrome and a Dead Boys roadie by the name of Fuji dancing to Devo's set. "They all laughed and watched us as we hopped up and down and clowned around, just being stupid and having fun. Then Devo went into 'Jocko Homo,' the long version, which at the time sounded horrible. Mark Mothersbaugh came out in his Booji Boy mask and jockey shorts, jumping around and making the crowd go even crazier. It was fun—we were even enjoying making asses of ourselves… . Then Fuji yelled in my ear: I dare you to pants him!"

Sensing his opening, Chrome yanked down Mark's shorts around his ankles and was promptly set upon by Devo's dedicated if not exactly tough fans. "The next thing I knew, we were being kicked and punched by the entire bunch of bunny-hopping nerds, who had suddenly turned into vicious, killer wolverines in a split second. They weren't really landing any good punches or kicks, but they were clobbering us with little wussie ones. We looked at each other and I yelled: Down! We both dropped to our knees and began crawling toward the bar, getting kicked a couple of times, but making a good escape."

In Chrome's view, there was never any ill will between the two bands, and the entire incident was nothing more than a drunken prank. "We ended up getting along with the Devo guys quite well; all the stories of a feud between us are bullshit. They grew on me over time and I finally had to agree with Ward that they actually had commercial potential. When they played CBGB for the first time, we promoted the show like it was our own, telling everyone we knew that they had to see this band."[58]

King Cobra would eventually ditch most of their hard rock covers in favor of original material, developing a leaner sound and changing their name (at the suggestion of Bators) to The Rubber City Rebels, with Ward Welch/Rod Bent rechristening himself Rod Firestone. The Crypt would stay open until November 1977, when The Rubber City Rebels moved to Los Angeles to pursue a major-label deal. Meanwhile, Devo would use their confrontation with The Dead Boys to their advantage, aligning themselves with a nascent musical movement while still standing apart from it.

"Exaggerated reports of the incident spread fast, causing Devo to be linked to the US punk music scene," Casale later wrote. "Commercially, it would turn out to be another case of the right thing for the wrong reasons."[59]

CHAPTER 6
JANUARY–JUNE
1977

*Like Henry Ford said about technology—there is nothing to be learned
from history anymore. We're in science fiction now. All the revolutions
and the old methods for changing consciousness are bankrupt.*
ALLEN GINSBERG

On March 12 1977, Devo unveiled *In The Beginning Was The End: The
Truth About De-Evolution* at the Akron Art Institute on East Market
Street, a few blocks from the university. The film was screened in the
basement and was followed by a performance from the band. The
choice of venue was strictly pragmatic, as Mark Mothersbaugh
recalled: "There was nowhere to show it because there was no such
thing as MTV."[1] Retreating from rock clubs for the night, the band
had returned to the more comfortable surroundings of their art-
oriented roots.

The screening was part of a program called *Concept*, which also
featured poet Alex Gildzen and painter Ed Mieczkowski and was
described as "an afternoon of music, discussion, and improvisation
devoted to the ideas and concepts of contemporary arts."
Mieczkowski was a Cleveland-based artist while Gildzen was a Kent
State graduate who went on to work in its University News Service.
Gildzen was on the Commons on May 4 1970, and later that year
wrote a poem entitled 'Allison' about Allison Krause. The newspaper
listing for the show carried a photograph of "DEVO, (the de-evolution
band)" smiling and waving, dressed in their coveralls and hardhats.

143

The day of the screening also marked the release of the band's first single. The fact that they didn't really understand the machinations of the record business hadn't stopped them. "We had no idea what a record company was or how it worked," Mark said. "We had no idea of what a recording studio would really be like … it all seemed so fantastic and confusing and beyond our reach for sure." Adopting a timely DIY spirit, the band recorded themselves on a four-track in a garage before locating a pressing plant, Queen City Records in Cincinnati, to transfer the recordings to vinyl. Queen City was known for pressing up records by local rhythm & blues acts, as well as such oddities as the *Christmas Wishes* album issued by the restaurant chain Eat 'n Park and an LP by four doctors called *The Fabulous Four Skins Sing Songs Of Medicine And Med School.*

As with the film stock used for *In The Beginning Was The End*, the manufacture of Devo's first single was funded by profits from Mark's Unit Services store. 'Jocko Homo' / 'Mongoloid' was the inaugural release on Booji Boy Records, and came packaged in a three-panel foldout sleeve designed by the band. The front cover shows a motley-looking four-piece Devo onstage, with Mark dressed in gym shorts and a tank top emblazoned with the word 'DEVOTED.' Jerry Casale and Bob Mothersbaugh are dressed similarly, but with the addition of the wraparound sunglasses and pantyhose they wore in the film. Jim Mothersbaugh sits to the left, behind his drums, calmly looking on. Instead of the band's name, the word 'DE-EVOLUTION' is superimposed over a symmetrically interrupted sinusoidal map of the earth in a font that would be more appropriate on a piece of lab equipment. The back cover has Booji Boy in a work shirt and a pair of novelty glasses made from oversize dice. The inside panel includes a progressive color bar of the sort printers would use for quality control in the top right corner, while there's a UPC barcode—still something of a novelty in 1977—on the bottom left hand corner of the back cover. "They're going to be on everything anyway, so rather than resist it, we used it as a design principle," Mark said. "It was from a tampon box, so if anyone ever tries to re-order the record using that identification line, they're in for a surprise."[2] The inside panels include lyrics and an introduction—"it's d•e•v•o.. from o•h•i•o!"— as well as images of goggles, snorkel, flippers, and the box that the Swim King 3-Piece Swim Set came packaged in. The box has been modified, however, with the word 'DEVO' and Japanese text cut-and-pasted onto it. The images are set over a repeated rubber-stamped background of a pair of dice and a fat Chinese man running with his braid trailing behind him.

By self-releasing their first record, Devo had unwittingly aligned themselves with the punk-rock scene, which would place a premium on the DIY ethic. Patti Smith had released her debut single three years earlier. 'Hey Joe' / 'Piss Factory' was the sole release on Mer Records, funded by her friend, photographer Robert Mapplethorpe. In 1975, Television's 'Little Johnny Jewel, Part One' / 'Little Johnny Jewel, Part Two' became the first offering on their manager Terry Ork's Ork Records, and Pere Ubu established their own Hearthan Records with the release of '30 Seconds Over Tokyo' / 'Heart Of Darkness.'

The A-side of Devo's single was a re-recording of Mark's 'Jocko Homo,' which while decidedly cleaner than the version that appears in *The Truth About De-Evolution* is still somewhat sterile. "It would seem fairly obvious what the production was," Casale later noted, acknowledging these shortcomings. "It was a combination of our degree of organization and the amount of money we had with what was available. So it represented really a random point in time."[3] It's also slightly faster than the version in the film, and while the drums remain muffled the hi-hat is much more prominent. The song begins in an odd 7/8 signature before shifting midway through to standard 4/4 time. Shortly after the time switch comes a new verse based around a joke that would be familiar to all children from the Buckeye State: "What's round on the ends, high in the middle? / O-Hi-O!" It's followed by a rousing, march-like bridge—"God made man / But he used a monkey to do it . . ."—before the song returns to 4/4.

The flipside, a relatively new Casale composition entitled 'Mongoloid,' is musically much more straightforward, almost predating post-punk with its stark, driving bassline. (The fact that the two sides were split between the two songwriters was most likely not a coincidence.) The mid-tempo 4/4 bass is soon joined by tribal drums and slashing guitar. Jerry would later describe the time signature as "a football half-time drumbeat, because what is like more Devo, more potentially unholy, than cheerleaders and marching bands at a football game, which always encourage some kind of group experience?"[4] The lyrics dealt with a mongoloid who was "happier than you and me," and who had a day job and "brought home the bacon / So that no one knew." The term 'mongoloid' had once been used by anthropologists to describe various Central and East Asian populations, and along with Caucasoid and Negroid was one of the proposed three major races of humankind. The term had since fallen out of favor in the scientific community, however, and had come to be used as a derogatory slur against the mentally retarded, and in particular people with Down's Syndrome.

The song—and lines like "one chromosome too many"—would cause something of a furor in Britain. A teacher's organization demanded to meet the band to discuss the motivation behind it, while the BBC reportedly banned the song from broadcast upon its re-release in 1978. Mark would later defend the song as an exploration of "why the value system of humans is about going out and getting a job, just mindless toil."[5] Casale, however, claimed he was employing a classic twist that filmmakers had been using for decades, likening the song to the movie *Bonnie & Clyde*: "Everyone comes in and thinks it's a funny, farcical film, with the banjo music and the bank robbing ... and then suddenly it gets real hardcore and heavy and they pull the twist ... It was like: No, no. You shouldn't make fun of mongoloids, because *you're* the mongoloid."[6]

With both a professionally pressed single and a film in their arsenal,

Devo relaunched their efforts at finding an audience outside of Akron/Cleveland. They would deliver the single to every record store they could find, while Jerry (posing as the band's manager) sent copies of both the record and *The Truth About De-Evolution* to any potentially interested party he could think of. "I sent it around to all the record companies," Jerry recalled. "I sent it to *Saturday Night Live*, where Dan Aykroyd promptly threw it in the wastebasket … Nothing happened whatsoever. Nothing. Nobody responded, nobody called back."[7]

At some point in 1976, however, Devo had submitted their film to the Ann Arbor Film Festival. In addition to being a showcase for aspiring filmmakers, the festival also had a reputation for taking artistic risks, including hosting The Velvet Underground & Nico— with their matchmaker Andy Warhol in tow—and their 'happening,' the Exploding Plastic Inevitable, in 1966. That same year, Yoko Ono screened her *Film No. 1* and *Film No. 4*. From 1964 onward, the festival had organized a traveling tour for its winners, which initially visited Los Angeles, Berkeley, and Paris. The tour later expanded to include many college campuses, including Kent State, which is undoubtedly where Devo first encountered it. *The Truth About De-Evolution* screened on the fourth day of the six-day 1977 festival, on Friday March 18, just six days after it premiered at the Akron Art Institute. It won the award for Best Short Film, and for the next few months it would be part of the traveling tour.

In the meantime, Devo continued to play live dates. If they had found their earlier pairing with The Dead Boys an odd one, they would not have to look much farther to find a considerably more suitable equivalent. Cheetah Chrome and Dead Boys drummer Johnny Blitz had previously played with Rocket From The Tombs, a band that had existed for less than a year and had disbanded before producing any studio recordings. (If they had, the critic Jon Allan assures us, their efforts would have ranked alongside the MC5's *Kick Out The Jams*, Patti Smith's *Horses*, and The Stooges' *Raw Power*.[8]) When the Tombs split, it was into two distinctly different factions:

147

Chrome and Blitz favored a straightforward approach closely aligned with the emerging punk scene, while singer David Thomas and guitarist Peter Laughner were interested in exploring much more experimental territory with their new group, Pere Ubu.

Pere Ubu were decidedly not punk in either the social or musical sense of the word. Thomas was the son of an architect and a professor who planned on becoming an English professor himself, or perhaps a microbiologist. He made no bones about his upbringing, noting: "All adventurous art is done by middle-class people. Because middle-class people don't care. ... If you sit down and make a list of the people you consider to be adventurous in pop music, I'd bet you lots that the vast majority of them are middle-class."[9] He had worked first as an art director and then as a record reviewer for the Cleveland magazine *The Scene* (under the nom de plume Crocus Behemoth) before forming Rocket From The Tombs in 1975. His writing was characterized by colorful yet nonsensical ramblings that usually had nothing to do with his subject. He eventually gave up writing and turned to music when he realized: "If I'm so smart, I should do this myself."[10]

Thomas took the name of his post-Tombs band from Alfred Jarry's proto-surrealist 1896 play *Ubu Roi*, using its opening line—"Merdre!" ("Shit!")—as the refrain on their 1977 single 'The Modern Dance.' In the play, the character of Père Ubu is usually portrayed as a grotesquely fat and vulgar figure of a man with a crown perched atop his head. Thomas himself cut an imposing figure onstage, as Devo would later note in an article for *Search & Destroy*. "Crocus weighs over 300 pounds and has hair like Curly from The Three Stooges. He dresses just like Ubu—ugly black raincoat, stands absolutely stiff, skinny tie and white shirt, and he just stands there and stares straight ahead, looks like he's crying the whole time he's up there. When he gets into it he'll rip his hair out like the Three Stooges, and he has a little horn and hammer with a big metal window weight—he bangs his hammer and screams, 'LIFE STINKS, LIFE STINKS!'"[11]

In November 1976, Pere Ubu began playing at the Pirate's Cove,

Cleveland's counterpart to the Crypt. Ubu bassist Tony Maimone was a bartender at a dive bar in the city's decaying, industrial zone on the banks of the Cuyahoga River. Just as the Crypt had seen better days serving the once prosperous rubber-mill workers, the Pirate's Cove had once done booming business for shipmen from the lake freighters delivering steel from the nearby mills. "Nothing was going on in the Flats in the 70s," Ubu drummer Scott Krauss remembered. "It was deserted. It was scary. People would say: don't go there."[12] It didn't take much to talk the Cove's owner into booking the band—he had nothing to lose. They went on to play nearly every week for a year, sharing bills with local and nationally touring bands. Devo were among the bands welcomed to the Cove, and had only to make a short trek up from Akron.

On paper, the two bands would seem to be eminently compatible. Pere Ubu used the term 'avant-garage' to describe their sound, which embraced both the three-chord primitivism of 60s bands like The Music Machine and The Stooges as well as experimental electronic music. While many would have seen Pere Ubu's integration of electronics into an otherwise traditional rock band format as revolutionary, Thomas never thought that was the case. "We had no programmatic urge or design to revolutionize rock music, simply to fulfill its manifest destiny," he later recalled. "In the early 70s that destiny was to integrate synthesized sound, abstract sound and *musique concrète* into music. Of course, by doing so we understood that we would change the course of music. Clearly some thought had to go into this, and 'strategies' had to be developed and evolved for this purpose. If you want to call that innovation, fine."[13] Like Devo, they were also influenced by Captain Beefheart, although Thomas would only admit to it in a roundabout way. "There's nothing of Captain Beefheart in our music," Thomas noted in 2007, "but he's ... influential because he pointed out there were other ways of solving the problem and approaching it or looking at it."[14]

In addition to guitar, bass, and drums, Pere Ubu also employed a

149

synthesizer player, Allen Ravenstine, who played a keyboard-less EML ElectroComp 200. Due to the nature of his instrument, Ravenstine's contributions were more akin to Brian Eno's frequently atonal blasts that punctuated early Roxy Music songs. But where others might be put off by the instrument's limitations, Thomas and his cohorts had a unique appreciation of it. "The analog synthesizer has always been central to the Pere Ubu sound, and one of the reasons it's central is because unlike a digital synthesizer it never sounds the same twice," he said. "You could leave it set up overnight without touching it, and the next morning it would sound totally different. That sort of unpredictability is important to the sound ... [because] you're always struggling to get the instrument to do what you want and it won't do it. I think that's a valuable quality."[15]

Mark Mothersbaugh recognized a kindred spirit in Ravenstine but was also aware of the differences between them. "We were doing slightly different things," he recalled. "He did things that were more ... John Cage-sounding." Mothersbaugh realized that many of Ravenstine's contributions weren't exactly tailored to the specific needs of each song and were, in fact, virtually interchangeable. "And he kind of did that from night-to-night, it wasn't always that specific," Mark continued. "But he was definitely on the right track."[16] Ravenstine took a circuitous route to electronic sound, and would later admit that his initial attraction to it "had a whole lot to do with smoking pot." He had a friend who used to rewire stock fuzz-boxes into oscillators capable of producing sound without an input device (such as a guitar). They eventually added lights to the boxes and took the contraptions into art galleries for performances, sometimes accompanied by other musicians, under the name Hy Maya. One day, somebody told him that "all those boxes come in one box, and it's called a synthesizer," prompting Ravenstine to immediately seek out one and buy it with money he'd recently come into from an inheritance.[17]

Ravenstine also used his inheritance to buy an entire apartment building not far from Cleveland State University, simply referred to as the Plaza, to save it from being torn down. For a time it housed all the members of Pere Ubu within its 36 rooms, along with an assortment of other likeminded artists and writers. According to the band's website, the building had originally been constructed "by a gang of industrialists from the Steel Age to house their mistresses. The courtyard featured a heart-shaped garden with a fountain at its center."[18] Unfortunately, the building was no longer in the most savory neighborhood. "The building I had was right on the edge of a ghetto," Ravenstine recalled. "I had guns pointed at me more than once when I was there. And that building would get broken into almost every night. And some people got robbed at gunpoint. I was scared a lot of the time. So I'm sure that was in there. With the sounds I made, some of those sirens and things ... the level of intensity to that place that was frightening."[19] Coincidentally, Mark Mothersbaugh was working as the live-in apartment manager at Harland Hall, a 29-unit building in Akron owned by his father (aka General Boy), who let Mark live there rent-free in exchange for providing basic upkeep of the building. Many of Mark's friends, including Jerry Casale and Rod Firestone, lived in the building at one time or another.

Like Devo, Pere Ubu started out as individuals with a similar intellectual conception of the world rather than musical compatibility. Their concept wasn't quite so clearly defined, however, as Ravenstine recalled: "The concept behind the band was that if you took a group of people that were like-minded in terms of their sense of ... what mattered, some sort of similar philosophy, and you gave them a bunch of instruments and you told them to make noise, they'd make something interesting."[20] They did have something approximating a manifesto, though:

Don't ever audition.
Don't look for someone.
Don't seek success.

Choose the first person you hear about.
Take the first idea you get.
Put unique people together. Unique people will play
    uniquely whether or not they know how to play.
Delay Centrifugal Destruct Factors for as long as
    possible then push the button.

These were the 'Ubu Rules,' and although both bands had written down their processes and aims—a highly unusual act for a rock band then, as now—their content would contain the seeds of a future rift between the two bands, although it might of course have had to do with something else entirely. "We're pretty good friends with Crocus," Devo noted in *Search & Destroy*. "Once, he got upset because we did a parody of him."[21] One night, Casale apparently took the stage dressed as a caricature of Thomas, with newspaper stuffed into his suit to greatly increase his girth. "One of the cardinal sins that Devo committed was they came to the Pirate's Cove and Jerry mimicked David—got a big suit on of some sort and got some outfit on that made him bigger," Ravenstine recalled. "That did not go well! So I don't think we had anything to do with them after that."[22]

It seemed that Thomas didn't approve of Devo's strange kind of wit. In a 1918 essay entitled 'The Taboo Of Virginity,' Sigmund Freud coined the term "the narcissism of minor differences," explaining that it is "precisely the minor differences in people who are otherwise alike that form the basis of feelings of strangeness and hostility between them."[23] While we would assume our strongest feelings of animosity are reserved for those who are the most unlike us, Freud argued that the opposite is true: we actually save that hatred for those who are most like us. Freud revisited the idea in *Civilization & Its Discontents* (1930), noting the animosity that is often present between "communities with adjoining territories," such as the Spanish and the Portuguese, or the English and the Scottish.[24] To this list we can add Akronites and Clevelanders. Our narcissism manifests itself in our feeling of uniqueness, and those that threaten our sense of being special end up as the target of our aggression—which could go some way in explaining the continuing animosity between Devo and Pere Ubu, or more precisely between Jerry Casale and David Thomas.

Devo continued to sing the praises of Pere Ubu, expressing an interest in producing the Cleveland band in a 1978 interview but "doubt[ing] it would be reciprocated."[25] Thomas summed up his opinion of Devo by saying: "I like passion. That's not something Devo were known for. They used to do a song that you might describe as poignant, called something like 'Words Get Stuck In My Throat.' As I remember, they dropped it. It's a side to their work that was stifled. I was disappointed." He was similarly unimpressed by the band's presentation. "I didn't really care for the whole mutant thing, though it was clearly well designed. Simply not to my taste."[26] (What Thomas may not have realized is that Devo had lifted 'Words Get Stuck In My Throat' from the 1966 Japanese monster movie *War Of The Gargantua*. In the film, American chanteuse Kipp Hamilton sings the Burt Bacharach-inspired tune—actually called 'Feel In My Heart'—in a Japanese nightclub before being snatched up by a monster and dropped motionless onto the dance floor. And so Thomas's favorite Devo song wasn't a Devo song at all.)

While there were similarities between the two bands, they saw their ultimate contributions to music very differently. Thomas, always a contentious and contrarian interviewee, saw Pere Ubu as a mainstream band, although it's unlikely that many others would have agreed with him; Devo felt the opposite. "We felt like we were what was new about new wave," Casale recalled, evoking a term that would soon become a buzzword. "It was raw and basic and self-contained, and we were creating our own image and doing things that you weren't supposed to do—you know, singing about subjects other than sex and love and drugs, certainly looking and sounding different in the way we put together our musical parts and staged our shows, so at least it was original."[27]

Thomas's view could not have been more different. "I am uninterested in 'making something new,'" he said in 2011. "I am interested in mainstream rock as the fundamental voice of the American folk experience. I am interested in exploring the narrative voice within the mainstream. Pere Ubu is mainstream rock. ... Pere Ubu does the same old thing. 'New' is a trap and a scam to dupe student-types and other naïve people."[28]

In 1970, Greg Shaw founded *Who Put The Bomp* (aka *Bomp!*), one of a growing number of self-professed 'oldies' magazines, most of which were aimed at record collectors and those seeking to gain more information about their favorite overlooked bands. Shaw made it clear that he was not interested in the past simply for its own sake, but more out of necessity, since "so little good rock & roll is being made nowadays."[29] He would have been happy to write about current bands making exciting music—if only he could find any. Instead, he looked to the past to find music that might serve as an inspiration to contemporary musicians, notably what he called the 'punk rock' bands of 1964–66: The Standells, The Kingsmen, The Shadows Of Knight, and so on. He was no doubt attracted to these bands' raw energy and simplistic, direct approach, which stood in sharp contrast to the excesses of early-70s rock music.

Shaw's message quickly spread from Los Angeles, where *Bomp* was based, to Detroit, home of *Creem* magazine, founded a year earlier. *Creem* writers Dave Marsh and Lester Bangs were similarly effusive about 60s 'punk' bands and felt a similarly vitriolic hostility toward contemporary 'rock stars.' Bangs's hyperactive, amphetamine-driven writing echoed the careening energy he was looking for in music. Many of the bands he and Shaw most admired would soon be collected together by *Creem* writer and future Patti Smith guitarist Lenny Kaye on *Nuggets: Original Artyfacts From The First Psychedelic Era 1965–1968*. (That Kaye used the loaded term 'psychedelic' while

Shaw and Marsh favored 'punk' conveys what a no-man's land these bands occupied at the start of the 70s.)

These magazines would also champion a select few contemporary bands, including The Stooges (who at the behest of David Bowie regrouped for one final album in 1973) and the MC5, and would also rehabilitate the reputation of the recently disbanded Velvet Underground, who had been virtually ignored during their lifetime. They would also debate the merits of the term 'punk' as it applied to the musically brash and visually bracing New York Dolls. Many of these bands were shortlived, however, and by the mid 70s most were out of commission.

Around this time, an oft-repeated story has the members of the recently formed Television happening upon a Bowery bar named CBGB & OMFUG (an acronym for the types of music it intended to showcase: Country, Bluegrass, Blues, and Other Music for Uplifting Gormandizers). When it opened in December 1973, it was not much more than a seedy neighborhood bar frequented by Hell's Angels and winos, but before it was even able to begin presenting acts in its intended genres, the enterprising members of Television persuaded owner Hilly Kristal to let them play, even going so far as to build the stage on which they would perform. What this account omits, however, is that Kristal was not entirely unacquainted with booking the occasional fringe musical act in addition to his favored folk music. From 1969 to 1972, Hilly's, the bar he ran at the same location, had played host to acts such as the provocative transvestite Wayne County and sparse and confrontational electronic duo Suicide.

The success of Television's run at CBGB was enough to convince Kristal to book more acts in a similar vein, including Blondie, the Ramones, the Patti Smith Group, and Talking Heads. While these bands were soon lumped together into a 'scene,' however, there were in actuality few similarities in their music. And with such abundant diversity on show, it should come as no surprise that there was no single agreed-upon label for the bands, although a number of critics made suggestions. In a *Village Voice* article about the three-week Festival of Unrecorded Rock Talent of August 1975, James Wolcott described a "New Rock Underground," which, he said, "represented a counter-thrust to the prevailing baroque theatricality of rock." Perhaps tellingly, however, Wolcott's article looks back to the 60s, a time when "rock bands flourished" as a result of a "genuine faith in the efficacious beauty of communal activity, when the belief was that togetherness meant strength."[30] A subsequent *Billboard* magazine article catalogued some of the other terms being used, including "underground rock," "urban rock," "arrogant rock," and the highly unimaginative "music that comes from CBGB."[31]

In January 1976, John Holmstrom, Ged Dunn, and Legs McNeil published the first issue of *Punk* magazine from a storefront in West Chelsea. It was one of the first publications of its type in New York City, but it was inspired not by events taking place at CBGB but instead by the discovery of an album—on a major label, no less—by a band from the Bronx, *The Dictators Go Girl Crazy!* The editors' stated aim was simply to "hang out with The Dictators." While they were oblivious to what was going on at CBGB, they shared a love of The Velvet Underground and The Stooges, as well as "television reruns, drinking beer, getting laid, cheeseburgers, comics, grade-B movies"—in short, the trash culture of a generation.[32] For McNeil, the term 'punk' represented "the thread that connected everything we liked—drunk, obnoxious, smart but not pretentious, absurd, funny, ironic, and things that appealed to the darker side."[33] As Holmstrom put it: "There was punk rock before *Punk* magazine, but Legs turned it into a movement, and my magazine gave it a forum. The media believed us, and punk rock as we know it was born."[34] (The Dictators, meanwhile, had disbanded by 1979, with guitarist Ross 'The Boss' Friedman going on to form the humorless Manowar, and bassist Mark 'The Animal' Mendoza enjoying multi-platinum success with Twisted Sister.)

McNeil and Holmstrom scored an editorial coup when they snared an unenthusiastic Lou Reed as their first interviewee and cover star on the same night that they first saw the Ramones at CBGB. The fact that Reed—the recently crowned 'godfather of punk'—was on the cover no doubt helped the term gain acceptance as the moniker of choice for the music emanating from the CBGB-centered scene. For his part, Greg Shaw felt vindicated that his prediction for a rock revolution had been proven correct "to almost the tiniest detail by the events of the past two years," while also noting how the word punk had evolved from its origins as "a quaint fanzine term for a transient form of mid-60s music."[35]

In 1975, an enterprising British boutique owner named Malcolm McLaren had become involved in the management of the flagging New York Dolls, and within six months had driven the band, whom he called "the new wave of rock'n'roll," to the point of splitting up by having them dress in red leather outfits and relocate to a trailer park in Florida.[36] After returning to England, McLaren applied much of what he had learned in New York to his new creation, the Sex Pistols—even going so far as to offer Dolls guitarist Sylvain Sylvain a place in the band. Assembling a band from an unpromising bunch of ne'er-do-wells who frequented his Sex shop, McLaren took Richard Hell's spiky hair and ripped T-shirts and the Ramones' buzz-saw guitar sound and wedded it to his interest in issues of class consciousness and Situationist-inspired publicity stunts. The fact that the Sex Pistols' 'Pretty Vacant' bore more than a passing similarity to Richard Hell's 'Blank Generation' was not a coincidence.

The first journalist to interview the band, *Sounds'* Jonh Ingham, got a strong sense of something new. "It wasn't called punk then," he said. "Malcolm was insisting that we call it new wave, like the French cinema."[37] The term 'punk' only began to spread overseas once the key New York bands signed record deals, and it gained widespread currency following the Sex Pistols' infamous expletive-laden appearance on Britain's *Today* show in December 1976. The incident was front-page news the following morning and set a precedent for publicity stunts that McLaren would continue to follow throughout the remainder of the band's existence. "The word ['punk'] only got a super wide circulation when the Sex Pistols made so much news in Britain and then the US," Richard Hell later noted. "Because of that, because the Sex Pistols were such a powerful phenomenon, the model of 'punk,' the definition of it, became the Sex Pistols."[38] By now, McLaren had abandoned his crusade for the adoption of the term 'new wave,' and by the time *The Great Rock'n'roll Swindle* was shot in 1978 he was claiming credit for creating an entire musical genre—but curiously not its name. "My name is Malcolm McLaren," he says in the film. "I have brought you many things in my time ... but the most successful of all was an invention of mine they called punk rock."[39]

It was into this milieu that Devo landed, headfirst, in May 1977. "We couldn't wait to get to New York," Jerry recalled. "We thought: they'll understand!"[40] The actual decision to play in New York came about in a quite circuitous fashion, however. Devo had earlier sent a demo to A&M Records, among others, but had not received a response. When the A&R head Kip Cohen saw *The Truth About De-evolution* as part of the Ann Arbor Film Festival tour, however, he remembered receiving a package by the same band. He located the package and called Casale in Akron in April 1977, offering the band $2,000 to play a showcase in Los Angeles. Casale later recalled that he "did a song and dance and some bullshit to delay it, because we didn't play really, we didn't have a set."[41] He told Cohen that his band was booked solid for the next three months—three months he would actually spend woodshedding the band into shape. In addition to endlessly practicing their 45-minute set, Devo took the time to write some new songs, one of which was 'Recombo DNA' (which remained unreleased until it became the title track on Rhino Handmade's rarities compilation of the same name in 2000). The song finds the band in an unusually upbeat mood, buoyed perhaps by their recent good fortune. "I got a good reason for stayin' alive ... 'cos I'm fallin' in love

/ With recombo DNA." It was also notable for its punk-like tempo and lack of keyboards, which meant it was tailor-made for the band's raucous live shows.

The final part of the band's plan before setting off for Los Angeles was to conquer New York. Mark put his printmaking background to good use to announce Devo's arrival. He figured out a way to use blueprint machines to make four-by-six-foot posters for 50 cents apiece, which they would print up and then change the dates on for each subsequent show. Their ability to produce such material led to some strange rumors, as Mark recalled: "People would look at them and say: Wow. My band is doing 8½-by-11 flyers at Kinko's. How are they doing it? They must be ad executives."[42] While the shows would continue to feature the band's self-styled costumes and choreography, they now had the added dimension of film, albeit in their own improvised fashion. Audiences would arrive to see a sheet tacked up on the stage, onto which the band would project their film using a rented 16mm projector before playing their set.

Devo's first show in New York was a Monday night at CBGB, a day of the week typically reserved for untested bands to audition. Members of The Dead Boys were in attendance, and Devo once again provoked a strong reaction. Blue Öyster Cult roadie and recently anointed Dead Boys MC Ronald Binder was among those present. "One night, we threw toilet paper rolls at another band from the Midwest trying to showcase at CBGB's—Devo," he recalled. "We humiliated them that night when they played to a capacity table. Little did we know that this band of geeks would have a hit, 'Whip It,' while Stiv and the guys would not go beyond a niche status."[43]

Some of the other musicians in the audience that night were rather more inspired by what they saw. Drummer Terry Bozzio had recently been dismissed by Frank Zappa and, after two albums with prog rock supergroup UK, was contemplating his next career move. He would go on to form his own band, Missing Persons. "I had seen Devo audition on a Monday night at CBGB's," he recalled, "and it was just amazing, with the full blown theatrical show, and it was one of those moments where I wanted to do something different and innovative."[44]

While Devo obviously shared some of the same impetus as the punk bands, their aesthetic was fully formed by the time they got to New York. As Mark Mothersbaugh would later recall, they showed up "like space aliens" with a "vocabulary that was particular to us. By that point, because we had been so insulated in Ohio, we were kind of like our own Midwestern Aborigine tribe that talked about spuds as comrades and 'high Devo' and 'low Devo.' And we were dressed in yellow plastic hazardous waste outfits instead of tattered blue jeans and T-shirts. So, it was kind of to our advantage to have had a chance to fester back in the Midwest before we headed east." [45] Punk rock's influence on Devo would be minimal yet plainly apparent. Casale had taken preliminary trips to New York to pose as the band's manager, shop around their single, and book gigs. He had seen the Ramones during one of those trips, and according to Mark had been struck by how fast the band played. "We thought our music would sound better faster. Until then we'd been playing at Ohio unemployment speed. Punk really inspired us to fire it up a notch or two."[46]

While CBGB was ground zero for what had become known as punk, Devo would play the majority of their New York gigs at Max's Kansas City. Once a favorite spot of Andy Warhol's and his entourage, it had also served as the epicenter of the glam-rock scene of the early 70s. It was also where David Bowie and Iggy Pop first met. Located off Union Square, two blocks from Warhol's Factory, it was "the exact place where pop art and pop life came together in New York in the 60s," as the artist put it. "Teeny boppers and sculptors, rock stars and poets from St Mark's Place, Hollywood actors checking out what the underground actors were all about, boutique owners and models, modern dancers and go-go dancers—everybody went to Max's and everything got homogenized there."[47]

Pere Ubu had played at Max's at least a year earlier, and were in fact the only non-New Yorkers among the eight bands to feature on the compilation album *Max's Kansas City 1976* (reissued in 1978 as *Max's Kansas City—New York New Wave*). Devo made their debut at the venue immediately after their second CBGB show on May 25 1977. Having worn their yellow HAZMAT suits at CBGB, at Max's they unveiled some new finds: high-waisted, billowy, knee-length Gurkha shorts (as worn by the Nepalese military units from which they took their name) and white suspenders. These baggy, pleated shorts were entirely out of step with prevailing trends of the 70s but predated the look of the 80s.

Devo would return to Max's for more shows during the summer, fall, and winter of 1977, one of which was attended by an aspiring music journalist, Byron Coley, who would later travel with the band on their first major-label tour just over a year later and write about the experience for *New York Rocker*. They had an intriguing way with introductions. "I personally fell in love with Devo during the summer of '77 at Max's Kansas City," Coley later wrote. "What made the show so special for me was the moment when Bob Mothersbaugh got so carried away with his solo on 'Smart Patrol' that he jabbed his guitar into my ear and actually drew blood. Ya hear that, babies? Blood! You think I'd spill the very essence of life over some band I hadn't taken a mighty big hankering to? Damn straight I wouldn't. When he jabbed the same guitar into my pal Strato's eye (blackening it for a long two weeks), I knew this was indeed the band for me. Their swell costumes and even sweller songs had me in their sway. Call me a fool, I call it rock'n'roll."[48]

Each of the band's forays to New York drew bigger crowds than the last, and their reputation increased correspondingly. The main booker at Max's, Peter Crowley, would later describe the band's performances there as "a giant showcase. They were already becoming famous and all that … but they were not identified with Max's as struggling beginners. They were already kings of the underground. By playing New York, they then got the international reputation."[49]

For their second appearance at Max's, Devo shared the bill with the equally misanthropic New York bands The Cramps—featuring transplanted Akron native Lux Interior—and Suicide. The latter group regularly caused genuine riots with their performances— including one in Belgium that had to be dispersed with tear gas— which featured Martin Rev's primitive organ and rhythm boxes and Alan Vega's confrontational stage demeanor. He would routinely taunt pugilistic audience members with a bicycle chain, and sometimes barricade the exits so audiences were forced to stay and listen. Suicide shows would culminate in the ten-minute 'Frankie Teardrop,' a harrowing tale of a desperate factory worker's murder of his wife and six-month-old child. "People would run, screaming," Television guitarist Richard Lloyd recalled. "The whole crowd at CBGB would go outside … it was dreadful. But that's their charm."[50]

The band's formation in 1970 preceded Devo's by a few years, but the impetus was the same. "The Vietnam War was going nuts with Nixon dropping bombs everywhere," Vega recalled. "Suicide was very much a reaction to all the shit that was going on around us." For all the nihilism and cynicism, however, one of the band's defining works was 'Dream Baby Dream,' which Vega described as being "about the need to keep our dreams alive."[51]

Before the show at Max's, the legendarily confrontational Vega let down his stage persona long enough to go and introduce himself to Devo in their dressing room. He was shocked at what he found. "I opened their door and they were all doing calisthenics," he recalled. "When they performed, they were almost like a calisthenic—all in unison with their movements onstage—like a machine. When I looked into their dressing room and saw them doing all their movements I just cracked up." Nonetheless, Vega got on well with the band, and remembered them signing a record deal shortly after the show. It was not the first time that had happened. "This was a test for the band: if the band could play to a Suicide crowd and get over it, then they got signed."[52]

Although Devo found acceptance within the burgeoning underground rock scene in New York, they realized that their unique worldview could not have been fostered there. In Akron, they had been allowed to develop in isolation, whereas audiences in New York had been able to watch bands like the Ramones and Talking Heads evolve over time. "When Devo finally popped and were able to drive in our Econoline van from Ohio to New York City and play shows, people were disbelieving that it could have even happened," Mark recalled. "They were like: how did we not know about this? … People were mystified. They wanted to know what Akron was."[53]

Jerry had a similar backhanded compliment for his hometown. "Devo couldn't have come out of LA or New York. Cleveland and Akron are like the boot camp to the world. If you can survive those places and still be a functioning human being, you can go anywhere. It's pretty brutal. It was industrial then, and it was very blue-collar, and it was very hostile to creativity. So the bands that had the balls to do something in the face of the rejection and threats really got strong."[54]

CHAPTER 7
JULY-DECEMBER
1977

Nobody knows anything.
WILLIAM GOLDMAN

Devo finally made it to the West Coast in July 1977. They made the journey at the behest of Kip Cohen of A&M, who had taken an interest in them after thinking that they could be the new Tubes (and a cheaper version at that). Cohen had signed The Tubes in 1975 after seeing a 'video demo' they had shot the previous year. The video showcased the band's live show, which would grow more outrageous over time. Back in 1974, however, it had consisted mainly of the band playing competent, progressive-rock-inspired fare while singer Fee Waybill adopted different outfits and mannerisms to correspond with the characters in the songs. For Gene Pitney's 'Town Without Pity,' he wore a black overcoat, boots, and a dog collar; for 'White Punks On Dope,' it was silver lamé pants, a blue sequined tube top, and body glitter. Eventually, the stage show would involve all manner of costume changes, props, and pyrotechnics as Waybill became characters like Quay Lude, country singer Hugh Heifer, and the crippled Nazi Dr Strangekiss; unsurprisingly, the band's tours hardly ever grossed any profits. It was while Waybill was in character as the chainsaw-wielding punk Johnny Bugger in 1977 that he broke his leg onstage, temporarily halting the band's career.

The Tubes had relocated to San Francisco after forming in another insular pocket of the country. "We grew up in a place called Phoenix,

Arizona which is an isolated desert city in the middle of a huge dust bowl," Waybill recalled. "You had to watch TV there, you see, because it was so oppressively hot. You were in the house watching TV all day long. ... Imagine what that does to a person. They grow up and they're totally nuts." Keyboardist Michael Cotten said the band hailed from "the first television generation," adding that television gave the youth of America access to "every piece of violence, commercialism, sex, and everything ... almost 24 hours a day."[1]

It was not just television in general but specifically advertising that made a strong impression on the band. Phoenix was often used as a test market as its geographic isolation made it relatively easy to gauge the effectiveness of new advertising before moving on to larger markets. According to Waybill, both McDonald's and Kentucky Fried Chicken tested their products in Phoenix first. "We were just bombarded throughout our whole life with one stupid thing after another. I guess it kind of jaded us to where we never take *anything* seriously!"[2] Mark Mothersbaugh would claim many of the same influences when he noted in 1978 that Devo came from "our nightmares ... television ... commercials."[3]

Predictably, The Tubes and Devo shared many of the same musical influences. They listened to "anybody weird," as Waybill put it—"anybody who wasn't going along with the program," notably Frank Zappa and Captain Beefheart.[4] In fact, when Kip Cohen first got in touch with Devo, The Tubes were about to release their third album, *Now* (1977), which features a cover of Beefheart's 'My Head Is My Only House Unless It Rains' (from *Clear Spot*), while the Captain himself plays saxophone on 'Cathy's Clone.'

Devo had not previously been aware of The Tubes but soon recognized a kindred spirit. "We got to realize they were deep into what we were doing," Casale noted. "We were encouraged."[5] He would soon acknowledge the debt Devo owed the band. "It wasn't until The Tubes came along that a group like us could get jobs," he said in 1978. "Before that, everything on the music scene was slick

165

and derivative. Wherever we got to play we had to sneak in and lie about what we were doing."[6] Unfortunately, The Tubes' approach to live performance and video was the exact opposite of what Devo had envisaged. The Tubes were first and foremost a live band who seemed largely uninterested in the possibilities of video beyond documenting their stage show; Devo saw video as a surrogate for live performance, freeing them from the constraints of a typical band's duties. The ultimate goal, as Mark later put it, was that there might be "five or six Devos out touring around the world, and it didn't matter who the personnel were."[7]

There were further key differences in the two bands' approaches. "With The Tubes, the music was incidental," Devo noted. "We're more musically oriented and more minimal. We even reduce the number of costumes or props and take it down to one focus, one relentless center."[8] (A year later, Andy Gill of the *NME* would agree with that assessment when he caught Devo at Newcastle City Hall on their first UK tour, describing them as "simple but effective, more so than the excessive organized routines of The Tubes, and far funnier."[9]) The Tubes came to realize their predicament as well. "It just got worse and worse and worse till people didn't even think of us as music anymore," Waybill recalled. "They just thought of us as a visual type of thing, which was no good at all. We didn't sell any records that way."[10] It took until 1981, and *The Completion Backward Principle*, for them to even make a dent on the mainstream charts.

Devo made their West Coast debut with two shows at the Starwood in Los Angeles on July 25 and 26 1977. Kip Cohen's reaction was not what they had expected. "He didn't stay to the end," Casale recalled. When Cohen summoned the band to his office on Monday morning, he ruefully informed the band of his decision by way of a labored analogy about how there could be "seven naked teenage girls in here right now … and maybe one of 'em's got a mole." Pressed to explain himself, Cohen told Devo they were "not my kind of girl." For Casale, the incident was "just horrific on every level. You couldn't make up a more horrible music biz moment." Cohen encouraged the band to enjoy the rest of their stay at the Oakwood Garden Apartments— "hang in the Jacuzzi, get laid ... take home a nice memory of LA." However, Casale and his bandmates were "so angry at the disgusting, ludicrous treatment that we received that we said: we're not going anywhere. We're going to figure this out."[11]

Fortunately, as one door closed, another had already opened when the first of the band's many celebrity admirers introduced himself backstage at the Starwood. According to Casale, Devo had been irritated at having to get changed into their stage clothes while people hung around in the dressing room area. "There was this one guy with chopped-up hair and little reading glasses sitting against the wall in the dressing room; he looked like he'd already lived a few lives. I asked who he was and he said he was Iggy Pop. I said yeah, right! He got really pissed off."[12]

To prove his knowledge of the band, Pop began singing Devo songs that had yet to be released, and in fact had not even been performed live. Pop explained that he and David Bowie had been listening to a tape passed to them in Cleveland in March, during a stop on the tour for *The Idiot*, for which Bowie filled in on keyboards and backing vocals (having co-written and recorded the album with Pop the previous summer). Pop and Bowie had been listening regularly to the album during the spring, while they worked on Pop's next album, *Lust For Life*, in Berlin, where they had moved in 1976 to overcome debilitating drug additions and other assorted demons. Neither believed the Devo songs were the work of an actual band, however, and as such had made no attempt to track them down. It was only when Iggy happened to see the band's name on the marquee outside the Starwood that he was finally convinced they were real. Accounts differ as to who had actually made the bold move of attempting to pass a demo tape to Iggy or his faithful keyboardist at the Agora Ballroom back in March, but whether it was Casale, one of his bandmates, or one of their girlfriends, the result was successful.

It seems unsurprising that Bowie and Pop would find a kindred spirit in Devo's admittedly rough demo tape. While Bowie was arguably at the forefront of every vital musical movement of the 70s, from psychedelic folk to glam rock to 'plastic soul,' by 1976 he was enamored with krautrock bands like Kraftwerk and Neu! Having spent several years in the USA, he found his attention had "swung back to Europe with the release of Kraftwerk's *Autobahn*. The preponderance of electronic instruments convinced me that this was an area that I had to investigate a little further." As much as Kraftwerk inspired him, however, he found their approach to making music very different to his own. "Theirs was a controlled, robotic, extremely measured series of compositions, almost a parody of minimalism," he later explained. "In substance too, we were poles apart. Kraftwerk's percussion sound was produced electronically, rigid in tempo, unmoving. Ours was the mangled treatment of a powerfully emotive drummer, Dennis Davis. The tempo not only 'moved' but also was expressed in more than 'human' fashion."[13]

Devo, meanwhile, would claim the German group as an influence but liken themselves to "Kraftwerk with pelvises." Explaining further, Jerry said that Devo "loved what [Kraftwerk] did. But there's no sexuality there. Devo was primitive and driving sexuality at the same time."[14] Mark would describe their approach in even more colorful terms. "We kind of felt like what we were doing was sort of like *The Flintstones* meets *The Jetsons*. We had like the Flintstones side of blues and rock instrumentation, and then the more modern side of electronics."[15] (It's also worth noting that, while many felt that punk was a vital movement in the progression of rock, to Bowie it barely registered. "The few punk bands that I saw in Berlin struck me as being sort of post-'69 Iggy, and it seemed like he'd already done that."[16])

Iggy had originally flown to Los Angeles to work with his friend, dancer and choreographer Toni Basil, on a *Saturday Night Live* special that had since been canceled. He invited Basil along to the Starwood to see Devo, and as she later recalled: "Our mouths never shut."[17] Basil was as interested in Devo's moves as their music. Meeting them backstage after the show, she asked who choreographed the performance, to which the rest of the band replied by pointing at Jerry Casale. "I'm laughing," Casale recalled, "because I would never consider it choreography, but she loved it and the next thing you know I was bedding down with her for a year. She crossed the rule with me, a guy always had to be at least 14 years younger than her— I was the first guy who wasn't."[18]

In fact, Casale was about to turn 29, perhaps pushing the upper limits of the acceptable age range for an aspiring rock musician. Basil, though, was nearly five years his senior and had a significant amount of experience in the entertainment industry. She had already served as assistant choreographer for mid-60s musical variety show *Shindig!* and the 1964 concert film the *T.A.M.I. Show* (featuring The Beach Boys, The Rolling Stones, and James Brown) for which she was also a go-go dancer. She choreographed The Monkees' ill-fated *Head* (1968), in which she danced with Davy Jones, and had small acting roles opposite Peter Fonda and Dennis Hopper in *Easy Rider* (1969) and Jack Nicholson in *Five Easy Pieces* (1970). In 1975, her street dance troupe, The Lockers, featured on the first season of *Saturday Night Live*: six African American males (among them Fred Berry) dressed in a curious combination of 70s style—oversize berets, sweater vests, and wide ties—and early hints at 80s fashion, in the form of impossibly baggy, pleated pants and bold primary colors. Basil herself appeared as a hip-hop Pierrot in conical hat, black jacket with white buttons, and billowing grey pantaloons.

Basil had been part of a close-knit group of artists and actors who congregated around the charismatic figure of Wallace Berman. Berman had been one of the original California beatniks of the late 50s whose one and only solo commercial show at the Ferus Gallery in Los Angeles in 1957 led to his sensationalistic arrest on obscenity charges. He never exhibited publicly again but instead organized underground showings for his widening circle of friends and admirers in the pastoral environs of Topanga Canyon, as isolated a location as one could find within the confines of Los Angeles. These West Coast artists had their own approach that differed markedly from their East Coast peers. As one critic later noted: "Removed by geographical distance from the critical culture that sustained (and then mortified) painting in New York, [Berman's] California community instead admired and drew influence from earlier Romantic and transgressive avant-gardes in Europe. In North Beach and Topanga Canyon, familiar Modernist techniques—Dada-derived collage and photomontage especially—took on a new vitality. Dada, Surrealism, mysticism, and pornography were the dominant influences; several seemed to be under the spell of Hannah Höch's dense collages in particular."[19]

Berman was an assemblage artist who initially exhibited found-object sculptures (some in the shape of a cross) before shifting his focus to two-dimensional collage. His main tool in these endeavors was a 40s-era copy machine, the Kodak Verifax. He collected these works along with poetry and art from likeminded friends in *Semina*, a hand-printed, freeform, loose-leaf journal of which he published nine issues from 1955 to 1964. Each run only reached into the hundreds, and the contents were packed into envelopes and mailed directly to friends, but it would count contributions from such writers as William S. Burroughs, Allen Ginsberg, Charles Bukowski, Michael McClure, Alexander Trocchi, Philip Lamantia, and David Meltzer. *Semina* was also an outlet for Berman's radical politics, which were not exactly in line with the popular sentiment of the day. As McClure put it, *Semina* was "un-American. In the fifties, when the magazine first began, it was against what in those days we called the American Way. *Semina* was a long way from the American Way. The American Way was the Korean War, the grey flannel suits, the military preparedness to wage war behind the Iron Curtain or the Bamboo Curtain."[20]

In addition to choreography and music, Casale and Basil would have also bonded over their shared interest in filmmaking. Casale would go on to direct nearly all of Devo's videos, while Basil would co-direct Talking Head's 'Once In A Lifetime' video with David Byrne in 1981. Although Berman's foray into collage-like filmmaking produced only *Aleph*, which he assembled over ten years between 1956 and 1966, he attracted a number of both mainstream actors and experimental filmmakers into his orbit, including Dennis Hopper, Russ Tamblyn, Dean Stockwell, George Herms, Bruce Conner, Robert Alexander, and Basil. Stockwell and Tamblyn appear in *Aleph*, while Stockwell and Billy Gray play at an outdoor table in Basil's *The Ping Pong Match* (1967–68). Her *Our Trip* (1967) is an experimental travelogue documenting a romp around Europe with friends Teri Garr and Ann Marshall, and Conner's *Breakaway* (1966) simply features Basil gyrating against a black background in increasingly revealing outfits—and finally none at all—while the camera's hyperkinetic edits transform the scene into a swirling disjointed dance. Stockwell's *Pas De Trois* (1964) even contains footage of Conner in the act of shooting some film.

The crowd that associated themselves with Berman came from remarkably diverse backgrounds, and would continue to pursue increasingly adventurous paths after his death in 1976 at the hands of a drunk driver. According to critic Ed McCormack, those artists "are now acknowledged as forerunners of hippie psychedelic art, funk and junk sculpture, new-wave painting, graffiti, punk, and various neo-Dada tendencies that would emerge in the 1960s, 70s, and 80s … Directly or indirectly, their influence still filters down to inspire young artist-hipsters struggling to create bohemian utopias of their own."[21]

Casale's chance meeting with Basil would not only put Devo into contact with some of the more adventurous Californian artists of the late 60s, but it would also provide a bridge extending back to the contrarian spirit of the late-50s beats—connections that the band would wisely draw upon before the end of the decade. For now, however, it was most likely another of Basil's credits that most impressed Casale. In 1974, she had choreographed David Bowie's *Diamond Dogs* tour, which Jerry attended at Cleveland's Public Auditorium that June. "I'd never seen anything as spectacular before," he said. "At the start, an eight-foot diamond descended to the floor of the stage. The front opened forward and Bowie jumped out wearing a Kabuki outfit, pulling dance moves reminiscent of Broadway. I lost count of the number of set changes and dance routines. It was seamless—an incredible fusion of rock music energy, theatrics, and disturbing asexual innuendos. The show solidified right then and there what I wanted to do with Devo. We'd spent way too much time smoking pot, talking about ideas and doing nothing about it. Here was someone who'd taken the time to do it for real."[22]

With the support of Iggy Pop and Toni Basil, Devo's prospects began to grow quickly. "We built up a fan base over that summer in California," Casale recalled. "It just started getting better and better and better, and of course what happens is a lot of people come forward, you know, managers, record company people, start getting interested 'cause they saw how many people we could draw."[23]

It is telling that Devo chose to relocate to Los Angeles, rather than New York, which is geographically much closer to Ohio. A precedent had already been set of Ohio bands moving to New York in search of greater opportunities, notably The Dead Boys (now managed by CBGB owner Hilly Kristal) and The Cramps, and others would soon follow, including Pere Ubu bassist Tim Wright, who joined no wave band DNA after moving to the city in 1978, and Chris Butler, who formed The Waitresses with several fellow Akron transplants in 1979. Only the Rubber City Rebels would follow Devo's lead and move to Los Angeles.

Jerry described the transition in typically colorful terms. "That was like going from a toilet to a sewer. You know: you have your personal toilet, then you move to the total sewer. We'd seen the picture postcards of LA and we believed it, and we came out and it was just one long stretch of sprawl and yellow sludge, you know? And it was horrifying. And we couldn't believe that all of Hollywood—highly touted as the Mecca to all musicians—looked like Cuyahoga Falls, Ohio, except worse. Yeah, it was just a bigger cesspool of a place."[24]

Nonetheless, inspired by their successful run in New York, Devo set their sights on conquering LA. "We came over really cocky, 'cos we'd gone to New York and kind of freaked people out," Mark recalled. "We had these yellow outfits and a whole vernacular and a set of songs that didn't sound like anything else they were hearing, so we quite quickly became a phenomenon in New York. So we left there going: we don't have a record deal and we don't have any money, but we're doing something right … we're going to take over Hollywood."[25]

Devo's initial booking at the Starwood led to gigs at more established venues, including the Whisky A Go-Go which had recently become the nexus of the Los Angeles punk scene. They played for free, purely in the interest of exposure. "We were nervous," Jerry recalled, "because these were the kids who decided who was good and who was shit." Even so, Mark Mothersbaugh's confidence had been bolstered enough for him to charge the crowd during the call and response section of 'Jocko Homo.' "We weren't sure if he'd get back on stage, because it was pretty rough and nasty," Casale later noted. "They pulled off all of his clothes except his boxer shorts; Mark looked like he'd been in a fistfight."[26]

One audience member they did manage to win over was Joan Jett, who had been a fixture on the LA scene since the formation of The Runaways in 1975, and prior to that as a regular at Rodney Bingenheimer's English Disco—ground zero for Californian fans of British glam rock. "I saw a lot of amazing shows—people like Billy Idol with Generation X, and Devo, who really surprised me," Jett recalled. "They had perfectly greased hairdos and glasses, but when they played, they were very dirty, and their energy was very sweaty."[27]

John Doe of X even remembers seeing their films before seeing any of their performances. "They sent some copies of their films—the Booji Boy films and stuff like that—to play before punk rock shows, before they ever came out to LA to play," he recalled. "'Whip It' was a little bit later, but the first stuff—'Jocko Homo' and 'Satisfaction'— those were great. They were delivering on the promise of what video could do."[28]

Devo shared bills with a variety of bands—some better suited to their unique aesthetic than others—but there was one that stood out. According to Mark: "We saw The Screamers and we thought: that's the real thing."[29]

Making their official debut at the Starwood exactly three weeks before Devo, The Screamers were unusual among rock bands in that they had no guitars. Instead, there were two keyboard players— Tommy Gear on ARP Odyssey and Paul Roessler playing a Fender Rhodes run through a fuzz box—alongside drummer K.K. Barrett and charismatic singer Tomata Du Plenty. At the time, their sound was dubbed 'techno-punk'; two decades later, the term 'synthpunk' would be retroactively coined to describe The Screamers and a handful of others.

While the band's machine-gun sonic attack could hold its own with the best of them on the punk scene, it was Du Plenty who served as the riveting focal point. He had grown up in Los Angeles before hitchhiking in 1968, aged 20, to San Francisco's Haight-Ashbury at the height of flower power. He fell in with a ragtag theater troupe named The Cockettes, described by John Waters as "hippie, acid-freak drag queens. ... It was complete sexual anarchy, which is always a wonderful thing."[30] The Cockettes had been formed in 1971 by someone calling himself Hibiscus—in fact none other than George Harris, the young man photographed putting flowers into the barrels of MPs' rifles outside the Pentagon in 1967, who had made a stunning transformation over the previous four years. As another Cockette put it, he looked "like Jesus Christ with lipstick."[31] While the Cockettes were undoubtedly a product of the 60s counterculture, they were fixated on show tunes from an earlier era. "Hibiscus told me I was the image of the young Mary Martin," Du Plenty recalled, referring to the star of *South Pacific* and *The Sound Of Music*. "Very disturbing."[32]

After a year in San Francisco, Du Plenty moved to Seattle, where he founded a group of his own, Ze (Fabulous) Whiz Kidz. When they opened for Alice Cooper at Seattle's Paramount Theater in July of 1971, they performed a 50s-themed musical called *Puttin' Out Is Dreamsville*; by the time they opened for the New York Dolls in 1974, they had morphed into a proto-glam band. "Tomata is a fascinating character," prominent Seattle graphic designer Art Chantry later said, "because he was the one who pioneered Northwest punk. He was producing honest-to-God DIY punk posters in 1972."[33]

After leaving Ze Whiz Kidz in 1972, Du Plenty moved to New York, where he performed in a cabaret show called *The Palm Casino Revue* across the street from CBGB at the Bouwerie Lane Theatre. *The Palm Casino Revue* also included scenester sisters Tish and Snooky, who were eventually recruited to sing backup in an early version of Blondie (and would later form The Sick Fucks). The rest of the *Palm Casino Revue* would stage performances at CBGB in 1974, including such productions as *Slaves Of Rhythm*, *Spit*, and *Savage Voodoo Nuns* (the last of which was part of a Halloween show with Blondie and the Ramones).

Du Plenty returned to Seattle in 1975 and formed The Tupperwares, who became The Screamers when they moved to Los Angeles the following year. "Their personas in The Tupperwares were already similar to what they'd become in The Screamers," Penelope Houston of The Avengers recalled, "except maybe they were a little more new wave and not quite so intense."[34] According to Tommy Gear, The Tupperwares started out as "sort of a lark. It was more in the context of an art expression of some sort rather than in terms of a serious band or real music." Their first performance in Seattle was before a showing of *Pink Flamingos* for which they were dressed "in unisex kind of jumpsuits. It had a ring of Devo about it, but this was quite a while before Devo."[35] (Coincidentally, Devo had opened for a screening of the same film that same year.)

The Screamers would become one of Los Angeles's most popular live bands, sharing bills with many of the city's punk and power-pop bands. They opened at least one of their sets by thanking "the first groups for playing you music from the 1960s and 1970s. Now we'll give you music of the 1980s."[36] They sold out multiple nights at the Whisky A Go-Go, and they headlined at the Roxy, becoming the first band to do so without a recording contract. Curiously, the band did not release any official recordings during their lifetime, even after original keyboardist David Brown co-founded the shortlived yet influential Dangerhouse Records. Rumor had it that they would only entertain offers from major labels, and that they were interested only in releasing their debut as a video album—a much more ambitious prospect. In a *Melody Maker* article, Jon Savage noted that The Screamers "remind me of Devo in the respect that they want REAL BAD to become stars, and no doubt they'll make it."[37] Unfortunately, they didn't. They hooked up with Dutch writer and director Rene Daalder, who cast them in his film *Population: 1*, but the results were dreadful, and would remain unreleased until 1986. It didn't help that Du Plenty was very much the star—in fact, most of the film feels like a one-man show, further hastening the band's demise. "I've seen the film," said keyboardist Roessler, who did not participate in it. "It's retarded." By 1980, The Screamers were no more, prompting Dead Kennedys front man Jello Biafra to proclaim them "the best unrecorded band in the history of rock'n'roll."

Devo were clearly impressed. "They were mesmerising, their songs were great, they were incredible performers, and girls went crazy for that band," Mark Mothersbaugh said in 2009. "I mean: The Germs definitely had something of interest to them. But I think The Screamers are the ones that deserved recognition as what could have been the most important band from that era. Their music was excellent but they were the band that we were watching thinking: that's it—that's the band. They should have been."[38] The rest of the band shared Mark's enthusiasm. "Devo loved The Screamers," Jerry recalled. "You see a band that you're creatively and intellectually inspired by and envious of, and we were like: why didn't we think of it? They were so way ahead of their time … they were using rudimentary synths and sequencers but with punk energy and aggressive lyrics and theatrical staging with German Expressionist lighting."[39]

Devo had reportedly invited The Screamers to accompany them on tour but the offer was rejected. Whether it was a decision based on aesthetics or simply a case of The Screamers being in the midst of falling apart was not clear. Despite the apparent similarities, Roessler for one felt that the two bands were polar opposites. "Devo's live performances were studies in deadpan delivery. Their costumes were uniform. Satirically or not, they were portraying a sort of futuristic hive-human." The focal point of The Screamers' live sets was Du Plenty's intense and impassioned theatricality. "Where Mark Mothersbaugh's face is expressionless, Tomata's is a neon billboard of conflict, joy, pain, tension and confusion, and this difference permeates the theatricality of The Screamers, their songs, their costumery and their aesthetic."[40]

While Devo had been talking from day one about getting rid of their guitars, The Screamers had actually done just that. In early 1979, Jerry told *Rolling Stone* that there would be "more synthesizer" on future recordings. "The guitars will eventually be eliminated. Once the big solo hippie stars blew it out with guitar riffs there was nothing left to do with them. We use them now as textures, punctuation."[41] For Roessler, "Devo's sound was original, [but] their instrumentation was typically rock-band; guitar, bass, and drums, with a bit of keys here and there." (By 1980, Jerry and Bob Casale had switched to playing most of their parts on synths, but lead guitarist Bob Mothersbaugh never made the transition.)

Crucially, The Screamers' relationship to punk was also very different. While Devo were hosted by punk clubs and accepted by its fans, their music didn't stray from its singular course. With the exception of increasing their tempos, they made few concessions to the movement as a whole. By contrast, The Screamers were determined to beat the punks at their own game, and some would argue that they did, even if it made them bandwagon-jumpers of a sort. "Devo was one of those bands that had sprung up around that period, sort of in a vacuum, but they were undeniably a punk band in the best sense of the word," Roessler recalled. "Their relationship to punk was very organic. I always felt like The Screamers, on the other hand—and I could be misreading this somewhat—came at punk from an absolutely mercenary stance: the 'winning by intimidation' factor; this is the next big thing; we'll jump on this bandwagon early and rule the roost. Not a very endearing position, but it makes me think of what Dylan did when he first moved to New York and got in the folk scene. Sometimes that distance and objectivity can be very freeing artistically. But are you going to say Dylan wasn't a folk artist when he started out, or that The Screamers weren't a punk band? Of course not."[42]

Roessler seemed to have as good a grasp on what differentiated the two bands—and what set Devo apart from the punk movement in general—as anyone. "If Devo are post-modernists, The Screamers are perhaps better considered modernists, harkening back to [Antonin] Artaud and the Theater of Cruelty, or maybe [Jean] Genet." Roessler's aligning of his band with the nihilistic playwright—also one of Richard Hell's key inspirations—further solidifies their link to punk, which Devo were clearly not part of.

Amid this flurry of activity in California, Devo found time to release their second single. '(I Can't Get Me No) Satisfaction' / 'Sloppy (I Saw My Baby Getting)' was released on Booji Boy Records in September 1977, its songs listed on the sleeve as '(I cån't gèt mé nö) SÅTISFACTIÖN' / 'SLÖPPY (I såw my baby getting).' Both came from the stockpile of songs the band had recorded back in Ohio.

'Satisfaction' traces back to the band's practice space from the winter of 1976–77, the band having been inspired by a musical form that had recently caught the attention of everyone from Eric Clapton to The Rolling Stones. "Our idea on that was 'Let's do Devo reggae,' believe it or not," Jerry said in 2001. They found "the reggae beat, which is almost a skip" by listening to Bob Marley records. "It's a backward kind of thing. We thought that was kind of funny. We thought it was a Jamaican sort of polka or something. We twisted the beat backward on 'Satisfaction,'" he added, likening the result to "some kind of nasty, mechanical, reggae polka."[43] Something had gone awry in the band's "reinvention process," in much the same way as it had when Talking Heads attempted to ape James Brown. (Heads front man David Byrne could have been talking about Devo when he described his band's "version of funk" as "skewed, herky-jerky, and somewhat robotic."[44])

The rest of 'Satisfaction' came together in a collaborative manner, beginning with Bob Casale playing what Mark Mothersbaugh described as a "Persian, goose-steppy guitar part," to which the others added "parts with frozen limbs."[45] At one point, he and Jerry were singing different songs—"Jerry tried singing 'Paint It Black' and I started singing 'Satisfaction'—but it soon became apparent that these disparate pieces added up to an impressive whole. "It was like this big machine—it was like some sort of stupid perpetual-motion machine clanking around the room that we couldn't stop, and it just kept happening for hours, the song, and we were all in spud bliss."[46]

The song's iconic status would also provide a crucial gateway into Devo's often intimidating worldview. Although it was not their composition, Mothersbaugh has called it "the quintessential Devo tune ... when people would say: what the hell are these guys doing? they could listen to that song and then extrapolate from there." It also served as the perfect example of what Devo liked to term 'positive mutations'—something that was infinitely easier to grasp in the format of a two-and-a-half-minute pop song. The song had a

179

personal relevance for Mark, too, having taught him an important lesson about rock'n'roll at an early age when his mother brought a friend from church to their house one day and they found him playing the Stones' 45 in their living room. The visitor expressed surprise that Mary Mothersbaugh would allow her son to listen to such a 'dirty' song. "And then they left the room and I had to listen to it like 100 times more, trying to figure out what she meant. Then it made me like the song even more, 'cause I'm like: wow, I missed out on the dirty part. What is it?"[47]

The single's B-side, 'Sloppy (I Saw My Baby Gettin'),' was credited to Devo, but it had actually been written by Gary Jackett, whose friendship with Jerry Casale extended back to their days at Kent State. The band had altered some of Jackett's lyrics and taken great liberties with the phrasing and music as well. (For the band's debut album, the songwriting credit would be revised to "Mark Mothersbaugh/Bob Mothersbaugh/Gerald V. Casale/Gary Jackett.") Casale later described Jackett as "a brilliant acid casualty ... where Charles Manson went into the evil zone, he went into the beatific zone." This may have gone some way to explaining the song's impenetrable lyrics, which concern the narrator's "baby" and her "brand new car." She turns to her boyfriend and says the word "sloppy," to which he adds: "I think I missed the hole." Casale later admitted that he and the others were never entirely sure what the song was about. "It just made us laugh. It's back to that scatological side, and sexual innuendo."[48]

The single's cover featured an image of the band in 3D glasses, black gyms shorts, dress shoes, and over-the-calf socks, as well as plastic breasts. Only the bare breasts on the two fishnet-clad models accompanying the band are real. Jerry later described the black-and-white shots of the band against a plain backdrop as "a parody of slickness. Those glasses were 3D glasses. Just Hollywood. A parody of sexuality—plastic tits."[49] The photos were by Moshe Brakha, who brought some unorthodox ideas with him, producing what the band felt were some of the best photographs ever taken of them. In addition to the plastic breasts—polymer love, indeed—he also shot the band in the same body bags that were last seen in *The Truth About De-evolution*, but this time with surgeon's caps and masks as well. The Israeli-born Brakha then surprised the band with his next suggestion for a series of shots that have never seen the light of day, for which he pulled out "this gigantic Nazi flag," as Mark recalled. "He's got us holding this Nazi flag for a few photos, and we're like: whoa, what's that about?"[50]

For their first single, Devo had been in charge every step of the way; this time around, they wisely enlisted some help. While simultaneously publishing his magazine of the same name, Los Angeles-based Greg Shaw had also started Bomp Records in 1974. Although Bomp was primarily concerned with retro power-pop bands like The Flamin' Groovies and The Shoes, the label would also handle distribution for Devo's single, freeing the band up from hawking their product to record stores themselves. Devo might not have been an obvious fit with the other acts, but Shaw admired their "originality and conceptual sophistication … and their early stuff was quite raw, after all." There was some discussion as to whether the single would be listed as a Bomp release or a Booji Boy record, but in the end the band won out. "This was one of those cases where Bomp was the only game in town," Shaw recalled. "They [Devo] needed to get a record out and nobody else was interested. I probably should've insisted on having it on a Bomp label but ended up letting them put their Booji Boy label on it. But we pressed and distributed it, and it had a really lovely (now super rare) picture sleeve."[51] (The label would also erroneously credit 'Satisfaction' to Devo and 'Sloppy' to Jagger–Richard.)

Bomp also took on distribution of Devo's earlier single, 'Jocko Homo' / 'Mongoloid,' but the band were dissatisfied with the services Shaw provided. As the usually taciturn Alan Myers later put it: "The only distributor we ever had for those records was Greg Shaw of

Bomp Records, and I think it would be an understatement to say he didn't do a very good job."[52]

Within days of their unsuccessful showcase in Los Angeles, Devo made their way north to San Francisco, where they played the Mabuhay Gardens restaurant and nightclub in the North Beach neighborhood, once the locus of the beat movement but now better known for its abundance of strip clubs. In December 1976, a fledging band called The Nuns convinced the owner to let them play on Monday nights. The band would take the door money while the owner would take the earnings from the bar (much as Television had done at CBGB). Others followed, and by February 1977 the club was exclusively booking rock bands, often those of the punk persuasion, the thatched booths and tiki lamps providing a unique setting for the often-aggressive performances.

At first the club and the scene it catered to was small and insular. "We made it totally unique and no one knew about it," said Nuns singer Jeff Olener. "It was a well-kept secret. And for the first six months of 1977 it was fabulous, because it was like your own private scene you had created. It was like wonderful, you know. It was artists, writers, photographers, filmmakers, musicians—all different cool people mixed up. There weren't very many punk bands because there really *weren't* any. So they kind of mixed in regular rock in the club as it got popular."[53]

San Francisco's nascent punk scene had somewhat different characteristics compared with those in other cities. V. Vale began publishing *Search & Destroy* in 1977 to document this subculture, funded by a $200 donation—half each from the poets Allen Ginsberg and Lawrence Ferlinghetti (Vale's employer at City Lights Bookstore). "It was wonderful: you had a scene which wasn't defined," he recalled. "Basically weirdoes and outcasts and artist types, post-beatnik types, were the main audience at the Mabuhay. I would also say the age was older; it wasn't as young as it was in England where you had Johnny Rotten and the people who were mostly teenagers. In San Francisco, when it started out, people were at least in their twenties and thirties. It was definitely an older scene. In a way that was kind of good, because it seemed to be a richer scene. There were a lot of people like Bruce Conner and lesser-known artistic rebels, which made the scene a lot more interesting. I can't compare it to New York because I wasn't there. I know that to begin with, a few people brought the seeds of it back from New York City, like The Nuns."[54]

Devo continued to open their shows with a screening of *The Truth About De-Evolution*. Dirk Dirksen, the booker at the Mabuhay, thinks this helped their swift rise. "Devo's film did a lot of good in terms of contributing to the mystique," he said. "I think the first evening we had them, they had 97 paid, and the next time it was 400 paid."[55]

Filmmaker Bruce Conner had moved to San Francisco in the late 50s and established strong ties with the city's beat community. He had started his career as an assemblage artist before moving into filmmaking, which he approached in the same manner that he did his three-dimensional art, by assembling films from secondhand ephemera that he found. His first film, the groundbreaking *A MOVIE* (1958), was a 12-minute-long juxtaposition of Ottorino Respighi's stirring and uplifting symphonic poem, *Pines Of Rome* (1924), with seemingly random footage of pin-up girls, Western movies, demolition derbies, tightrope walkers, a mushroom cloud, and scuba divers. Conner would go on to make more than 20 such films in the course of the next 50 years. He was also no stranger to hostility. *REPORT* (issued several times in different edits between 1963 and 1967) paired audio reports of John F. Kennedy's assassination and funeral procession to visuals of Kennedy as well as stock footage of film leader countdowns, sporting events, television commercials, bullfights, and the scene in which the monster is brought to life from *The Bride Of Frankenstein*. It was intended as a meditation on the media's exploitation of Kennedy's death, but was not always taken as

183

such by viewers. Conner recalled incidents where incensed audiences "unplugged the projector and took away the screen."[56]

Conner was ultimately interested in taking this marginalized form of film to a wider audience that may not have spoken the language of artists and critics. "I've always known that I was outside the main, mercantile stream," he later said. "I have been placed in an environment that would have its name changed now and again: avant-garde film, experimental film, independent film, etc. I have tried to create film work so that it is capable of communicating to people outside of a limited dialogue within an esoteric, avant-garde or a cultish social form. Jargon I don't like."[57]

The peripatetic filmmaker had also crossed paths with the city's psychedelic music scene of the mid-to-late 60s by providing light shows for Family Dog productions at San Francisco's Avalon Ballroom. However, his introduction to the city's latest musical movement came from an old friend and fellow protégé of Wallace Berman. "In 1977, Toni Basil called me and said: you gotta go to Mabuhay Gardens tonight and see the world's greatest new rock band, Devo," he recalled. "So I went there and I liked the show; the place was pretty interesting. I started going back to see if I would find another band just as interesting." Conner became a regular at the club, despite being in his mid forties at the time, and he regularly took photos of the bands, some of which ran in *Search & Destroy*. "There were a number of events there, some of which I photographed. Most of my photographs are of San Francisco and California punk bands; some of the bands were obscure and only played once. There are pictures of Toni Basil and Devo, and a few others that are better known."[58]

Conner was so impressed with Devo that he applied his collage filmmaking technique to a video for the band's song 'Mongoloid.' He combined 50s television advertisements, science-fiction film clips (including a scene from *It Came From Outer Space*), and scientific documentaries with abstract animation and original film work. (Devo

184

would later use a similar technique for their 'Beautiful World' video in 1981.) Conner called the film "A documentary film exploring the manner in which a determined young man overcame a basic mental defect and became a useful member of society. Insightful editing techniques reveal the dreams, ideals, and problems that face a large segment of the American male population. Educational. Background music written and performed by the Devo orchestra."[59] The film had its premiere at the Mabuhay Gardens on December 7 1978, making it Devo's second official music video.

Mark Mothersbaugh thought the video was a perfect fit for the song, later noting that Conner had picked "some of the best, most amazing looking, insipid, insane images from 50s television commercials" to go alongside the music. "There was some woman on top of a ball of a deodorant roll-on where she's stuck to it and she's on her hands and knees, and she's frightened 'cause she's like trying to get unstuck from a ball of deodorant. Somebody making it for you … it couldn't be better."[60]

Another San Francisco character with whom the band would soon cross paths was Patrick Gleeson, who had founded Different Fur Studios (originally named The Different Fur Trading Company after the sartorial preferences of friend and poet Michael McClure) in 1968. Gleeson was an early adopter of synthesizer technology, which led to him recording and touring with Herbie Hancock in the early 70s. Prior to that, he had experimented at the San Francisco Tape Music Center, the brainchild of Morton Subotnick and Ramon Sender, in the mid 60s. When asked what had first inspired his interest in electronic music, he cited a trip to Mexico in 1963, during which he was introduced to "a new drug called lysergic acid diethylamide. That was the beginning. From that, I found out two things: one was that I was OK, and secondly, that everything has to do with music."[61] In addition to production and releasing his own solo albums, Gleeson and composer Terry Riley also provided the soundtrack to Bruce Conner's 1976 film *CROSSROADS*, which consists solely of footage of the nuclear blast of Operation Crossroads.

Gleeson would approach Devo after a show at the Mabuhay Gardens to suggest they record at his studio while they were in San Francisco. The band decided to take him up on his offer, recording versions of 'Come Back Jonee' and the appropriately synth-heavy 'Shrivel-Up' at Different Fur, although Jerry would later indicate that he was not entirely enthusiastic about working there. "You can imagine how hungry Devo was for the studio, and rather than looking at the motivation behind the carrot dangled, Mark decided: let's go for the *carrot*."[62]

Several years later, while David Byrne and Brian Eno were working on *My Life In The Bush Of Ghosts* at the studio, Gleeson would introduce them to Bruce Conner, too, and Conner would go on to direct clips for two tracks from the album, 'Mea Culpa' and 'America Is Waiting.' The latter's repurposed footage of children playing at war, juxtaposed with mobilizing soldiers, cowboy movies, and appliance commercials, caused Sire Records to decline using the film for promotional purposes and instead relegate it to the art-house circuit. Nevertheless, V. Vale would subsequently describe Conner as "the father of the MTV-identified music video."[63]

San Francisco seemed to be the perfect milieu for Devo, with its free mixing of artists from different disciplines and a demographic old enough to remember the artistic and political convictions of the 60s. Although they were initially paired with straightforward punk bands like The Avengers (who later opened for the Sex Pistols' final performance, at San Francisco's Winterland Ballroom, on January 14 1978), they would eventually share bills with more likeminded acts, including Tuxedomoon, who were as much an art collective as a band. Multi-instrumentalists Blaine Reininger and Steven Brown had met in an electronic music class at City College of San Francisco, while Brown had previously been part of The Angels Of Light, the more spiritually minded offshoot of The Cockettes formed in 1971 by Hibiscus, who wanted to present free performances unlike those by his earlier group. Singer Winston Tong came from a more conventional theatrical background, having appeared in a production of *Hair* in 1970, while Bruce Geduldig was a full member of the band whose sole obligation was incorporating Super 8 film projections into their live shows. Their debut album, *Half-Mute*, would eventually come out on Ralph Records, the imprint of the Bay Area's other great multimedia band, The Residents.

Tuxedomoon credit their opening slot for Devo at the Mabuhay (January 6 and 7 1978) with increasing their profile and respectability. Their newfound association with rock music proved important. "From that point on we were beginning to be treated with a new respect in this club and by people in general," Reininger recalled. The band's first single, 'Joeboy The Electronic Ghost' / 'Pinheads On The Move,' was released around the same time. "We admired Devo a lot from the beginning," Steven Brown said. "And of course there was an affinity between songs like 'Mongoloid' and our 'Pinheads,' for example. We were on the same wavelength for a minute."[64] Reininger would later pinpoint the moment their paths diverged and Tuxedomoon began to take on their signature noirish qualities. "[Glenn O'Brien] wrote about us in his column for Andy Warhol's *Interview* and said something like: if you can't find the B-52's in your local record store, then Tuxedomoon's 'Pinheads On The Move' will serve as a fine temporary substitute. I guess our sound and our shtick was a little goofier back then … But not so long after that, there was a palace coup and the rest of the guys in the band stood me up against a wall and said: we're going to get serious now! And we did. We shed the Residents/Devo-style postmodern humor real quick."[65]

Like Devo, Tuxedomoon found themselves sharing bills with punk bands and playing punk clubs without ever identifying with or taking inspiration from the scene. "I had long since cut my hair and was well aware that most of the culture I had been inspired by had been commodified and watered down," bassist Peter Principle later said. "I really am still an old hippie. But I love energetic and dynamic and electric and so as things took off I realized that something I could do was to make music myself again, and this was how I ended up doing so." He did not identify himself as a punk, however. "We didn't support punk for any reasons other than it was there and needed a venue. I liked other types of music and performance as well. As you can see my interests then and even to this date are directly related to a stream that surfaced in the 60s."[66] Tuxedomoon even shared Devo's dissatisfaction with American politics, which is partly why they left the country in 1980, never to come back. The band-members first relocated to the Netherlands, and then Belgium, and are now spread among various far-flung locations, including Greece and Mexico.

This dedication to incorporating visuals into rock performance extended to other bands on the San Francisco scene. The Units would later be dubbed 'synthpunk,' but at the time their intention was simply to be "a synthesizer band that rocked out."[67] To this end they had two synth players, Scott Ryser and Rachel Webber, in addition to a drummer. In fact, Ryser and Webber had first met at a Tuxedomoon concert at the Mabuhay. Ryser began as a filmmaker prior to becoming a musician. "I was making films before I got involved with music," he said. "The early movies had actors and plots. Then I got into film collages, which lent themselves to fast-paced music. I chose to create my own soundtracks. Later, the films were an integral part of The Units' live shows." Ryser's films incorporated scenes from diverse genres, including "educational, technological, pornographic, family-home movies—scenes taken out of context and redirected," and provided a backdrop for their unexpectedly energetic performances.[68] "Most people consider synthesizers and the musicians who play them to be cold and emotionless," Ryser said in 1980.[69] "I've got to move when I'm singing."[70]

"We were already playing shows in the late 70s when I first heard of and saw Devo live at the Mabuhay in San Francisco," Ryser later recalled. "You have to remember, this was before MTV and the internet ... the punk scene was very regional. It wasn't easy to see or hear early punk bands from opposite coasts unless you traveled across the country." He instantly recognized Devo as kindred spirits. "My first reaction when I saw them live was: shit, they are doing kind of what we are doing, only they are better at it. They have perfected the black humor critique of how our culture worships conformity and technology." He also noted the differences between the two bands, and the sly and skillful way that Devo got their political points across. "I think Devo took a more comedic approach than us ... they were able to critique art as commodity ... while still making money off it as a commodity! Kind of like Jeff Koons, they packaged their critique in a great pop culture way, and frankly, the packaging helped it sell better to the masses. We took a weirder, more alienated, 'outsider art' approach to it." Sometimes, however, the commentary could be a bit too buried. "I continually struggle with the idea of the relativity of things, and of the parts of something versus the whole of something ... and whether or not you feel the part that you are playing in that whole is helpful, valid, or rewarding. So for me, it's hard to reveal an artistic revelation about our culture and consistently present it in a humorous way. Sometimes I don't want to disguise the anger and loneliness. I guess I'm probably better at writing tragedy!"[71]

In time the video component of many of these bands soon fell by the wayside. Just as breakdancing and graffiti had once been as important to hip-hop as the music, prerecorded and live visuals were, to some, integral parts of this developing musical scene. "For a split second, film and performance art were a part of the cultural revolution of punk," Tuxedomoon's Steven Brown recalled. "Z'ev ... Mark Pauline ... NON ... even Devo in the beginning, with their Bruce Conner films. What happened was the tyranny of music over the other arts. It's apparently still easier today to make waves with a music CD than, say, a new film. ... For Tuxedomoon, our shows were always 'scripted and choreoed' after our own fashion. The point is there were video artists and performers like those mentioned coming in on the wave of energy then."[72]

Just how well Devo could fit into the punk scene at the Mabuhay was seemingly never in doubt, however. "Let me tell you something," Ryser said. "We ALL considered Devo to be a 'stick it to the man' PUNK BAND!"[73]

On September 12 1977, the US Court of Appeals for the Sixth Circuit Court ordered a retrial, reversing the lower court ruling of two years earlier, which had cleared the defendants charged in the damage suit resulting from the Kent State shootings. The ruling stated that at least one member of the jury had been "threatened and assaulted by a person interested in its outcome." Judge Donald Young, who presided over the trial, had been accused of being biased against the plaintiffs due to their political beliefs, prompting one author to write: "What the judge was doing in the courtroom was as great an affront to civil liberties as what the guardsmen had done on campus."[74] Due to the judge's actions, a new trial for the federal civil cases was ordered, meaning Governor Rhodes as well as several state officials and National Guardsmen would have to stand trial once again.

Having spent three months in California, ping-ponging between Los Angeles and San Francisco, building momentum all the while, Devo returned to New York to play Max's Kansas City in November 1977. It was their third run at the venue. By now, Iggy Pop had informed his friend and fellow Devo fan, David Bowie, of his dealings with the band, and Bowie was there to greet them. Bowie had released *"Heroes"*, the second installment in his Berlin trilogy, exactly one month earlier, on October 14. He would not begin the tour to support it, dubbed Isolar II, until the following March, but was busy promoting the album. He was in New York to provide narration for a recording of Sergei Prokofiev's *Peter & The Wolf*, originally composed in 1936 to introduce young people to classical music. (Bowie later claimed he had taken on the project as a Christmas present for his young son, Zowie.)

After chatting with the band backstage after their first set, Bowie made his way onstage to introduce the second. With the band's movie screen as his backdrop, he addressed the packed house: "This is the band of the future. I am producing them in Tokyo this winter." Having only just met Bowie, Devo had not had any discussions with him about the recording of their album, although their admiration of him was no secret. "We'd done some interviews, and people said: who'd you like to have produce you guys?" Mark recalled. "Of all the people I could think of, I thought it would either be David Bowie or Brian Eno. I liked their music, and I thought maybe they would understand what we were trying to do."[75]

Bowie was indeed a fan. When asked by an interviewer a short time later if there was anyone he was interested in working with (having earlier claimed to rarely listen to "anything that's currently in vogue"), Bowie replied: "There's one band that I can mention. I like them very much indeed. They're an unrecorded band in America called Devo. I've been listening to them for a long time, since they sent me their tapes, and I hope if I have the time at the end of this year to record them." In an effort to sum up their approach, he described them as being "sort of like three Enos and a couple of Edgar Froeses [of Tangerine Dream] in one band," seemingly missing out on the *Flintstones* half of the *Jetsons* meets *Flintstones* analogy. "Most peculiar. That's very nut-shelling of what they're like."[76]

Despite their surprise, Devo were delighted by Bowie's announcement. "I remember we were standing there onstage thinking: that's great, cause we live in an Econoline van right now and that's where I'm sleeping tonight," Mark recalled. "Tokyo sounds great, I'll bet you don't sleep in a van." Bowie also had Brian Eno and guitarist Robert Fripp with him that night, and there seemed to be some "bickering" between them after Bowie publicly claimed the band as his own. Almost immediately after making his announcement, however, Bowie was forced to qualify it. "The only caveat to this," he told the band, "is if I get this part in this movie, I'll

191

be in Berlin filming and we'd have to wait till spring or summer."
Bowie was vying for the role of Paul Ambrosius von Przygodski in the
film *Just A Gigolo*, eager to establish himself as an actor following his
recent role in *The Man Who Fell To Earth*. "He called the next day,"
Mark added, "and said: I just got the part for this movie."[77]

However, Eno had been just as interested in producing the band,
declaring them "the best live show I have ever seen." He may have
had an even more intellectual approach to the band than they did to
themselves, which would surely bode well for their potential
collaboration. He explained his attraction to the band by describing
"what ... always happens when you encounter something new in art—
you get a feeling of being slightly dislocated, and with that are emotional
overtones that are slightly menacing as well as alluring. With me, that's
almost a code word. I am very interested in knowing why that happens,
and why that is happening now, and I spend as much time in that sort
of reflection as I do in the work. You see, in this work, you arrive at
attractive positions for which sometimes you have no defenses. Trying
to find that out—the whys and wherefores of creativity and fashion,
generally—is very interesting to me." Some of Eno's rationalizations
echoed what Devo had long been saying, such as: "When you make a
piece of work, you are postulating a little world of your own, with a set
of rules, and you try to see how they work. Then, how do they apply
to real life?" Some of his other concepts would prove anathema to
Devo's method of working, however, such as his use of Oblique
Strategy cards to create "accidents as a part of the work."[78]

The night after the show at Max's, Eno took them to dinner and
presented them with a counter-proposal. Their first album—like *The
Velvet Underground & Nico*—would be recorded before the band had a
contract with a record label, as Jerry recalled. "He said: I'll do this
right away. I'll take you guys to Germany and I'll pay for the record so
that you don't have to sign too onerous of a record deal because
they'll hear what they're gonna get before they start negotiating. And
that sounded really good. And we did it."[79]

PART 3
WIGGLY
WORLD
(1978–79)

CHAPTER 8
JANUARY–MAY
1978

We are often told that we are incoherent, but into this word people try to put an insult that it is rather hard for me to fathom. Everything is incoherent ... There is no logic ...
TRISTAN TZARA

If the buzz surrounding Devo had grown steadily since they made their debut in New York nearly six months earlier, Bowie's announcement set off a full-fledged bidding war. Island Records declared an interest in the band, and the label's founder, Chris Blackwell, paid a visit to the band in Akron during the blizzard of winter 1977–78. So too did Dave Robinson of Stiff Records. Shortly thereafter, Virgin Records founder Richard Branson offered to fly the band to Jamaica to discuss a possible deal.

Branson was something of an entrepreneurial prodigy, having started Virgin with a pair of business partners at the ripe old age of 22. Virgin's inaugural release was *Tubular Bells* by Mike Oldfield, a proggy new age classic, which like *Dark Side Of The Moon* seems to periodically re-enter the charts as each new generation of adolescents and college kids discovers marijuana. Virgin would also find success as one of the few British labels willing to sign German krautrock bands such as Tangerine Dream and Faust in the early 70s, further solidifying its cachet and credibility. It was also the sort of label that would sign Captain Beefheart knowing full well that he wasn't at the peak of his powers. On the release of his *Bluejeans & Moonbeams* in 1974, one staff member remarked: "It was such a kick for us to have a record by Captain Beefheart on Virgin. We were a very new label at the time. ... The records, musically, were disappointing, but even a bad Beefheart record was better than most of what was available, in our opinion."[1]

Virgin would eventually sign the Sex Pistols, a move considered financial suicide by some since the band had been dropped by both EMI (where they lasted three months) and A&M (where they held on for all of one week). Despite being booted by the labels, the band got to keep the rather hefty advances that they were paid, prompting manager Malcolm McLaren to declare his manifesto "cash from chaos." Their one and only album, *Never Mind The Bollocks, Here's The Sex Pistols*, was released by Virgin in October 1977; the band would break up three months later after a performance at the Winterland Ballroom in San Francisco, at which point the four of them went their separate ways: guitarist Steve Jones and drummer Paul Cook to Rio de Janeiro to record two songs with the infamous Great Train Robber Ronnie Biggs; bassist Sid Vicious to New York to attempt a solo career; and front man Johnny Rotten back to London, via Branson's place in Jamaica.

Devo briefly crossed paths with the Sex Pistols after that final show, having played the more intimate Mabuhay Gardens several days earlier. They were sleeping on the floor of the offices of *Search & Destroy* magazine, which hosted something of an after-show party on the evening of the Winterland performance. They seemed to spend more time in the presence of Sid Vicious than any other Sex Pistol, whose behavior they found to be nothing short of fascinating. Mark Mothersbaugh would later recall watching Vicious gradually push a bottle of beer closer and closer to the edge of a table, looking around to see if anyone was paying attention before eventually sending it crashing to the floor. "He did it three or four times, and then he realized he wasn't gonna get anybody upset, so he quit."[2]

That winter had been one of the worst in Ohio in recent memory. "I remember it because Northeast Ohio was under a blanket of snow about 30 inches deep," Mark recalled. "We got a call from Richard Branson ... he says, hey, wanna come down to Jamaica? And I'm looking outside at the snow—I'm wearing a winter coat to try to eat breakfast in this cold apartment—and I said, yeah, I'll come down to Jamaica."

While Mark and Bob Casale accepted Branson's offer, the most business-minded member of Devo, Jerry Casale, declined. "I already knew what was going on—he was tempting us," he later noted.[3]

When Mark and Bob #2 arrived in Jamaica, they were greeted by Branson and his entourage and presented with unprecedented amounts of Jamaican marijuana. Their previous experiences with the drug had been limited at best. "In Ohio, we would sit around with enough pot to fill up a thimble, and we'd stare at it all day," Mark recalled. "We would finally roll this pencil-thin joint, and like eight people would all desperately try to get a little buzz off of this really bad pot. We'd all be like: I think I'm high. Maybe I'm high. Yeah, I might have felt something. My throat's definitely feeling raw. It was that kind of thing."[4]

Mark and Bob smoked plenty of what Branson was offering before the conversation turned to the newly disbanded Sex Pistols, and then to Johnny Rotten. "We think he's great," they said. "We think he should totally change what he's doing and do something new."[5] It was at this point, according to Jerry, that Branson revealed his "brilliant idea ... I've got Johnny Rotten in the next room, I've got *Melody Maker* and *NME* across the hall and if you say so, we're going to go out to the beach and get pictures of you guys together and announce that Johnny Rotten is going to be the lead singer of Devo."[6]

"We were a unit," Jerry noted. "Five punk scientists with a plan. We didn't need a guy who didn't realize anarchy and rebellion were obsolete except as cartoon consumer hooks."[7]

In hindsight (and with a clear head), Mark realized that he could have handled the situation differently. "In retrospect, I wish we'd said sure, let's go down to the beach and make an announcement—just for the fun of it," he told *USA Today* in 2009. "I've thought about it since … that would've been interesting if we'd done an album, *Devo Featuring Johnny Rotten*. They just made it sound really permanent."[8] Elsewhere, Mark recalled telling Branson that Rotten needed his own band, or perhaps "a corporate image of his own. Then the next thing he did was Public Image Ltd."[9] Rotten made it back to London without ever meeting Mark or Bob. In fact, he was most likely unaware that Branson was attempting to broker such a deal.

In late February 1978, in an interview with *Melody Maker*—Devo's first with the British press—Jerry Casale attempted to illuminate the differences between Devo and punk. "We are a corporate image, we are entertainment for the corporate state of the world in the eighties."[10] In July, John Lydon (as Johnny Rotten was now known) would christen his band Public Image Ltd, later claiming to have been inspired by Muriel Spark's novel *The Public Image*.

On June 25 1980, Lydon and PiL guitarist Keith Levene appeared on Tom Snyder's NBC talk show, *The Tomorrow Show*, which played host to a number of punk and new wave bands, including Elvis Costello, Iggy Pop, and the Ramones. When the amiable host inquired about Lydon's new "band," the singer took offense—"We ain't no band. We're a company. Simple. Nothing to do with rock'n'roll"— while Levene referred to PiL as "a communications company."[11] Lydon's contemptuous protestations then became increasingly (and unintentionally) comical. Pressed by Snyder as to what exactly made them a company and not a band, Lydon finally laid out their interests as "videos, movies, soundtracks for films"—hardly a radical agenda for a moderately successful band. PiL weren't actually operating as a corporation but were rather trying to pass themselves off as a multimedia project—and not a very imaginative one at that. And it was a promise that they wouldn't keep.

After leaving Roxy Music in 1974, Brian Eno initially confined his solo recording career, and increasingly busy production schedule, to his home base of London, but then gradually began to move his operations to wherever in the world he found inspiration. In 1974 Eno attended a performance by Harmonia, who were something of a German rock supergroup, consisting of Dieter Moebius and Hans-Joachim Roedelius of Cluster and guitarist Michael Rother of Neu! Two years later, he visited the band at their studio in the remote village of Forst in Lower Saxony, four hours outside of Berlin. This was most likely the first collaboration between an English (or American for that matter) musician and members of the insular krautrock community. "Brian came to our house to learn from us," Moebius recalled. "We didn't go to him to learn from him. He didn't know what to do really I think at this moment. He was at a dead end of the street."[12]

Eno brought three blank tapes with him to record these informal sessions, which were eventually released in 1997 as *Tracks & Traces*, credited to Harmonia '76. "The idea was to continue working together," Rother recalled, "but that didn't happen."[13] Eno, of course, went straight from Forst to Hansa Studios in Berlin, to commence work on David Bowie's album *Low*. In between work on *Low* and the next two albums in Bowie's so-called 'Berlin Trilogy,' *"Heroes"* and *Lodger*, he would book lower-budget projects at Conny Plank's studio in rural Neunkirchen.

Plank was the one figure who tied together the disparate strains of adventurous German music dubbed 'krautrock' by the British music press. Kraftwerk and Neu! (from Düsseldorf), Cluster and Ash Ra Tempel (Berlin), and Holger Czukay of Can (Cologne) would all seek out Plank's distinctive sonic stamp. Eno would record two more albums with Moebius and Roedelius at Conny's studio in June 1977 (the eponymous *Cluster & Eno* and *After The Heat*, credited to Eno Moebius Roedelius). He would also mix parts of his solo albums *Before & After Science* (the last of his more conventional rock albums) and *Ambient 1: Music For Airports* (the first of his much less structured ambient records) at the studio. (In fact, Eno formulated his concept of ambient music while waiting at Cologne/Bonn Airport, which coincidentally was designed by Paul Schneider-Esleben, father of Kraftwerk founder Florian Schneider.)

That winter, Eno took Devo to Plank's. If they had harbored visions of standing by the wall while the guns shot above their heads, however, these would soon be replaced by the cold reality of a converted Victorian farmhouse in an isolated area. Plank's tracking room was once the hog pen. "We were stuck in the country ... with this sophisticated recording equipment set up and there was no place to go," Bob Mothersbaugh recalled. "The only thing you could was go to the recording studio and work 20 hours a day."[14]

Initially, the pairing seemed promising; Mark would later reveal that he had found a photograph of himself standing by a lake, holding hands with Eno. They appeared to hit it off with Plank, too. "He looked and dressed like a Viking," Jerry recalled. "He laughed and played and worked hard like a mad scientist. We amused him, and he amused us."[15] Holger Czukay, who was mixing an album of his own at the studio, would later note that Devo seemed "as if they had come in from outer space."[16] Although Bowie had promised to come to the studio on weekends, his visits were limited by illness. "He did show up at the studio a few times, but he was sick and he just laid in the back of the studio semi-conscious," Mark recalled. "So Eno wound up producing us."[17]

If Devo and Eno shared a mutual admiration for each other's work, they would soon find that the methods they used to achieve those ends could not have been more different. Eno was famous for his love of experimentation. He would often enter a studio with little or no material, preferring instead to compose and record on the fly. "I started coming to the studio with less worked-out pieces, and eventually with nothing at all," he later explained. "I would just start working with that thing, 'the studio,' as the instrument. I'd say, OK, let's start with a drone or single repeated piano note. What happens if I put an echo on that? What happens if I make that echo wobble by sending it through a tape recorder with a bent capstan?"[18]

Devo, on the other hand, had spent countless hours practicing and refining their songs, right down to the specific sound of each instrument, obsessively recording multiple versions of each song and compiling a library of tapes to use as reference. Eno later expressed his frustration with the band's methods in no uncertain terms. "Anal is the word," he said, describing the band's inability to experiment as "terrifying" and recalling how they would dip into the "big chest of recordings they'd already done of these same songs" to demonstrate the types of drum and guitar sounds they wanted to achieve. For Eno, this seemed "impossible," "foolish," "stupid," and simply a waste of time. "I'd be sitting there at the desk, and there are EQs, echo sends, all those kinds of things, and my hand would sort of sneak up to put a bit of a treatment on something, and I could feel Jerry Casale bristling behind me. It was awful! He would stand behind me all the time, then lean over and say, why are you doing that? As if you can know why you do something before you do it, always!"[19]

It didn't help that Devo had been recording themselves for at least three years by this point. They had decided to re-record all four tracks from their two previously released singles with Eno, although they dropped the "O-Hi-O!" part of 'Jocko Homo' because, as Jerry later explained, the album was due to go on sale in "two-thirds of the world, and we questioned whether it was necessary to put something so geographically parochial on it."[20]

Eno dutifully persisted in his attempts to add flourishes to Devo's material. "He was a really great guy, but the odd thing about it was that he kept wanting to play on the record," Mark recalled. Devo, by their own admission, had become "maniacally possessive" of their work and were resistant to almost all of Eno's suggested contributions. "He would play a synth part, and we'd kind of pretend, oh, that's nice, Brian!"[21]

In addition to playing synthesizer and singing on the songs, Eno had other methods he would employ while making a record—a series of "tricks and subterfuges." "When I'm recording a track, for instance, I will have randomly chosen a spool of tape from my not-well-labeled tape library, and as I'm recording, the tape will also be going somewhere on the 24-track. Later, when I play back the tracks, I'll hear the random tape as well. It sounds like junk at first, but soon I'll have discovered a point where they click—something fits the sounds I've made with the random tape. Eventually I'll edit out where it doesn't work but I'll have kept about 30 per cent of it and the change is felt."[22]

One of these tape loop tracks did, in fact, make the final mix of Devo's debut album. "I remember once we were all holding pieces of tape that were 20 feet long and going around the spindle of some echo machine," Mark recalled in 2010, explaining how Eno came to integrate a tape of some "Balinese monkey chanters" into the call-and-answer section of 'Jocko Homo.' "I don't know where he recorded them, but it sounded really good, and he *timed* it. That wasn't easy then. You didn't have digital gear, but he timed the monkey chants to play in sync with the song, so we kept that. That was great."[23]

Eno's vocal harmonies on 'Uncontrollable Urge' would prevail, and so too the cascading electronic pulses (generated by the Eventide Harmonizer used to such great effect on Bowie's recent albums) that cross the stereo field midway through 'Too Much Paranoias,' but the majority of Eno's contributions went unused. In many cases, one or other of the band would slowly slide down the fader on his parts during the mixing process. "We'd be looking straight ahead, acting like nothing happened," Mark recalled, "and I could feel his eyeballs going into the side of my head, like, what the fuck are you doing?"[24]

Eno's use of Oblique Strategies cards only increased the tension between band and producer. He had created the cards with his artist friend Peter Schmidt in 1975; each one provided a non-intuitive suggestion for working through difficult creative situations. The first card in the deck states "Honor thy error as a hidden intention"—and that was one of the more straightforward suggestions.

"Devo being the smartass intellectuals that we were, we thought the Oblique Strategies were pretty wanky," Jerry recalled. "They were too Zen for us. We thought that precious, pseudo-mystical, elliptical stuff was too groovy. We were into brute, nasty realism and industrial-strength sounds and beats. We didn't want pretty." As far as Devo was concerned, Eno's ideas were the total antithesis of what they intended to do with their songs. "We were married to what they were. We were driven by anger."[25]

Mark even went as far as taking a blank card from the deck, drawing a rat on it, and putting it in a mousetrap in the corner of the studio. "I thought they were silly," he recalled, "like fortune cookies, but I wish I hadn't done that."[26]

With the benefit of hindsight, the band-members would come to realize that they were not easy to work with. "We felt like we had to protect everything we did," Mark said in 2010, noting that they would soon gain a reputation for being "terrible" to work with. "We were probably really obnoxious ... in the old days."[27]

Although their contact with Eno ended after the recording of the album, Devo were keen not to burn their bridges with him, and for good reason: he loaned the band $30,000 to record their first album. "Him and David Bowie came over to Germany with us," Mark recalled, "and I'm grateful, I'll always be grateful to them for helping us do our first record."[28]

The same can't be said for Patrick Gleeson, with whom the band had recorded versions of 'Come Back Jonee' and 'Shrivel-Up' at Different Fur Studios in San Francisco. On the final album, Gleeson was credited only for engineering, but evidently thought that a production credit would have been more appropriate. "That would get into a question of what production is," Jerry later noted. "Just because somebody is in a studio, and it's theirs, and they're there—suddenly Patrick was calling himself a producer. That wasn't the case. The tracks were recorded there, they were mixed in Conny Plank's studio with Eno."[29]

Before leaving Germany, Devo would strengthen their connections to the country's music scene even further when Kraftwerk—who, like Devo, were averse to sharing the stage with another band—suggested screening *The Truth About De-evolution* in place of an opening act on their forthcoming tour. "They said, we're gonna go on our first tour, and we would like to play your film," Mark recalled. "So, in the spring of '78, they took the Devo movie as their opening act."

Meanwhile, although Bowie had not exactly been involved in the recording of Devo's album, his endorsement still affected the way the band was viewed. On the day they finished work on their album, somebody brought in a copy of the latest issue of *Melody Maker*, dated February 25 1978, the cover of which featured a photograph of Devo taken the previous year at the Goodyear Tire & Rubber Museum in Akron, Ohio. "We're all posing around these pipes and valves and dials and acting like we're scientists working in a factory," Mark recalled.[30] Although the picture took up the front page, the headline read "BOWIE DATES—and his protégés Devo (pictured left) are coming too."

It was apt that Devo had recorded their debut album in Germany, even if they didn't end up there by choice. ("We were told to," Jerry revealed at the time. "We didn't know what we wanted. It was just as easy to be told where to come."[31]) German music had been undergoing a renaissance since the late 60s, albeit one that was largely ignored by the English-speaking world. While the movement's origins can be traced back to both the Munich-based Amon Düül commune in 1967 and the founding of the Zodiak Free Arts Lab in Berlin in 1968 by Hans-Joachim Roedelius (later of Kluster/Cluster and Harmonia) and Conrad Schnitzler (later of Tangerine Dream and Kluster), it wasn't until 1972 that the British music press took notice. When they did, they gave it the dismissive appellation 'krautrock,' possibly inspired by the Amon Düül track 'Mama Düül Und Ihre Sauerkrautband Spielt Auf.' (Faust would subsequently record a song with the intentionally cheeky title 'Krautrock' in 1973.)

In December 1972, Ian MacDonald's three-part 'Germany Calling' series appeared in the NME and profiled the likes of Amon Düül, Guru Guru, Kraftwerk, Neu!, Can, Tangerine Dream, Cluster, Amon Düül II, and (his obvious favorite) Faust, along with lesser known acts such as Witthüser & Westrupp and Floh De Cologne. MacDonald had mixed opinions about the bands, and was unimpressed with Kraftwerk, calling their music "hard without convincing structure, heartless with no redeeming dignity, and ultimately a numbing bore." It was hard to know what he made of Can, who he said "epitomize a central contradiction of German rock, play some good and some awful music, and look unusually happy for a bunch of incipient schizophrenics. At the very least they're honest and articulate and cannot be ignored."[32] His beloved Faust, however, were "a single-handed justification of all the ballyhoo that's been kicked up about krautrock in recent years." He described the schizophrenic 'Meadow Meal,' an eight-minute collision of atonal clanging and scraping, eerie chants, and fuzzed-out psychedelic rock, as "the first genuine example of rock that Britain and America could not only never have conceived, but which they would, at present, find technologically impossible to emulate. This is truly avant-garde music, played with a panache and an amiable humor duplicated by no other German band."[33] MacDonald shared his last word on the genre four months later, in an article entitled 'Common Market Rock,' in which he stated: "In the wider view, however, German rock still seems to be missing its own point: which is that it can only really succeed in the area outside the Anglo-American zone, in which it has arrived too late and with neither tradition nor originality sufficient to rise above the earnest plagiarism. We don't ask for phony nationalism, *Herren und Damen*. Just something new and real."[34]

MacDonald was only partially right in his assessment. The

krautrock bands never truly found a wide audience outside of their native Germany, but they became a key influence on many other musicians. This influence would be felt most strongly in Britain, but would take somewhat longer to penetrate America. Devo, however, had become aware of Kraftwerk back in Akron, and immediately saw some similarities in approach. "Well, of course, we were first working in obscurity in basements, and when we first became aware of Kraftwerk, we were kind of crestfallen in a way that somebody beat us to it," Jerry recalled. He was also quick to see where the two acts differed. "We love what they did. But there's no sexuality there. Devo was primitive and driving sexuality at the same time. It was using cerebral concepts and synthesizers."[35] It wasn't until Devo arrived in California that they were introduced to another of krautrock's leading lights, Neu!, by Iggy Pop. "It's 1984 Nazi Music," Jerry noted in 1977. "GOOD Nazi, TOTALITARIAN music that takes your body over but you want it to!"[36]

If the krautrock bands had one unified goal, it was to create a music that was uniquely their own. Perhaps not coincidentally, they were, like Devo, the indirect product of war. If 1977 was the year zero of punk rock in Britain, 1945 was the true year zero in Germany. "For 20 years, we had got rid of culture," Can's Irmin Schmidt later explained. "It wasn't just towns that were bombed; culture was bombed, too, and you can't rebuild culture." The young German musicians had no desire to continue in the footsteps of their parents, many of whom simply refused to talk about the war after Germany's surrender. "We were born after the war," Kraftwerk's Ralf Hütter noted. "It is not much of an incentive to respect our fathers."[37] The bands were equally uninterested in emulating the blues-based rock music that was arriving direct from America (and secondhand from England), no matter how much they might have admired it. "We were pretty much aware that we weren't raised in the Mississippi Delta, or we weren't raised in Liverpool, and it was certainly not our identity," Kraftwerk's Karl Bartos recalled in 2008.[38] Hütter concurred. "After the war, German entertainment was destroyed," he told *Creem* in 1975. "The German people were robbed of their culture, putting an American head on it. I think we are the first generation born after the war to shake this off, and know where to feel American music and where to feel ourselves. We are the first German group to record in our own language, use our electronic background, and create a Central European identity for ourselves."[39] As a result of others' actions, then, the young German bands could only look forward. "There was nothing for our generation to look back on; there was only the future," said Flür. "The future was a land of hope, heroes, security, music and fashion."[40] Jerry Casale realized as much in 1977—most likely before he knew that Devo would record their first album there—when he remarked: "I think we have to look to Germany at this point. Germany—I think—has totally avoided the hippie 60s."[41]

Just as the German bands had realized the disingenuousness of aping outside influences, Jerry had also made an intellectual decision to stop playing his beloved blues. He would later explain how the origins of Devo lay not in initially aimless, nonverbal jam sessions but in a conscious artistic stand. Jerry had grown up on R&B and blues and was self-taught, while Mark was a schooled musician whose leanings were more toward technically proficient progressive rock. But they made a conscious choice to abandon these influences to forge something unique. "I brought the primal ape energy and he brought the white man mathematical/architectural energy," Jerry recalled in 2008. "We decided to go beyond our genres on purpose."[42]

Some German bands, like Neu!, used repetition with slight variations and a gradual, building propulsion to break free of traditional rock idioms. Neu! began when guitarist Michael Rother and drummer Klaus Dinger replaced Kraftwerk co-founder Ralf Hütter who had temporarily left his band in 1971. "When I jammed with Ralf Hütter it was so apparent that we had the same idea for melody and harmony which was definitely not American, not blues, it was a European music," Rother recalled. "There's a German expression called *stunde null*, hour zero, and that was more or less my situation."[43]

Before Rother and Dinger could record as Kraftwerk, however, Hütter returned to the band, so they continued as Neu! Iggy Pop later explained their impact. "The drummer was playing in a way that, when you listened to it, allowed your thoughts to flow. Allowed emotions to come from within and occupy the active parts of the mind I thought. It allowed beauty to get there. The guy had somehow found a way to free himself from the tyranny of stupid blues, rock, of all conventions that I'd ever heard. Some sort of a pastoral psychedelicism."[44]

Others used emerging technology to point to a new direction. Karlheinz Stockhausen was based in Cologne and had been incorporating electronics into his compositions since the mid 50s. These works proved to be very influential on two of his students at the Hochschule für Musik Köln (Cologne University of Music), Holger Czukay and Irwin Schmidt, who later formed Can. In 1967, Czukay attended a performance of his mentor's *Kurzwellen*, which consisted of five musicians playing shortwave radios as well as traditional instruments. Before inviting American expatriate singer Malcolm Mooney to join the band in 1968, Can incorporated random shortwave frequencies into their sets instead. Kraftwerk's Florian Schneider and Ralf Hütter were also music students who would have been exposed to electronic music through their studies. Hütter remembers first hearing synthesizers in the mid-to-late 60s, not only through his academic exposure but also through film soundtracks as well, and he finally bought a Minimoog in the early 70s.

Musician and writer Wolfgang Seidel explained the appeal of these sounds by noting that electronic music "is a music without any tradition at all. The experiments that took place in the 1960s were only known by a small audience. We think of Stockhausen as the originator of electronic music, but people like Pierre Schaeffer—these were names that very few people were aware of, or the early experiments in electronic music of people like Luigi Nono. It was a high culture, avant-garde elite who knew these artists. For the 16-to-18-year-old youth the access to electronic music was very different, the tradition that existed there was from science fiction films."[45] (Seidel was speaking about the krautrock bands, although he could just as easily have been talking about Devo.)

Many of these bands also began their careers within the confines of the art world before assimilating themselves into popular music. "We were very lucky," Ralf Hütter recalled. "At the time there were electronic music concerts, happenings, the Fluxus group, etc. It was very normal; we played on the same circuit, the galleries. When we began we didn't have any engagements in the traditional music world, we were engaged in the artistic world, galleries, universities."[46]

German audiences were much more receptive to these new sounds than their American counterparts. "Germany is very open to new music," Hütter noted. "It is not like America, where there is a strong entertainment thing. Everything in America is measured by its entertainment value. If you do not draw a sell out, then you are nobody."[47] The only band to truly break out of Germany and reach a global audience, of course, was Kraftwerk, but that breakthrough came only after they had devised an all-encompassing aesthetic that tied together their various artistic concerns on their landmark fourth album, *Autobahn*, in 1974. (They have subsequently disowned their first three albums, *Kraftwerk*, *Kraftwerk 2*, and *Ralf und Florian*—and don't even ask about their pre-Kraftwerk album, *Tone Float*.)

As Professor Diedrich Diederichsen later noted, it was precisely this unifying aesthetic that made Kraftwerk's success possible. "The ideal thing was that in *Autobahn* it really had a subject matter that combined all the ideas they were thinking of," he said. "That was the genius thing about it. All of a sudden they had a subject matter; so far they were these conceptualists [that] were thinking about ideas of how to be an artist or how to be a musician in the pop world with all of these visual artists' concepts around. But they didn't have a concept matter, they didn't have a subject matter."[48] That their subject matter of driving on the autobahn also represented speeding away from the past—in terms both of Germany's tragic history and rock music's stifling Americanisms—was poetic justice.

Punk's aims, meanwhile, have typically been summed up as a desire to return rock to its most basic framework, making abundant room for spontaneous excitement in the process. Punk was given credit not only for clearing out the excesses of bloated and self-indulgent 70s rock but also for inspiring a myriad of other styles to spring up in the wake of this housecleaning. Once punk cleared the way and served as an example of the do-it-yourself spirit in action, others were free to follow in their footsteps exploring ever more adventurous avenues. Or so the story goes.

Before this revisionist history became accepted as fact, however, punk was merely considered another part of a larger, more encompassing new wave. (Only when the latter term was anointed as a marketing vehicle did a chasm develop between the perception of the two terms. While punk became something to be defiantly proud of, new wave was subsequently seen as a corporate scheme that no one would willingly align themselves with, particularly after it fizzled out.) But the idea of the simplest musical statements taking historical precedence over anything less rudimentary simply does not hold water. While the 'post-punk' bands—many of whom clearly predated their supposed punk influences and/or disavowed punk as an inspiration altogether—were obviously not preoccupied with virtuosity or concept albums, neither were they ever necessarily interested in a reductive, back to basics approach.

The goals of the new wave of bands that emerged in America and Britain in the mid-to-late 70s seems not to have been to return rock music to its three-chord roots but rather to strip out the all-pervasive blues influence that had become so ubiquitous. The Rolling Stones, Jimi Hendrix, Eric Clapton, Led Zeppelin, and the like were all essentially playing an amped version of electric blues, albeit with very different lyrical themes and a much more overt sexual energy. These building blocks of 60s rock had not only been played out but also felt wholly inappropriate to these musicians, who were more interested in looking forward than backward. (Coincidentally, when Black Sabbath ditched the blues influence after their first album—harmonica and all—they similarly founded a new genre, heavy metal.) It's not surprising that this approach would first take hold in Germany, a country that had no choice but to look forward after the war. The British followed, and the Americans—having the closest ties to the blues tradition—held out the longest, at least in any regions not on the coasts.

When the initial flush of punk (and the attendant press coverage) began to wane, it was not surprising that many turned to the krautrock bands for inspiration. In the late 70s and early 80s, British groups Ultravox, Eurythmics, and Killing Joke, as well as Australians Hunters & Collectors, would make the trek to Germany to record at Conny Plank's studio.

When Johnny Rotten appeared on the Tommy Vance show on London's Capital Radio on July 16 1977—less than a month after the release of 'God Save The Queen'—with a stack of records to play on the air, it was one of the first signs of defection from the punk camp that Malcolm McLaren had so carefully constructed. Rather than the New York Dolls, Stooges, Dr Feelgood, or even Chuck Berry, Rotten indulged in a dizzying array of obscure reggae and dub (Culture, Dr Alimantado & The Rebels, and Augustus Pablo), difficult art-rock (Nico, some of John Cale's more inaccessible work), traditional folk (Third Ear Band and an uncredited 'Drowsy Maggie'), and, of course, Captain Beefheart. He also played Can's 'Halleluhwah,' from *Tago Mago*. While Can's influence on Public Image Ltd's work is readily apparent, there is a much more direct influence from half of Neu! For the second side of their final album, *Neu! '75*, Klaus Dinger stepped out from behind his drum kit and assumed guitar and vocal duties.

His approach to the guitar was worlds apart from Rother's subtly shifting phrases. Dinger's chunky chords and elongated snarl on the stomping 'Hero' would eerily predate Rotten's work with the Sex Pistols and Public Image Ltd by at least two years. Even his dismissive lyrics, seemingly aimed at someone successful and out of touch, bore Rotten's trademark cynicism ("You're just another hero riding through the night ... Fuck your progress, fuck the press / Fuck the company ... Your only friend is money").

Prior to decamping to Germany to record with Eno, Devo had had another serendipitous encounter. While the band had released their first two singles on their own Booji Boy Records imprint, they hadn't exactly flown off the shelves. "We couldn't give them away back home," Mark recalled. "I'd get in a car and go from Akron to Cleveland and I would go into a record shop and say, hey, need some more Devo records? And the guy would walk down to the last little spot he had in his store, under 'OTHER,' and he'd go, nope, still got the one you brought in last week. And I would go, OK, and I would get in my car and go to the next record store."[49]

Copies of the two singles had, however, made their way to West Village institution Bleecker Bob's, and it was here that an English record company owner had found them. Stiff Records had formed in 1976 in London and had been documenting the city's homegrown talent as it transformed from pub rock to punk and new wave. While the label's bread and butter was acts like Nick Lowe, The Damned, Elvis Costello, Wreckless Eric, and Ian Dury, it had also licensed Richard Hell's 'Another World' single from Ork Records and proposed to do the same with Devo's singles.

After finding the singles, label founder Dave Robinson offered to release the records in Europe. Devo had agreed to let Stiff reissue the singles with the stipulation that they be presented exactly as Devo had designed them in their original runs. (As it transpired, the Stiff version of 'Satisfaction' would omit the fake boobs and scantily clad women and replace them with another shot from the same session, featuring the band, in bodybags, superimposed with cartoon letters spelling the band's name and the lower half of a woman's face in the corner of the frame.)

Although Devo began talks with Robinson prior to leaving for Germany, 'Mongoloid' / 'Jocko Homo' would not see a European release until February 1978, with 'Satisfaction' / 'Sloppy' trailing a month later, by which time the band were in Neunkirchen with Brian Eno. Their reception in Europe was a lot more enthusiastic than it had been in Akron or Cleveland, however. The 'Mongoloid' / 'Jocko Homo' single—which the band "couldn't give away" at home— reached number 51 on the UK singles chart, while 'Satisfaction' / 'Sloppy' made it to number 41—the highest position the band would ever reach on the British charts, beating even 'Whip It' (number 51 in 1980).

The band's swift ascent of the charts would prompt swipes from other bands similarly outside the mainstream yet harboring commercial aspirations themselves. One such act was Siouxsie & The Banshees, whose front woman Siouxsie Sioux and bassist Steve Severin (both former members of the Bromley Contingent) had appeared alongside the Sex Pistols during their infamous interview with Bill Grundy on the *Today* show in December 1976, where they looked more Roxy Music glam than Sex Pistols punk. (It was only when Grundy made advances on Sioux that the playfully inebriated interview turned into an obscene tirade from Pistols guitarist Steve Jones.) In July 1978, Banshees drummer Kenny Morris complained: "Some people have often said things like, how come you've had all this trouble and a group like Devo hasn't? The fact is Devo are such a comfortable package. It's all there, all their strangeness that isn't. It's all dead comfortable." Sioux concurred, adding: "As much as they're trying to go against what's normal, they're making rules and taboos for something that's abnormal, which is ridiculous." Severin was the most scathing of all, declaring: "If you take all the hype away and take what all these groups put on vinyl, even that is just rubbish."[50] (The Banshees needn't have worried. Their debut single, 'Hong Kong Garden,' released the following month would crack the UK top ten, peaking at number seven.)

Devo's presence in Germany, the release of their first single in the UK, endorsements from Bowie and Eno, plus the rumors of an intense bidding war from multiple major labels led to the group becoming the darlings of the British music press. Despite having never played a show in Europe or released more than a couple of singles (or perhaps because of these facts), Devo were now the band everyone was talking about. In typically hyperbolic fashion, *Melody Maker* enthused: "Everyone is tipping them for mega-stardom, and rumors circulate daily about million-dollar contracts and inter-company rivalry to secure their names on the dotted line. ... So why all the furore? Quite simply, Devo are extraordinary."[51]

While Devo were busy putting the finishing touches on their recordings with Brian Eno, Stiff Records had been readying the release of their second European single. At the behest of Dave Robinson, Devo had agreed to play a short run of British gigs to promote the records. They would make a quick detour north from Germany before heading back home. The first of these shows was at a club called Eric's in Liverpool, where chaos ensued before the band even began playing. A reporter for *Melody Maker*, vying for a good view of *The Truth About De-Evolution*, which was given its customary pre-performance screening, complained that the film was "completely obscured by the pogoing hordes clamped tight around the stage front." When the band appeared, they, too, were "little more than a rumor in the crush."[52] The frenzied atmosphere was exacerbated by the club's unusual setup. To protect the stage from projectiles—human or otherwise—it was enclosed by chicken wire. "They had us caged in and we never saw what the room looked like," Mark recalled. "There were just kids hanging from the ceiling down to the floor. We were in a square box." The chicken wire also served another unintended purpose, with Jerry recalling members of the audience "hanging on the chicken wire, spitting at us." The club's owner helpfully explained that the fact that the audience "gobbed you so much" meant "they really liked you guys."[53] (The stage setup bore a striking similarity to the country bar in *The Blues Brothers*, co-written by and co-starring Devo's friend, Dan Aykroyd.)

Stiff had another motive for bringing Devo to the UK, with the tiny upstart label interested in joining the bidding war to sign the band to a multi-album deal. "We were approached by every snake in the world, promising a lot of weird things and then pulling them away," Jerry recalled. "And we were then in that bidding war stage where you're the new girl in town, every guy wants to fuck you."[54] While Stiff's initial offerings were a distinctly British version of amped-up retro-soul, promptly dubbed pub rock, the label had also gained the distinction of releasing the first punk-rock record, The Damned's 'New Rose' / 'Help!' on October 22 1976. While Stiff wasn't able to offer Devo the kind of money that major labels were tempting them with, it could offer something else—the kind of credibility that comes with signing to an up-and-coming indie. After signing The Damned, Stiff had transformed pub-rock veteran and nine-to-five computer programmer Declan MacManus into an unlikely success story as the bespectacled new-wave balladeer Elvis Costello.

It seemed like a well-matched pairing, but when the two parties finally met they found they weren't so compatible after all. "We took our do-it-yourself ways and went with Stiff to get distributed in Europe," Jerry recalled. "And, of course, we were sold a bill of goods that these guys were outsiders, they were cool, they weren't like establishment suits, they were on our side, they didn't live high on the hog, therefore they weren't charging you for everything, therefore you'd make money quicker and keep more of your money. And what's funny was it was just like pigs in hippie clothes."[55]

Dave Robinson—who was indeed old enough to have tour-managed Jimi Hendrix in the 60s—later claimed that Devo had "whinged, whinged, whinged" from the moment they arrived in the UK. "I realized that I really didn't fancy having them. I like elephants, but I wouldn't like to own one."[56]

While some would contend that Devo were a punk band, when they came into contact with a truly grassroots label such as Stiff, they mixed as well as oil and water. Bob Mothersbaugh, for one, dismisses any claims that the label was ever actually a contender. "We never considered signing with them other than just—it was too expensive for us to ship our self-produced 45s to Europe so we, like, leased them to Stiff Records," he explained in 1979. "That's that."[57]

It was around this time that Toni Basil's friend and sometime collaborator, Dean Stockwell, introduced Devo to one of the most prominent figures of the late-60s hippie scene. Stockwell was so sure that Neil Young would like Devo that he sat him down and played him their entire recorded output to date. "I had a little fuckin' cassette player," he recalled, "and I'm thinkin', Jesus, I'm nervy, tryin' to ask Neil to listen to somebody else's music. But I just knew. I said, man, you gotta listen to this, and I played him 'Mongoloid' and 'Satisfaction.'"[58]

Young liked what he heard so much that he asked Devo to participate in a film that he was making. He was not a trained filmmaker, and his only previous directing experience was with 1972's *Journey Through The Past* (which he made under the pseudonym Bernard Shakey), an odd mix of performance footage of Young, CSNY, and Buffalo Springfield interspersed with seemingly random footage of whatever he found worthy of pointing his 16mm camera at. While the film may have had art-house aspirations, its *cinema vérité* style was ultimately clunky and alienating. The non-musical sequences were edited with little regard for flow or insight; at one point Young and his girlfriend are shown stopping for a roadside picnic, sitting on his car, and wordlessly staring into the distance for over ten minutes. There's also a zombie-like hippie wandering around Las Vegas in a graduate's mortarboard cap and gown who eventually pulls out a hollow Bible containing a cross-shaped syringe and shoots up by the sea. And then there are the horsemen in what appear to be black Ku Klux Klan robes carrying elongated crosses and circling a mysterious obelisk on a beach. The film was almost universally panned by critics and met with uncomprehending stares from anyone else who managed to see it.

Despite this inauspicious beginning, Young was currently at work on his second feature length film, *Human Highway*, which like his previous film had no script but did at least have some semblance of plot and characters. The film opens with Booji Boy surveying a barren, post-apocalyptic landscape, reciting parts of a poem from *My Struggle* entitled 'How Many Ropes Must A Poor Monkey Climb Before He Can Sleep In His Tree?' We then meet Young Otto (Dean Stockwell), who has inherited a small gas station and diner located next to a nuclear power plant. Young plays a dimwitted mechanic named Lionel Switch, who dreams of becoming a rock star. Since the business is failing, Young Otto decides to burn down the building and collect the insurance money. Before he can enact his plans, however, Switch's rock-star idol, Frankie Fontaine (also played by Young), stops by the garage to have repairs done on his limousine. Switch accidentally drops a wrench on his head while doing the repairs and is knocked out cold. While unconscious, he dreams he is a famous musician backed by a band of wooden Indians. When he wakes from his fantasy, a nuclear war begins and the entire cast is seen ascending to heaven.

Young cast a number of his close friends in the film, including Russ Tamblyn (who plays Lionel Switch's best friend, Fred Kelly), Dennis Hopper (diner cook Cracker), and Sally Kirkland (waitress Kathryn). He would later brag that the film was "made up on the spot by punks, potheads, and former alcoholics." Filming stretched out over four years, and the total bill eventually topped three million dollars, which Young paid for out of his own pocket. It was as much an excuse to party with his friends as anything else. "The plan was: there was no plan, no script," Stockwell has said. And it was within this rapidly devolving environment that the fresh-faced band suddenly found themselves. "Devo was like the crew of the *Starship Enterprise*— we just watched the behavior of people in Los Angeles and couldn't believe it," Jerry recalled. "It was really like observing another reality as an alien being, like the nerd that finally gets let into the prom." Unsurprisingly, Dennis Hopper was the worst offender, with Jerry describing him as a "totally frightening" mix of his characters in *Apocalypse Now* and *Blue Velvet*. "He wouldn't let you alone. He'd chase you around the set, givin' you his rap, whether you wanted to hear it or not: Devo, you think yer shit doesn't stink, don't ya. And Dean Stockwell would be behind him, laughing at everything he said—heh, heh, heh—this evil laughter, like Ed McMahon. You never knew what the hell was going on. A lotta mind-fuck games."[59]

Devo's initial perception of Neil Young was that he was emblematic of another era, and they had their doubts as to how compatible their separate visions would be. "We just thought he was the grandfather of granola," Jerry recalled, but they soon realized that they had it wrong. "He was really far out. I mean really loopy, almost like a mad scientist."[60] The band soon discovered that they had a lot more in common with Young than they would have guessed. "He acts completely low-key, soft-spoken, anti-intellectual, no idea what's going on—if you didn't know who he was, you might think he was kind of a moron," Jerry later noted. "Though when you think about it, he's really kind of a Devo character himself. Although his music was totally different, his personal iconoclasm and skepticism about the world and organized authority was just the same as ours."[61]

Young wanted to cast Devo in his film as nuclear waste workers in Linear Valley, appropriately enough. He also offered them the opportunity to play a song of their choice in the film, and gave the budding filmmaker Jerry carte blanche to write and direct a segment. The band decided to do a cover of 'Worried Man Blues' (rechristened simply 'Worried Man'), an old folk song recorded by everyone from The Carter Family to The Kingston Trio to Johnny Cash. While the lyrics of the verse usually concerned waking up with shackles on your legs and being separated from the girl you love, Devo made them more current. "Everyone's going to parties / They're all laughing, having fun," Mark sings, "Everything is fucked up / It's all coming down." Devo took their roles seriously, outfitting themselves in coveralls and hardhats, designed by Jerry, fitted with boxes containing a "self-generating circular air supply" and surgical tubing that extended into the nostrils. But while visually arresting, they had the unintended consequence of causing irritation—and ultimately bleeding—to the wearer's nose. Mark had to see a dermatologist after his nose became infected, while the oil-based makeup the band-members applied to their faces to resemble dirt caused their skin to break out. As Jerry later put it: "We always tended to do very masochistic things that seemed to be integral to the Devo aesthetic."[62]

Devo are shown loading barrels of radioactive waste onto a pickup truck, at which point they are joined by Booji Boy, who delivers a monologue that seems more hippie than punk. "I don't know what's going on in the world these days," he says. "It seems that everybody's just got everything turned around. People don't seem to care about their fellow man. They're all going for that big ice-cream cone in the sky! They haven't figured out what happens when your eyes get bigger than your belly. Like an ostrich who eats his pizza with his head stuck in the sand. If they can't see it, it isn't there. And you know, it really *does* take a worried man!"[63]

Human Highway took a very different approach to *Journey Through The Past*. This time, Young was influenced by the low-budget monster movies of his youth whose financial limitations imparted on them their own unique aesthetic. "Cheap Japanese horror-movie kind of things?" Young said. "I like that vibe. I like something that's so *unreal* that you could believe it—where the set is obviously phony. Jerry Lewis movies, Japanese horror movies, *The Wizard Of Oz*—it's all in there."[64] (Coincidentally, Young's friend and co-star Russ Tamblyn had starred ten years earlier in the Japanese monster movie—and Devo inspiration—*War Of The Gargantua*, for which he was billed as Rasu Tamburin.)

The film was shot on stylized sound stages with unnaturally bright colors, giving it a defiant air of artificiality. (Devo's suits were painted an eerie red in post-production using rotoscoping techniques.) A similar look would pervade the cinema of the 80s, most notably Francis Ford Coppola's *One From The Heart* as well as cult classics like *Pee Wee's Big Adventure* and *Terrorvision*, while many of the actors Young employed would reappear in the similarly surreal work of David Lynch (Stockwell and Hopper in *Blue Velvet*, Tamblyn and Charlotte Stewart in *Twin Peaks*).

Devo also appear in a dream sequence in the film, in which Lionel watches the band play 'Come Back Jonee' at San Francisco's tiny Mabuhay Gardens. Lionel, dressed in a beige cowboy suit and carrying an acoustic guitar, attempts to push his way through the riotous crowd to the stage, presumably to sit in with the band. The film then cuts to a shot of Lionel on a concert stage, taking a bow to enthusiastic applause. Jerry would later confirm the veracity of the Mabuhay Gardens footage. "The crowd was jumping up and down, and right at the climax of the frenzy he came running in with an acoustic guitar and people knocked him down and didn't even know who he was."[65]

Young also invited the band to Different Fur Studios where they played a new song of his called 'Hey Hey, My My (Into The Black).' The film footage shows Young clad in a strange clash of punk and hippie fashions—a Sex Pistols T-shirt, suspenders, mirrored sunglasses, and his famous guitar strap emblazoned with peace sign and pot leaves—while the band are wearing matching black 'DEVO' T-shirts and pinhead masks. Mark is shown sitting in a playpen with his Booji Boy mask on, playing his Minimoog on his lap and singing the song in a high-pitched voice. Uncomfortable with the line "Is this the story of Johnny Rotten?" he sang "Johnny Spud" instead. The song is stretched out over almost ten minutes, and has the ragged feel of a first-time collaboration between two parties. The musicians fall out of time as guitars and synthesizer slide into cacophonous maelstroms of sound while the rhythm section provides a solid, unwavering grounding. Young finally collapses into a heap beside the playpen, furiously twiddling the knobs of the synth, which are the only sounds to be heard for the last minute of the performance.

It was during this session that Young found the title of his next album, *Rust Never Sleeps*. Accounts differ as to exactly how he first heard the phrase; some have it that Mark added it to the end of a line, others say that the band chanted it while playing, that it was written on Mark's T-shirt, or even that it was scrawled across Booji Boy's diaper. (Jerry would later claim that it originated from an advertising campaign he worked on for a rust-removal company back in Akron.) However Young first heard the words, he adopted them as his own. In his hands, 'rust never sleeps' meant maintaining his relevancy in the face of the crop of punk and new wave bands storming the castle walls.

Human Highway would not see a release until 1982, although Young's version of 'Hey Hey, My My (Into The Black),' recorded with his band Crazy Horse, appeared on *Rust Never Sleeps* three years earlier. When many finally saw the movie, they assumed Young and Devo were performing a twisted interpretation of the song, not realizing that it was in fact the earliest version of the track.

Mark Mothersbaugh, for one, was decidedly unimpressed when he eventually came to view the film. "In all fairness for Neil, I think he's actually a pretty interesting guy, but he wasn't right about everything all the time," he recalled, admitting that he was initially embarrassed for Devo to be associated with it. Over time, however, his attitude softened, and when he saw the film again years later he concluded that it was "really fucked up and … kind of cool."[66]

Young's next film, also entitled *Rust Never Sleeps*, was a document of a concert on the tour in support of the album at San Francisco's Cow Palace on October 22 1978. It was not a straight concert film, however, but what Young called a "concert fantasy," a characterization justified by the stage sets, which feature ridiculously oversized amplifiers, microphones, and road cases. This equipment is shown being set up at the start of the film by roadies dressed in brown, hooded robes reminiscent of the scavenger Jawas in *Star Wars* (released the previous year). They then hoist a road case from an amplifier to reveal a sleeping Young, who opens the concert with an acoustic set that includes a version of 'Hey Hey, My My (Into The Black)' renamed 'Hey Hey, My My (Out Of The Blue).' Before 'Like A Hurricane' (augmented with a synthesizer that descends to the stage disguised as a white, winged bird), a masked figure wearing a yellow HAZMAT suit with 'DEVO' inscribed on the chest takes to the stage, only to be carted away by roadies. Young even gave the film audience Rust-O-Vision 3D glasses, although they were of the red and blue variety rather than Devo's preferred grey.

Even if many of Young and Devo's values were surprisingly similar, there were still areas where they had their differences. Devo's later habit of advertising their admittedly offbeat merchandise on the inner sleeve of their albums—a place where other bands would put nothing more interesting than song lyrics and band photos—caused Young some consternation. "We treated the record jacket like the back of a cereal box," Mark later recalled, adding that their manager, who also managed Young, had told them "Neil said it wasn't cool that you guys were merchandising buttons and T-shirts and plastic suits on your album cover."[67]

CHAPTER 9
JUNE–DECEMBER
1978

We are what we pretend to be, so we must be careful about what we pretend to be.
KURT VONNEGUT

With their first album completed, Devo now had to settle on one of the potential offers they had received from record labels. The process would be longer and more complicated than they could have possibly anticipated. Being whisked away to Europe with one of the world's top producers had increased their desirability exponentially. "The spudboys' European transplant worked credibility wonders with record bigwigs," Jerry later recalled. "Telephone madness interrupted every session at Conny's Teutonic country bunker. But lunchtime callbacks saved us from gruesome lunches composed of cheese and mystery meats resembling 70s Monsanto floor-tile designs."[1]

Devo had already met with Chris Blackwell from Island, but the realities of dealing with a European label were too costly. Impressed as the band were with the label, they were not happy with the idea that "reduced foreign royalty rates" would include the USA, which accounted for around 60–70 percent of all record sales in the world. "We really liked Chris, though," Jerry noted.[2]

Meanwhile, David Bowie was evidently keen not only to produce Devo but to sign them to a record deal with Warner Bros through his 'media-production' company, Bewlay Bros. When the band met with Bowie's lawyer in Los Angeles, however, it soon transpired that the deal would be more beneficial to Bowie than Devo. "It turned into a seven-album production deal with David Bowie collecting 50 percent of all monies received for seven years, seven albums," Bob Mothersbaugh recalled. "We were, like, gonna be David Bowie puppets."[3]

Warner Bros was in many ways the best option among the labels Devo were talking to, but the downside, according to Jerry, was that much of that money would go to Bowie. "After siphoning off a hefty 'production' fee, Bewlay Bros intended to pass the scraps onto Devo. However we would be responsible for paying back the entire nut," he recalled. "Devo no like!!"[4]

It was Virgin's Richard Branson who eventually came through with the most attractive offer, despite the band's earlier rebuffing of his offer to have Johnny Rotten join Devo, and their later claim that Branson only became interested in them when he heard that Bowie wanted to produce their debut. Crucially, Branson also promised that he would help Devo establish a film company. Satisfied with the terms, Devo signed on the dotted line—only for Warner Bros Records to respond by serving the band with a lawsuit.

Acting manager Bob Lewis would later claim that, had he not been a continent away from the band at the time, he would have implored them not to sign the Virgin deal. It turned out that Brian Eno had not in fact paid the entire bill for Devo's debut album, since Warner Bros had evidently paid for the band's equipment to be shipped to Germany, which the label saw as a tacit agreement of a worldwide record deal. "English barristers assured Devo that was nonsense," Jerry recalled, "and then proceeded to lose the case. There we were with no money, an album that had been in the can for six months, with fighting between the two record companies preventing Devo from performing or doing anything."[5]

While the band waited for the legal mess to be resolved, Branson offered a stopgap solution: an advance on a publishing deal, which the band could live on for a time. The situation was finally resolved when Warner Bros secured the rights to release the band's records in the USA, Japan, Australia, and Canada; Virgin retained the rights to Europe, but on a modified contract not nearly as good as the original. "Branson sat down with Warners and they all decided they'd cut the deal that worked for them and just tell us what it would be," Jerry recalled. "It wasn't a good deal at all."[6]

One of the worst side effects of these combined deals was what it meant for the band's publishing rights. According to Bob Lewis, who was still acting as the band's de facto manager back in Akron, Devo had signed away 50 percent of their publishing in perpetuity in exchange for the sum total of $70,000 from Branson.[7] Despite Virgin's insistence that it would make Devo's presence felt in the big leagues—"something with an influence, rather than being just another art band which fizzles out," as Mark put it—and continue the fight with Warner Bros, the band felt duped. "We ended up with this real shit middle position, having two record companies that were both pissed at us for doing our own contract rather than working through lawyers and a manager."[8] Mark would later make clear his regret at being "stupid enough to trust" Branson. "He had my publishing for a long time. I probably paid for a couple ashtrays on one of his spaceships."[9]

Despite their seemingly shrewd business sense, Devo now had two record deals—which was not what they bargained for—and something of a reputation to boot. They had also gotten off on the wrong foot with Warner Bros, which was not always enamored with the band's attempts at maintaining a delicate balancing act between artistic integrity and commercial viability.

"It's not that easy to warm up to them," Warner Bros publicist Les Schwartz later admitted. "With a record company that prides itself on how great they are, and on what they can do for a band, when they are confronted with a band such as Devo that comes complete with a package, with an art concept—Here's our art, here's our concept, here's what we want for publicity; you don't tell us, we'll tell you what we want—I think that puts a lot of people off. So I think, early on, that might have been a sore point."[10]

It was also around this time that Devo decided to hire a professional manager to take on the role handled until now by founding guitarist Bob Lewis. They opted for Neil Young's manager, Elliot Roberts, whose Lookout Management company also handled such heavyweights as Joni Mitchell and The Cars. The band would colorfully claim that they chose him based on his responses to a questionnaire sent out to a host of potential managers. "Elliot was the first to answer the questions correctly," Jerry said. The band reportedly had 'applicants' complete the second half of Devo lyrics and maxims like "Wear gaudy colors or (avoid display)." According to Jerry, Roberts had been filled in on the band's idiosyncratic philosophy by Young, and had "boned up" on the answers to the questions. "Neil called me at four in the morning and asked me if I'd heard of this band called Devo," Roberts recalled. "He said it was the best music he'd ever heard."[11] Suitably impressed by Roberts's response to the questionnaire, Devo went to see him in Hollywood. "His office was all wood-grained, laid back and mellow," Jerry continued. "Just what Devo needed!"[12]

There was also another motivating factor behind Devo's choice of Roberts. "We had tried for two years to get ourselves on *Saturday Night Live*," Casale recalled. "We'd been sending videos and music to Dan Aykroyd and John Belushi, and they were probably just throwing it in the trash." When the band met with Roberts, they asked him if he could get them a spot on the show, to which Roberts replied in the affirmative. "OK, then," Devo replied, "if you get us on *Saturday Night Live*, we'll sign with you."[13]

Bob Lewis knew that his days with the band were numbered from the way they had been after the recording sessions with Eno. "Listening to the way that Jerry was talking," he recalled in 1997, "it was apparent that he was acing me out. Warner Bros had simply told Jerry that their manager was now Elliot Roberts. I talked to Mark about it, and he said that Jerry was the boss. It wasn't a high-pressure thing; it was just a quiet resignation on the rest of the band's part. Mark said, he's got to do what he has to do, and so do you."[14]

Lewis would not take his dismissal lying down. He filed a lawsuit against Devo, citing theft of intellectual property and claiming that he had had a hand in the creation not only of the name Devo but the concept of de-evolution, the characters, the design, and virtually every aspect of the Devo universe. The case went to trial and would drag on for two-and-a-half years before finally being settled out of court when Lewis received a reported six-figure payout.

Within a year of signing to Warner Bros, Devo had become embroiled in two lawsuits. But there was also the business of making records to think about, and now that Devo had signed with the label it was time to devise a marketing plan for their debut album. While Devo had positioned themselves as anything but a typical rock band, however, the Warners marketing department had evidently failed to take note.

At a meeting with Warners, Devo were presented with a marketing plan that consisted of little more than life-size cardboard cutouts of the band-members to be placed in records stores. "Record companies had enjoyed this long run up through the 70s where they didn't have to do anything," Mark later noted. "They just pressed a record and put it in a store and it would get gobbled up." Unimpressed with the strategy, the band asked what the budget would be to fund such a campaign. Then, when they were told it would cost $5,000, they asked if they could use the money to make a film instead. The marketing executives said they'd never heard of such a thing, but when Devo reminded them that they had already made short films for 'Jocko Homo' and 'Secret Agent Man,' the label relented. "They gave us the money and we made the film 'Satisfaction,'" Mark recalled. "They just thought we were crazy."[15]

With the budget in place, Devo made arrangements to work with

Chuck Statler once again. They secured a location in downtown Akron's Old Strand Theatre that spring and blocked out the day to shoot. The stage was covered in black plastic and a white backdrop was lit with green and white exposed klieg lights while the band performed the song in their yellow chemical waste suits. Playing with broken strings and mutilated guitars, they presented a visually arrested picture despite having not yet worked out their choreographed moves. They may have given in to "the biz," as Jerry later put it, by appearing as a band ("something we thought regressive and never wanted to do"), but they counteracted the straight performance aspect by intercutting it with "a series of interludes showing frustrated attempts at fulfilling desire." Booji Boy reappears, this time to stick a fork into a toaster, marking the second of many onscreen deaths. The scene would result in the clip being banned by British television. "That was our first lesson on devolved consciousness," Jerry later noted. "Many more would follow."[16]

Elsewhere in the video, Mark is seen in the backseat of General Boy's car, being scolded for "tryin' to make some girl," and again later on a couch, post-prom, trying to do the same before being threatened by a mother in nightgown and curlers wielding a rolling pin. Perhaps the most indelible image, however, is that of the lanky, shock-headed dancer Spazz Attack in a near convulsive state—a stunning counterpoint to Devo's controlled (or even repressed) movements.

Devo met and immediately christened Spazz Attack in Los Angeles. He was born Craig Allen Rothwell III and was famous on the burgeoning punk-rock scene for being able to flip forward from a standing position and land on his back without causing himself serious bodily harm. He had been the lead singer with Arthur J. & The Gold Cups, the house band at the famed LA punk club the Masque, and was another protégé of Toni Basil, who in fact began dating Rothwell after her relationship with Jerry ended in the fall of 1978. Despite this, Rothwell would have a long association with the band, appearing in a number of videos and touring with them as the masked Booji Boy. Later, the band would make the strange claim that Booji Boy's real name was, in fact, Craig Allen Rothwell, before explaining how Rothwell, "obsessed with the idea of genetic mutation," had "submitted to a botched operation in an effort to land a media deal with Big Media. Viola! Boogie Boy—a bizarre adult infant freak with pre-adolescent sexuality and Yoda-like wisdom."[17]

Three months after their first UK dates, Devo returned to the country to play an altogether different sort of gig, this time at the urging of Virgin Records boss Richard Branson, who had booked them to play the Knebworth Festival, a massive outdoor concert on the grounds of a 15th century British estate. Devo were both ill matched to the bill and ill prepared for the performance. "We didn't know what Knebworth was," Mark later claimed, "we just said, OK, we'll do it."[18] Devo found themselves sandwiched between Phil Collins's jazz-fusion side project Brand X and Tom Petty & The Heartbreakers, playing to a crowd of approximately 70,000. (Genesis were the headliners.)

Devo's problems began when they neglected to hire a road crew, deciding instead to do the job themselves. They dressed in their blue firemen's work suits to set up their gear and did their best to blend in with the other roadies on stage. When their slot arrived, they ran offstage through the mud to their trailer to change into their new stage clothes, which consisted of white paper suits, skateboard helmets, and kneepads. The Knebworth stage was massive— exponentially larger than anything they'd played until that time— and the band were removed from the crowd by a fenced-off area in front of the stage. "Almost immediately, this hail of projectiles comes toward the stage," Jerry recalled. "But of course, the distances are so great that the people are actually hitting each other." The band were met not only with a flurry or beer cans and fruit but also with that perennial favorite of the cultured, outdoor concert: wine bottles. One of these, thrown with a force not quite sufficient to reach the band, instead hit an innocent spectator, inflicting a head injury that required 16 stitches. After that, Jerry recalled, the audience members in the front started fighting with those further back. "There was this gnarly, angry, pseudo-hippie riot going on where people are screaming at us and fighting with each other, pissed off, while we tried to play. We kind of got off on it because it was so absurd."[19] The band evidently enjoyed not only the reactions they had provoked but also the aesthetics of the scene. "It looked so good," Jerry said. "It was like playing hell."[20] In the midst of the chaos, Richard Branson sat cross-legged, nodding along to the music.

Another problem came from an unanticipated difference in mains voltage, which left the band's amps sounding "like transistor radios," as Bob Mothersbaugh put it. "That's as loud as they would get. We had to play in front of a couple of hundred thousand people and all you could hear was the vocals and the drums."[21] The band valiantly soldiered on, trying to make the best of the situation even displaying a measure of humor. At one point, Jerry took off his bass and used it to knock a few bottles back into the crowd. "Don't you have anything we can use?" he shouted. After the show, the band put their blue suits back on and returned to the stage to clear away their equipment. "All these roadies were saying, wait, weren't you just onstage playing a show?" Mark recalled.[22]

At least one member of the jaded British music press was won over that day. "As I headed for the backstage area," Dave Fudger of *Sounds* wrote, "I remembered that I'd hoped I'd be disappointed when I saw Devo in a conceited, conservative English sort of way. You know: how dare these eccentric colonials try to show *us* the future of rock'n'roll? But, by George they've got it! And they'll be back when the album comes out for a tour."[23]

Shortly after the Knebworth show, Devo issued one last single before the release of their major-label debut. 'Be Stiff' was a song penned by Jerry Casale and his soon to be estranged friend, Bob Lewis. This version was recorded by Brian Eno at Conny Plank's studio in Germany, while the B-side, 'Social Fools,' was another from Devo's deep well of self-recorded tracks (but presented here in a different version from the one eventually released on *Hardcore Devo, Vol. 1: 1974–1977*). The single ushered in Devo's tradition of including otherwise unreleased, non-album B-sides on their British singles. The cover features an illustration of Puerto Rican golfer Chi Chi Rodriguez, which Mark had found years earlier on some golf-ball packaging by the Kent Sales & Manufacturing Company. Rodriguez is pictured in his trademark straw porkpie hat, superimposed over a giant golf ball and a bright yellow background. Mark had been particularly impressed with how the image mimicked an astronaut's head in front of the moon; he had included the same illustration in *My Struggle*, above the caption "Fig. 329, Man is what man thinks."

Although the song was one of Devo's most sexually oriented to date, the lyrics were assembled in such a free associative manner— "Cucumbers ripe and rude / Bend over fixed to shoot"— that it was hard to take offense. It was also the band's best showcase yet for Bob Mothersbaugh's prowess on guitar. (He has described the track as "one of them where you just get to beat on the guitar for a long time."[24])

The song dates back to at least 1974, but seemed apt for release on Stiff Records (whose provocative motto was "If it ain't Stiff, it ain't worth a fuck"). It turned out to be something of an anthem for the label, which organized a package tour—the Be Stiff Route 78 Tour— in October and November 1978. Stiff had each of the acts on the tour (including 16-year-old Akronite Rachel Sweet) tape a version of the song one afternoon during a soundcheck using the label's mobile recording unit. Mickey Jupp & The Cable Layers played a 12-bar blues interpretation, Jona Lewie & Two's Company turned it into a country song, and Wreckless Eric & The Four Rough Men incorporated elements of Jimi Hendrix's 'Purple Haze' into their version.

It's not clear whether Devo authorized the project, or if they ever received any royalties from it. Either way, they would soon express their dissatisfaction with the label after Stiff bundled its three Devo singles into an EP, also entitled *Be Stiff*, with striking cover art by in-house designer Barney Bubbles. "Once [a] record company [has] access to your music and you're not around to see what is going on, they can do anything they want to," Mark said, adding that *Be Stiff* was released "without our permission." The 'Be Stiff' single had not been given a US release, however, leading Mark to say: "The only good thing about [the EP] is, for hardcore Devo fans, there were a couple cuts not available anywhere in the US."[25]

Before Devo could release their debut album, there was one final hurdle to overcome. The band's version of 'Satisfaction' altered the music of The Rolling Stones' original to such a degree that they needed to get the approval of none other than Mick Jagger himself before they could proceed with including it on the album. (The labyrinthine copyright laws of the time would not have required any special permission from the songwriters had Devo faithfully replicated the music, but since it had been altered so radically, the Stones had the right to halt the song's release.)

A meeting was arranged at the offices of Jagger's manager, Peter Rudge, whom Jerry would describe as "this amazing high-powered slime-bag who wore three-piece saddle-rough suits with the paisley ties and the pin stripes and everything." Rudge's office, located several blocks from New York's Central Park, was evidently befitting its high-powered tenant, with oversized stuffed chairs, a fireplace, and an afghan rug. By the time Jerry and Mark showed up to the mid-afternoon meeting, Jagger was well into a bottle or two of wine. After shaking hands with the band and exchanging pleasantries, Jagger refilled his glass, turned around, and said: "OK, let's hear it then." Mark popped in a cassette of the song and prepared for the worst.

"Mick sipped his wine, and then got up and looked like he was going to turn it off," Jerry later recalled. "But he put his wine down and his head started bopping and then he went into a full Mick

Jagger dance, right there. It was incredible. He said he liked it, and we were so elated."[26] At the end of the song, Jagger told them: "You little cuties look a lot different than your pictures."[27]

Casale and Mothersbaugh were still on cloud nine when they returned to Los Angeles to share the good news with their manager, Elliot Roberts, but Roberts showed no trace of surprise. "I told Peter Rudge to tell Mick to say he liked it because you guys might really hit it big because you are about to be on *Saturday Night Live*," he explained, "and you could make him a lot of money."[28]

Q: Are We Not Men? A: We Are Devo! finally saw release on August 28 1978 in the USA through Warner Bros, with the UK edition coming out on Virgin Records four days later, on September 1. The album begins with the same chords that open The Beatles' 'I Want To Hold Your Hand,' a track the Fab Four played on their debut run on *The Ed Sullivan Show*, which fittingly was the original impetus for Mark to take up rock music. The choice of chords was not unintentional. "Nothing's really new," Mark later noted. "Especially when you're in the parameters of rock music. So we just make conscious references to things." Almost unbelievably, John Lennon himself caught the reference and once parroted it back to Mark. After a set at Max's Kansas City, Mothersbaugh was sitting in the passenger seat of the band's Econoline van, waiting for the club to clear out so he could finish unloading their equipment and begin the long drive back to Akron. A drunken Lennon (accompanied by Ian Hunter, formerly of Mott The Hoople) then stuck his head into the van and proceeded to sing 'Uncontrollable Urge' extremely loudly from about six inches away. "He knew it was a mutation of him," Mark recalled. "He sang it for me right there with alcohol stinking spittle right into my face. I was in shock and about as high as you can get for the rest of the night. I couldn't believe it."[29]

While many have assumed that the song is about urges of the sexual variety, sex is never explicitly mentioned in the lyrics, and Mark has consistently denied it. The matter would become a comical point of contention in 2006 when the song was performed by child actors, dubbed Devo 2.0, and released by Walt Disney Records, which insisted it was about a "snack attack." Mark's original intention was much less specific. He would claim the song was simply about "angst, unfocused energy, that thing angry young men go through. People have to go out and kill a lion or lynch somebody or sell a lemon to an unsuspecting old lady, have sex with the waitress at the local drive-in—whatever it is you have to do to prove you're a man. It's something different in every culture. You have that energy and you want to do it; it's talking about that phenomenon."[30]

To convey this feeling of tension seeking release, the band's tightly controlled precision is contrasted with the wild vibrato of Mark's vocals. He delivers his lyrics in a yelping bark that is in many ways the opposite of the band's mechanistic performance. Before each verse, they lock into a repeated single chord, over which Mark sings a dozen increasingly frenzied "yeahs." Rather than building to a chorus, the song then returns to the same place; only after the verse does a chorus emerge, and even then it is considerably more subdued. This denial of release itself is almost perversely sexual, harkening back to a Freudian form of subjugation. Devo were clearly rejecting the liberated, over-sexualized cock-rock of the likes of Led Zeppelin and the free love baby boomer hippies that had enabled it, but drawing instead from the repression that those rock musicians had so proudly thrown off.

'Uncontrollable Urge' also features one of the few vestiges of experimentation that producer Brian Eno so encouraged during the recording sessions. The chiming sounds heard during the outro were generated not by a synthesizer but by a guitar amplifier. Bob Mothersbaugh had stumbled upon an odd German amp at Conny Plank's studio and found that it produced these sounds when he touched the end of a guitar cable plugged into the amp. "That buzz or grounding sound," Bob recalled, "was one of the better parts I came up with."[31]

The album's second track deals with more repressive elements, this time the brand of homegrown evangelism that had sprang up in the band's own backyard. 'Praying Hands' was inspired by Reverend Ernest Angley and his church in the Grace Cathedral located in the suburbs of Akron. His weekly television show, *The Ernest Angley Hour*, was a mainstay of Ohio television programming in the 70s. "The essence of all those raps—and Reverend is best at it—is giving in, submission," Jerry explained. "He always says, give in, let Jesus enter you." When an interviewer characterized the song as "as open an attack on religion as has recently been in pop music," Jerry seemed to agree, boasting that it was certainly better than 'Religion I' and 'Religion II' from Public Image Ltd's recently released *First Issue*. His quarrel with Angley and his ilk was tied to one of the core beliefs of the Devo philosophy. "People delegate their responsibility as individuals—as thinking living individuals—to a force that's mystical and greater than themselves," he said. "Religion is just an organized means of doing that. Of people no longer being responsible for their own actions."[32] The song begins in jaunty 6/4 time and alternates between that and a more conventional 4/4 rhythm. Mark admonishes the listener to wash their hands and brush their teeth while Jerry orders them to "assume the position / Go into doggie submission."

'Space Junk' is another song about the dangers of modern life drawn straight from the media. It was supposedly based on a 1975 article in the *Akron Beacon–Journal* about high-tech debris returning to Earth, although the band then personalized the details by focusing on a character called Sally who is hit by the titular material while "down the street in the alley." The song builds as Mark iterates the locations where the junk "keeps coming" and is slowly joined by the sound of distorted voices suggesting random radio frequencies (a form of audio junk). For all the speculation, however, the band failed to accurately predict the details of the much-ballyhooed Skylab's re-entry the following year, for when the space station returned to Earth in pieces amid much media coverage it did not land in "Cuba, Angola, Saudi

Arabia on Christmas Eve" but rather in Western Australia on July 11 1979. "Well, you know, we warned 'em," Mark noted.[33]

The next track, the shortest song on the album, is 'Too Much Paranoias' (perhaps not coincidentally a line from the Sex Pistols' 'Holidays In The Sun'). It is also the most dissonant moment on the record, leading off with the sort of mangled chords that would seem to be more at home alongside the band's early *Hardcore Devo* material. Mark directly and blatantly quotes a popular Burger King commercial of the time ("Hold the pickles, hold the lettuce / Special orders don't upset us / All we ask is that you let us serve it your way") while also referencing McDonald's ("I think I got a Big Mac attack"). A large part of the song is taken up by nothing but random scratches of guitar and cascading effects derived from Eno's Eventide Harmonizer. This dissonance segues directly into the album's most subdued and subtly nuanced track, 'Gut Feeling,' which begins with lilting arpeggios on guitar that are gradually joined by bass, drums, and a stately electric piano. After a full two minutes, Mark's vocals emerge, while the beat changes to double time for the chorus, ratcheting up the tension even further.

"It's an organic song that depends on five people trying to incrementally shift gears almost mathematically," Jerry later explained. "You increase your speeds from the beginning to the end together at a certain rate and that's all subjective and it has to start slow enough and end fast enough and increase in between smoothly"—although, in a live setting, "it never does."[34] The lyrics appear to be the sort of direct put-down of an anonymous 'you'—"I looked for silver linings / But you're rotten to the core"—familiar from Bob Dylan songs such as 'Like A Rolling Stone' and 'Positively 4th Street.' By the end, the band has worked up into a frenzy, with Bob #1 adding some guitar feedback and Mark letting out a fiendish howl. Before the entire thing descends into chaos, they launch straight into 'Slap Your Mammy,' Devo's fastest song, and the closest they ever got to straight punk rock (in fact, the 2/4 drum beat seems to anticipate hardcore more than emulate punk).

The band once again gleefully mine the rapidly aging back catalog of rock'n'roll for 'Come Back Jonee,' which recasts the archetypal figure of Chuck Berry's 'Johnny B. Goode.' In Berry's song, Johnny discovers that "he could play the guitar just like ringing a bell," prompting his mother to predict that "maybe someday your name will be in lights." Berry continued to utilize the (most likely autobiographical) character in less well-known songs, including 'Bye Bye Johnny,' in which he's leaving Louisiana by Greyhound bus and headed for Hollywood to "make some motion pictures." By the time of 'Go Go Go,' Johnny has found success playing at "the weekly record hop." Devo's Jonee, perhaps unsurprisingly, meets a much more grim fate. "Jonee jumped in his Datsun / Drove out on the expressway / Went head-on into a semi / His guitar is all that's left now." For all the similarities with Berry's song, however, Mark would later cite another iconic John as the inspiration for the lyrics Jerry added to this particular piece of "neo-fascist *Bonanza* American music": "It was sad remembrances of JFK."

The closing track, 'Shrivel-Up,' is more synthesizer-heavy than the rest of the album—no doubt inspired by Patrick Gleeson, since it was one of two tracks recorded at his Different Fur Studios—and as such points toward the direction and sound Devo would pursue on the follow-up. Lyrically, it is another warning about things that are prohibited once again going against the grain of rock's all-encompassing permissiveness, although the band still find time to reference yet another hamburger chain, the line "buy 'em by the sack" having been lifted from a jingle for White Castle's diminutive 'slider' burgers.

The album's cover artwork, meanwhile, is based around the Chi Chi Rodriguez illustration that graced the 'Be Stiff' single. Although Rodriguez himself had cleared the image for use by the band, however, Warner Bros had reservations about using the face of a recognized celebrity on the cover. When the label suggested airbrushing the picture to make it look less like the golfer, Mark offered another solution. An image had just run in a newspaper of a composite of the facial features of the previous four ex-presidents— Ford, Nixon, Johnson, and Kennedy—and Mothersbaugh suggested replacing Rodriguez's face with the same morphed image. The resultant picture shows an oddly stilted, yet passable, version of the suburban everyman. Far from looking happy, however, he seems strangely uncomfortable, resembling a mannequin more than a satisfied, successful sportsman.

With the album's release the public at large finally had a chance to assess the band that everyone had been talking about in the comfort of their own homes. The critical response was predictably galvanizing. *Trouser Press* went so far as to run three articles by three different authors titled 'YES!' 'NO!' and 'MAYBE!' Cole Springer's 'YES!' pegs Devo as a band "reflecting American society today" and "very concerned with rejecting and destroying all the false values and propaganda foisted upon us during the 60s. They strongly feel that the last decade was a 10-year wrong turn in our nation's history." 'MAYBE' by Ira Robbins (one of the magazine's founders) slyly compares the band to such throwaway fare as The Ohio Express and The 1910 Fruitgum Company. "Not unlike the Kasenetz-Katz bubblegum bands of the 60s, Devo is providing crassly commercial insubstantial pap for the teen generation; fortunately they possess the same ability to please that made songs like '1-2-3 Red Light' so unavoidably charming." Steven Grant makes his case in 'NO!' that it's all been downhill since their first single—"in other words, before they had begun ... So far, Devo has proven themselves to be a one-joke band; pity that people are taking so long to get the joke." Grant dismisses them as a gimmick without the caliber of music needed to back it up, concluding: "Sooner or later, the novelty of the whole thing is going to wear off, and Devo will have to prove themselves through their music or join the ranks of either Tiny Tim and Napoleon XIV or Kiss."[35]

In *Melody Maker*, J.B. declared the album "one helluva fine debut.

It may not seem so at first. You'll have to play it loud and often for the power and surprising intricacies to strike home."[36] From *Rolling Stone*, meanwhile, came the first in a series of contentious statements about the band. After praising Devo's version of 'Satisfaction' as "a startling gesture, yet a surprisingly convincing one," critic Tom Carson claimed that there was "not an ounce of feeling" anywhere on the album, adding that "the only commitment is to the distancing aesthetic of the put-on." He was, however, spot on in his assessment that the record is "a brittle, small masterpiece of seventies pop irony, but its shriveling, ice-cold absurdism might not define the seventies as much as jump the gun on the eighties."[37] The *NME* was unimpressed, with Andy Gill calling Devo's debut "a damp squib of an album,"[38] while Lester Bangs dismissed it as "Tinkertoy music."[39] In the *Village Voice*, Robert Christgau concluded: "If this isn't Kiss for college kids, then it's Meat Loaf for college kids who are too sophisticated to like Meat Loaf. ... In small doses it's as good as novelty music ever gets, and there isn't a really bad cut on this album. But it leads nowhere." (He did, however, give it a grade of B+.)

Devo seemed to have shared the critics' ambivalence about the album. For a band who had exerted complete control over their creative endeavors, ceding any of that autonomy—even to a producer whose work they respected—had proved a difficult transition. "If you just play the songs we recorded on a TEAC tape recorder in our basement, which were released on Stiff Records, and compare them with the versions of the same tunes we did on our first album: they get drained of their essence," Mark concluded. "Those songs turn out consistently better live and on demo tapes."[40] (The band's fans evidently agreed, and Devo quickly became a favorite target of bootleggers, who circulated numerous recordings of their live shows.) Once again, Devo would paint themselves as misunderstood outsiders even in relation to one of their most significant influences, lamenting the impact of "conflicts with outside people" and dismissing the overall sound of the record as "Devo shoved through a keyhole."[41] In an interview with *Surfin' Bird* magazine published a few months after the album's release, Mark made what would become a recurring statement for the first time when he claimed that he and his bandmates "weren't entirely satisfied with Eno's production."[42] Over time, however, he would come to view the album as his favorite. "I still love that album," he said in 2010. "I like all the albums, but I like that one the best."[43]

Around the same time, Mothersbaugh finally issued *My Struggle* in a run of 700 copies through the vanity press Neo Rubber Band Publications. The book now included a 12-page introduction written by 'Chinaman' (Jerry Casale's alter ego) that careens wildly across disparate subjects, making reference to numerous works and authors—some real, some presumably fictitious. He relates aspects of these to elements of Booji (here consistently spelled 'Boogie') Boy's work, only some of which actually appear in the ensuing text. He also fairly successfully preempts any criticisms that could be leveled at the book. "BB's significance lies in the divine purposelessness of his work. The work represents an untutored read-out on all particles passing through his chamber. … His work is waste, but it is a healthy and nutritious waste that is hard to find." Before any parallels can be drawn to the authors who have obviously inspired such writing— William S. Burroughs, Thomas Pynchon, and Kurt Vonnegut among them—Chinaman preemptively name-checks them as well.

In 1981, Jerry claimed that the book was "about everything. It's a kind of uncensored, free association on perception of the world as it really is."[44] Mark himself presumably had the book in mind years later when he referred to "the part that's inside you that you don't understand. I've had artwork through my life that I felt was like a very kindred spirit to people that talk about stream of consciousness artwork where you don't know why it happened." He would also recognize how his work had changed since he first assembled the book. "For the satisfaction of connecting up with an audience, which to me is important for an artist, I think I'm more successful if I have something—some grain of preconception of where I'm going and why."[45]

As Devo's debut album came under scrutiny, so did their unified concept of de-evolution. While opinions of the music varied, their defining theory often fell on deaf ears, when it wasn't being rejected after the most cursory of analyses. *Melody Maker* summed up the band's philosophy as "K-Tel Dada affectations meet Fritz Lang's scenario for *Metropolis* with special effects by Walt Disney, i.e. so much beating of the air with vacuous verbal broadsides that confuse and conquer."[46]

In the *Village Voice*, Robert Christgau dug a little deeper, but still wasn't particularly impressed with what he found. "The Devo Philosophy is no less coherent than the *Playboy* Philosophy, opposing the most commonplace boho-modernist no-nos—conformity, technocracy, etc," he wrote. "And if what they're for is harder to pin down, isn't that always the way? In the latest dispatches from their spokesman, General Boy, distributed to journalists as well as fan-club members, the call for 'devolution' has given way to talk of 'positive mutation,' both of which come down to the same vague thing, the underlying theme and chief commercial appeal of post-hippie sci-fi all the way to Doris Lessing—namely that weirdos (*just like* you kids holed up in your bedrooms reading and listening) will save the world (or at least yourselves). But it's always been hard to tell whether Devo thought the world (or the weirdos) worth saving; like Frank Zappa, another provincial aesthete who waited too long to go to the big city, they purvey a sour satire in which audience is sometimes indistinguishable from target. This is a band which has always reveled in contradictions. Deploring conformity, they wear uniforms and hustle more groupie gear than anybody since Kiss. Skeptical of technology, they're on their way to an all-keyboard look and favor sets that closely resemble Gary Numan's."[47]

Anyone paying attention, however, would find—behind the matching outfits, choreographed stage moves, nonsensical videos, and tightly wound sound—a clearly discernible message. Jerry Casale would explain it most lucidly when he summed up the concept of de-evolution as "entropy, things winding down, systems falling apart. And again I don't think it's a matter of opinion if you want to take that on a political level, an economic level, a cultural level, even a physical, biological level. Human beings are on a downslide. They're falling apart. There's many new diseases and there's no center. There are no firm issues or something holding whole groups of people together that make them live for something outside themselves."[48]

The band's militantly political roots would largely remain buried, however, with Devo later blaming their misperception on their label. "Our record company was very confused about who we were," Mark recalled. "They wanted us to be like 'Weird Al' Yankovic or something silly. And Devo wasn't silly. Devo was the opposite of that. Devo had a message."[49] Or, as Jerry explained to Dick Clark on *American Bandstand*: "We do give straight answers, but nobody believes them."[50]

Although he dismissed much of the de-evolution philosophy, Robert Christgau had paid more attention to Devo than most. A few months before the release of the band's debut album, he had traveled to Ohio to file a report on the music scenes in Akron and Cleveland. Devo's initial interviews with the British press, as well as the success of Pere Ubu, had sparked an interest in Northeast Ohio, and for a time it seemed as though it might be America's next great music scene. A native New Yorker, Christgau recalls how he "looked at a map and ascertained that Akron was about 40 miles south of Cleveland and 10 miles west of Kent. Something was obviously going on out there."[51] His *Village Voice* article included profiles not only of Devo but also of fellow Akronites The Bizarros and The Rubber City Rebels (who had just released a split album together entitled *From Akron*), and Chris

Butler's new band Tin Huey, as well as Cleveland's Pere Ubu and The Dead Boys.

Two months later, Britain's Stiff Records would release *The Akron Compilation*—complete with a scratch-and-sniff rubber-scented sleeve—which featured many of the aforementioned bands. The cover art prominently features the 'Shine On America' mural seen in *The Truth About De-Evolution*, but shown here in a further state of disrepair, two years having passed since the film was shot. The album sold poorly. Asked why that was at a Stiff Records staff meeting, press officer Nigel Dick replied: "'cos it's crap." Interest in the region was shortlived. "I think everybody was interested in the concept, you know: this is the new Liverpool or the new Manchester or the new Seattle," Dick recalled. "Yeah, Akron's where it's at. And I guess frankly it wasn't."[52]

Before interest in Akron and its surroundings had dried up, however, Christgau used his report to discard one term for the musical genre he found there and adopt another one. He explains that he had previously favored the term 'punk' to refer to any music indebted to Lou Reed, adding that he had considered the term 'new wave' to be "a pretentious evasion … but Akron-Cleveland is so clearly influenced by King Crimson as well as by Uncle Lou that it's broken my will." He cites Cleveland's WMMS radio (once dismissed as hopefully conservative by Devo for its reaction to their performance opening for Sun Ra) as "one of the few FM rock stations in the country that might still be called free form or at least progressive," and acknowledges that a music scene that embraces both American proto-punk and English art-rock demands a new title. "So, I give up," he writes. "This is New Wave. And since most American listeners sympathetic to punk also admire Robert Fripp, say, or at least Bowie and Eno, I must admit that the synthesis makes sense."[53]

The attempted shoehorning of a number of disparate bands into the increasingly restrictive category of 'punk' had not always been successful, and many of the bands included were quick to point this out. Despite regular appearances at San Francisco punk club the Mabuhay Gardens, Tuxedomoon's Steven Brown would say that he felt "absolutely no connection with that scene at all." His bandmate Blaine Reininger went further, noting how "the punk movement claimed to be an anti-intellectual one, when it counted within its ranks quite a few people who appreciated using their brains."[54]

Perhaps unsurprisingly, Pere Ubu's David Thomas emerged as the most vociferous critic of this movement, which he saw not as an organic development but one that was engineered or at least quickly co-opted. "We never considered ourselves as part of the punk movement," he said in 2006. "Most of the great bands of that period, like Television and Talking Heads and Pere Ubu and The Residents and a number of others, all preceded that punk invasion, as it were. Because punk is a foreign form. It was developed to sell clothes—it was a commercial operation from the very beginning. It was encouraged and taken over by Sony Corporation and Ford Motors and everybody else—whatever record company you want to mention—because you could sell clothes with it, you could sell cars with it. You can't sell clothes off [Television's] Tom Verlaine's back—nobody wants to wear the clothes that Tom Verlaine wears or David Byrne—you'd have to be insane to wear that stuff. The whole attitude of punk is that it was a reactionary force designed to short-circuit an evolving wave of third-generation rock music in America which was literate and intellectual and not at all devoted to selling blue jeans."[55]

By Thomas's estimation, the first generation of rock music would have been its initial emergence in the 50s. "By the time of [The Beach Boys'] *Pet Sounds*," he explained to *The Wire*, "rock had moved into a mature emotional phase, and by the early 70s, when the third generation was getting involved, it had reached the point of unabashed, unashamed literacy." This is squarely where he would place his own band. "Where else do you think Television and Talking Heads and Pere Ubu came from? It was that third generation."[56] He traced these bands' formative years back to the previous decade. "It was this sort of third generation rock youth that came up with all the lessons learned from the 60s, The Velvet Underground, Soft Machine, and Magma, all those great bands where rock was moving into a mature, literate phase. You have very intelligent kids who were schooled in [William] Faulkner and everything else. They were literate and ambitious and didn't want to do things that were dumbed down. They felt that rock was capable of achieving wonderful things in truly artistic ways that speak to the human condition."[57]

The Residents would probably have agreed with Thomas's assessment. "The Residents sprang more from the fact that psychedelia dead-ended," one of the band's spokesmen, Homer Flynn, said in 1993. "The people who were doing experiments in that direction stopped when they had barely scratched the surface."[58]

As well as its literacy, there was another key component of this third generation. "A number of technological developments were going," Thomas said, citing the introduction and development of the analogue synthesizer. "Pere Ubu and groups like it were a very clear-cut next step in the line rock music was taking."[59] Thomas saw the punk phenomenon as a means of relegating his band to cult status when he felt that they rightly deserved to be part of the mainstream, explaining how he felt the division between what his band was doing and radio rock of the 70s was "intensified by the punk movement. And that's why I hold such a grudge against punk music."[60]

While Pere Ubu never reached the commercial heights Thomas would have liked, other bands would find the means to achieve material success in the coming decade while honoring their avant-garde roots. They would have to wait, however, for the media's infatuation with punk—be it positive or negative—to pass.

Use of the term 'new wave,' meanwhile, extends back almost as far as 'punk rock,' although it was virtually unheard of outside of rock criticism and even then used only sparingly. Dave Marsh used the term 'New York New Wave' in the title of a 1973 article for *Melody Maker* about bands such as the New York Dolls and Blue Öyster Cult.

Then, as 'punk' began its ascent, 'new wave' seemed to accompany it every step of the way. The differences between the two terms were nearly imperceptible, with many journalists alternating between the two terms within the same article, only adding to the confusion. Contradicting the modern view that new wave was a faddish offshoot of the more resilient punk, Greg Shaw wrote: "The new wave, as a revitalization of rock'n'roll and its audience, will be with us a long time, and is broad enough to encompass any number of fads or trends, of which punk rock has merely been the first."[61] In this sense, 'new wave' was never meant as a well-defined musical style but rather a groundswell of bands that had a similar attitude and willingness to break with past traditions. This seems to be what Patti Smith had in mind when she wrote: "It's gonna be a celebration of the whole new scene, the whole new wave."[62] New wave as a music also suffered from not having any clearly defined historical precedents (as did punk in the form of the tracks collected on *Nuggets*), further adding to its nebulous nature, while its very name was borrowed from a different medium altogether.

French cinema's *Nouvelle Vague* began at the tail end of the 50s and rose to prominence in the 60s. It was started by a group of critics who had been writing for the film magazine *Cahiers du Cinéma*. Jean-Luc Godard, François Truffaut, Éric Rohmer, Claude Chabrol, and Jacques Rivette all began their careers as journalists railing against the prevailing trend of pompous and expensive costume pictures dubbed '*cinéma de qualité*' ('cinema of quality'). They found the films' plotlines stifling and divorced from the often-chaotic yet exciting energy of everyday life. "There are two types of movie critique," one critic later noted. "There's one which could be advertised as 'good home cooking,' made for people who think cinema is not a religion, but merely an agreeable pastime. Then there is this intelligentsia who write criticism in an exalted fury. This intelligentsia believes they are in a state of war. Whether they approve or condemn, they are always furious. They judge films through the lens of the cinémathèque."[63]

Eventually, despite a lack of formal training, these writers ventured into making their own films. They worked on shoestring budgets, usually with non-professional actors and hand-held cameras, shot on location and outdoors, and utilized natural lighting. Their films were riddled with technical imperfections—for which they made no apology—and often these shortcomings came to be accepted as stylistic innovations, meticulously imitated by their followers. Jarring jump cuts became a particular hallmark after Godard was forced to cut nearly an hour's worth of footage from his film *Breathless* (*À Bout de Souffle*). "People try to put everything into their first film," he later admitted. "So they're always very long. And I was no exception to the rule."[64] Perhaps due to his famous impatience, Godard violated the most basic rules of continuity editing. Rather than trying to hide his edits, he made them plain to see. He also tended not to use scripts, preferring instead to inform his actors of the plot (which he often made up as he went along) at the beginning of the day and let them improvise their dialogue in an effort to achieve a more naturalistic tone. "All you need for a movie is a gun and a girl," he famously quipped. His actors would frequently and unexpectedly address the camera directly, shattering any suspension of the viewer's disbelief, while his plotlines were commonly unresolved or ambiguous, which led to accusations of a contempt for his audience.

Filmmakers such as Godard were also unafraid to incorporate a number of sly references to literature, politics, and even advertising into their work, although their favorite allusions of all were to other films. The anti-hero in *Breathless* (played by Jean-Paul Belmondo) repeatedly mimics the gestures of Humphrey Bogart, while the closing scene of Chabrol's *The Unfaithful Wife* pays homage to the corresponding moment in Alfred Hitchcock's *Vertigo*. Jacques Demy's *The Umbrellas Of Cherbourg* and *The Young Girls Of Rochefort* were obvious tributes to the Hollywood musical, while Jean-Pierre Melville's *Bob Le Flambeur* and Jules Dassin's *Rififi* did the same with the classic American gangster film. And let's not forget that Richard

Hell based his look on a mixture French symbolist poet Arthur Rimbaud, Theatre of Cruelty playwright Antonin Artaud, and "the kid in *The 400 Blows*, the Truffaut movie."[65]

In a broader sense, however, it was the qualities of emotion over technical expertise, turning limitations into assets, and a playful plundering of the past that Sire Records president Seymour Stein saw paralleled in the CBGB bands. Stein had co-founded Sire in 1966, achieving early success with bands like Barclay James Harvest and Focus, but he was one of the first record executives to see the commercial potential in many of these new groups. He felt the only impediment to marketing these acts to Middle America was their association with the term 'punk,' and was convinced that if he could rebrand this emerging genre its chances of commercial success would be greatly enhanced. Sire had signed the Ramones in January 1976 (after reassurances their debut album would be 'beyond cheap' to record), Talking Heads in November, and then Richard Hell & The Voidoids and The Dead Boys early the following year. In the autumn of 1977, Sire launched a promotional onslaught for its fall catalog of albums—*Talking Heads 77*, The Dead Boys' *Young Loud & Snotty*, the Ramones' *Rocket To Russia*, and Richard Hell & The Voidoids' *Blank Generation*—with the catchphrase 'Don't Call It Punk' printed on T-shirts, bumper stickers, and posters.

At the same time, Sire released a promotional record with the catchy title *New Wave Rock'n'Roll: Get Behind It Before It Gets Past You*. It was packaged as two seven-inch, 33rpm records containing eight songs, two per side each from The Dead Boys, Talking Heads, The Saints, and Richard Hell & The Voidoids. Inside the gatefold sleeve, an anonymous writer dubs new wave "a pretty fancy term for the new rock'n'roll. In less self-conscious times it would have been called something like 'That wild Big Beat sound that's got teenagers hoppin' and boppin' all across the USA!' There was nothing radically new about it when Elvis first brought it to the world's attention, nor when The Beatles changed it around and made it 'the Liverpool Sound.'

Whether you call it new-wave music or punk rock, it's the same music: honest, unpretentious, energy-charged rock'n'roll. For the curious and the uninitiated, this EP should provide a comfortable, useful point of entry. The introductions are handled by Talking Heads, Richard Hell, The Dead Boys, and The Saints, representing the premier (fall, '77) release of Sire Records through Warners."[66]

A year earlier, Warner Bros had agreed to distribute Sire Records, greatly expanding the number of stores that stocked its releases. By 1978, Warners had bought 50 percent of the label, and it would acquire the rest in 1980. In a similar fashion, Warners had purchased Leon Schlesinger's cartoon studio, Looney Tunes, in 1944, and taken ownership of such characters as Porky Pig, Daffy Duck, and Bugs Bunny, who was adopted as the company's corporate mascot. This backstory would have gone some way in explaining why Sire Records' 'Don't Call It Punk' campaign prominently featured Bugs in a black leather jacket, torn jeans, and sneakers. If Sire was attempting to make new wave palatable and non-threatening to a mainstream audience, however, it was doing so to the detriment of its long-standing fans. "New wave was really a term for people [like] college kids," Legs McNeil of *Punk* magazine later noted. "I remember everyone at the time said, I don't like the Ramones but I like the Talking Heads. It was safe. New wave was safe."[67] John Lydon echoed McNeil's sentiments when he described new wave as "watered down. That was the complete corruption of everything. It was when everyone tried to be nice all over again. Don't be nice, it's the kiss of death."[68]

Meanwhile, Elliot Roberts had finally come through on his promise to get Devo on *Saturday Night Live*, something Jerry had set his sights on years earlier, sensing that the band would be a natural fit with the show's subversive and often absurd brand of humor. At the time, however, he was the only one who thought so. He had gone so far as to send copies of Devo's singles and films not only to the show but also to individual cast-members, but his follow-up calls would be stonewalled. The best he would ever get was a terse "yes, we're considering it."[69]

Roberts had leveraged his management of Young to maneuver Devo onto the show. The show's creator, Lorne Michaels, was an admirer of Young but not of Roberts's new clients. "He basically dangled Neil Young to get Devo on *SNL*," Jerry recalled. "Lorne Michaels wasn't a fan at all."[70] (Young wouldn't appear on the show until 1989.)

While *SNL* was more likely at the time to feature MOR mainstays like Jackson Browne, James Taylor, or Paul Simon, the show was also known to feature more adventurous fare, including Frank Zappa, the Grateful Dead, and even Sun Ra, who appeared two episodes before Devo in 1978. Even so, Devo were one of the first of the younger generation of bands to guest on the show, the sole prior exception having been Elvis Costello & The Attractions, who appeared as a last-minute replacement for the Sex Pistols during the previous season. (Drummer Pete Thomas wore a homemade T-shirt daubed with the words 'THANKS MALC' in reference to the Pistols' manager.)

Devo's network television debut came on October 14 1978 as part of the fourth season of *Saturday Night Live*. The band's first segment was a performance of 'Satisfaction,' for which they wore their yellow HAZMAT suits and cardboard 3D glasses, with the stage (and much of the drum kit) covered in black plastic. Bob Mothersbaugh spends nearly the entire first minute of the song with his arms by his side, twitching to the beat. At the end of the song, the band-members jump in unison to the final note and freeze in place. Only Jerry breaks the stillness to raise a hand to wave and then take a bow. It was a remarkable piece of television, quite unlike anything else on the airwaves in 1978. And it was all the more noteworthy for airing one week after The Rolling Stones had appeared on the show to perform a shambling medley of songs from *Some Girls* (an album regarded by some as a reaction to the punk incursion).

Devo return later in the show with 'Jocko Homo,' which is preceded by the first minute of *The Truth About De-Evolution*—the quality and character of which does indeed prove to be a seamless fit with the rest of the show. During an extended bridge, Jerry and the two Bobs put their guitars away and move to the center of the stage before stripping off their suits to reveal matching black DEVO T-shirts and gym shorts with bright orange knee and elbow pads. (Alan Myers manages impressively to perform this feat while keeping a steady beat on the kick drum). The band then picks up where they left off (with Bob Casale now on synthesizer) as Mark tears his suit off while lying prone on his back. They then launch into a resuscitated 'Ohio' verse, for which Mark and Jerry do a spirited back-and-forth leap, apparently burning off nervous energy. While the audience is still applauding, Jerry announces: "Duty now for the future." At the show's end, as the credits roll, Mark is shown wearing his Booji Boy mask and crawling around onstage, seemingly terrifying the cast, while the rest of the band-members stand stock still and salute.

It was only after the show finished, however, that the night's most memorable exploits took place. Jerry Casale was backstage with Bill Murray and Elliot Roberts, preparing to sample from the first gram of cocaine he had ever bought. Just as he had finished laying out two celebratory lines, John Belushi burst into the room, still wearing his Blues Brothers suit. Jerry offered his new acquaintance a line, but Belushi clearly had other ideas. "In a flash he pulled a glass straw out of his suit jacket inside breast pocket, grabbed the vial, and snorted the whole thing in one long elephant inhale, leaving the two lines on the desk," Jerry recalled. "I was slack-jawed." Belushi then produced a roll of $100 dollar bills, offering a couple to Jerry, who turned them down. Belushi then did a hand wave and 'knuck, knuck' laugh reminiscent of Curly from The Three Stooges, "spun on his heels, and darted from the room."[71]

Devo were scheduled to embark on a modest first tour within days of their *Saturday Night Live* appearance, but found that their appearance on the show had exponentially increased their visibility overnight. Before, they had played to a maximum of 400 people at Max's Kansas City. Now, the clubs they were booked to play were quickly selling out, and they were forced to reschedule to bigger venues. The tour would encompass 22 cities in the USA and Canada, as well as a detour through Europe to play an additional eight cities in Germany, France, Belgium, and the UK. They would remain on the road until the following January.

Devo's *SNL* appearance was indicative of what fans could expect from a full-length performance. Their stage show was as thought-out as every other aspect of their presentation. "Devo in the beginning was really deliberate and controlled every single moment," Jerry recalled. "There were no arbitrary movements. We either did nothing or something we thought of doing. No walking around between songs, no communication with the crowd. Nothing. Almost like a machine that just turned on and off." They also refused to break up the pace of the shows with the requisite slower songs. "Part of the insanity of Devo was the tempo assault."[72]

The band picked up further unlikely fans along the way, including another fellow client of manager Elliot Roberts. "I love them," mellow folkie Joni Mitchell announced. "They are like Dadaists to me. Everything that they express is a complete reaction against everything that we stood for. But they do it so well, theatrically speaking, and with a great sense of humor." Unfortunately, Mitchell was unable to separate the band's music from their visual presentation. "Now, as far as putting on a Devo album? It wouldn't be something I would do. It's the visuals that make them fresh and fascinating to me."[73]

Devo's second music video, for 'Come Back Jonee,' would prove in many ways to be very similar to their first. Instead of being shot at an empty theater in Akron, however, they are shown this time in front of a live audience in Los Angeles. A quick call from Roberts had ensured the use of the Roxy for an afternoon. The band's yellow Tyvek suits were replaced with what they called "Third Reich cowboy costumes" and sunglasses (although Mark seems to be wearing the same swimming goggles he had on for 'Satisfaction'), while the cut scenes this time feature not Spazz Attack or Booji Boy but a group of "aging cowboy bowlers."

Jerry would later describe the video as "our first response to our new home." Even though Warner Bros had given the band a budget of $7,500, it was still in many ways a homegrown affair. Mark had designed a poster for the occasion, offering fans the chance to "Be In A Movie with Devo at the Roxy ... Dress Devo!! Younger, the better!!" They had hoped to get 200 responses, but on the day of the shoot there were 700 fans lined up outside the club.

If the response to the casting call had exceeded Devo's expectations, so too did the audience's enthusiasm. The band were interested in capturing the high energy generated by their live shows—which were quickly becoming legendary—but they got more than they bargained for. The shoot had to be cut short after four hours when the overexcited crowd stormed the stage and snatched hats straight from the band-members' heads, as well as buttons and medals from their uniforms, making it impossible to continue filming.

The only segments not shot in Los Angeles were the bowlers. Chuck Statler found "three or four aging alcoholics" in an unemployment line in Minneapolis and hired them to "put on cowboy hats and bowl." Devo had a deep fascination with the sport, calling it the "ultimate image of blue collar America and so fitting for Devo."[74] ('Come Back Jonee' would also find its way into the Ramones' own B-movie, *Rock'n'Roll High School*, providing the soundtrack to a scene in which Principal Togar and his toadies speed through the streets of Los Angles in their souped-up motorcycle and sidecar.)

By 1978, Seymour Stein found that his attempts to rebrand his stable of bands had proved successful only in some cases. In addition to the Ramones, Talking Heads, Richard Hell & the Voidoids, and The

Dead Boys, Stein had also signed The Rubber City Rebels after they commandeered an empty billboard on Sunset Boulevard, turning the white background into a giant postcard, complete with stamp and postmark, crudely addressed to "RUBBER CITY REBELS, AKRON, OHIO 44313, ATTN. BLITZ PROD." Stein saw the billboard one night while driving by, caught their show at the Whisky A Go-Go, and within a week had signed the band to Sire. Unfortunately, the band's contract was terminated before the label had issued any of their recordings.

Meanwhile, despite Stein's best efforts, radio programmers were simply not buying his claims that bands like The Dead Boys were new wave rather than punk. "Sire was pretty much disillusioned with what was going on with punk rock because radio was not going to play it," the Rebels' Rod Firestone later recalled. "They pushed the Ramones as hard you could push, and radio was just like, no! They were playing Talking Heads, Blondie—very new-wavy kind of stuff. They weren't going to play hard rock like The Dead Boys and Rubber City Rebels. Sire signed us, Radio Birdman, and DMZ, and never put any of our records out."[75] (In 1980, with considerable help from Doug Fieger of The Knack, The Rubber City Rebels would sign to Capitol Records for the release of their sole album.)

The Dead Boys' Cheetah Chrome would later recall meeting with Stein after the release of the band's second album, *We Have Come For Your Children*, in 1978, during which Stein told them: "I bet a lot of money on punk rock. I was wrong." Bassist Jeff Magnum remembered Stein saying punk "can't go on … there's no money and people ain't buying your stupid records."[76] (The situation was not helped when, several months later, former Sex Pistol and punk poster-boy Sid Vicious was charged with the murder of his girlfriend, Nancy Spungen.) Janis Schacht, National Director Of Publicity for Sire Records in the late 70s, confirmed that this widespread blacklisting extended to bands bearing no punk influence at all. "The punk radio stigma affected all Sire acts, including Renaissance, Climax Blues

Band, and The Paley Brothers," she said. "They were all clumped together in the punk bins."[77]

One of the more outrageous conspiracy theories attributes the quashing of punk rock not to Stein but to President Jimmy Carter. Varying accounts have Carter circulating a memo or making comments to a group of record company executives during a jazz concert on the White House lawn. According to Los Angeles punk producer Geza X, Carter had told labels: "We don't want this punk rock thing to happen like in England, bringing back all the problems of the 60s and everything like that, so we're going to give you these big tax breaks if you don't sign any of these bands." As far as Geza was concerned, major labels had been "ordered not to sign any punk rock bands. So that was why that incredibly vital scene with just the most maxed out, killer bands never got any deals." Jello Biafra of The Dead Kennedys had heard the same thing. "I could be wrong about this, but I think it was Robert Fripp who claimed that he'd seen something, information somewhere, where President Jimmy Carter … laid it out that the corporations should not be signing punk rock bands because, quote, we don't want another 60s," he recalled in 2007. "Right around the time, I saw that—poof—no more underground bands were getting signed unless they put on the little pink neckties and called themselves 'new wave.'" According to Biafra, the last "true punk band" to sign to a major label in the USA was The Dickies in 1978, and that would remain the case until Warner Bros acquired Hüsker Dü in 1985.[78]

When asked about this rumor by an obviously sincere radio DJ, Bob Mothersbaugh's response was that he didn't think that the American government was able to exert such influence—not that it wouldn't try. "I really don't believe that Jimmy Carter could put pressure on Warner Bros," he said. "I mean, that's a big corporation. It's as big as Jimmy Carter."[79]

That said, there was a clear change in atmosphere, as *SoHo Weekly News* and *NY Rocker* writer Roy Trakin noted. "What was really interesting was the early controversy over the terms new wave and punk," he said. "I remember I used to asterisk out the 'U' in Punk, as though it were a dirty word. Then at one point, new wave became a dirty word, because it symbolized the commercialization of punk."[80]

While it was clear that new wave wasn't punk, however, no one was entirely sure of just what it was. Everyone seemed to have their own definition, including director David Lynch who shared his idiosyncratic view with his friend Peter Ivers on an episode of *New Wave Theatre*. "Pete, it's a truck going down the highway at 70 miles an hour," he said. "And in the back of the truck there's a hundred smiling cows. Except one of them has got its head stuck through the floor of the truck and its nose is grinding on the highway. And the smell and the scream—that's new wave."[81] *Slash* writer and Catholic Discipline singer Claude 'Kickboy Face' Bessy voiced a popular stance that it didn't exist at all. In Penelope Spheeris's documentary *The Decline Of Western Civilization*, which was filmed in 1979–80, Bessy proclaims: "I have excellent news for the world. There is no such thing as new wave. It does not exist. It's a figment of lame cunts' imagination. There was never any such thing as new wave. It was the polite thing to say when you are trying to explain you are not into the boring old rock'n'roll, but you didn't dare to say punk because you were afraid to get kicked out of the fucking party and they wouldn't give you coke anymore."[82] Esteemed music journalist Greil Marcus agreed, going so far as to describe new wave as "a code word not for punk without shock, but for punk without meaning."[83]

As the newly minted new-wave movement drew the wrath of dyed-in-the-wool punks, it was simultaneously doing what most punk bands had failed to do—make commercial inroads. (Some would argue that this was, in fact, part of its very definition.) The Cars' 'Just What I Needed' reached number 27 on the *Billboard* Hot 100 in June, followed by Talking Heads' cover of Al Green's 'Take Me To The River' (number 26) in September and culminating with Blondie's transatlantic chart-topper 'Heart Of Glass' the following January.

Some enterprising musicians saw this new genre as an opportunity. While they may not have been able to pass themselves off as punks without being unmasked as frauds, jumping on the new-wave bandwagon was a considerably easier proposition. Some came to the party unwittingly. Declan MacManus was happy for Stiff Records to rename him Elvis Costello and retool his image, which led to him becoming an icon of new wave. Others arrived at the same point through cold calculation. "I don't want to sing tuneless, disaffected rants," Sting writes in his autobiography. "I sing tender love songs. That's what I'm good at. But I also realize there's an opportunity in the chaos, and that I am perfectly able to morph, adapting what I do to suit the current climate without necessarily compromising the integrity of my songs. I can establish some sort of position, some kind of defensible space, and when the dust has settled, run my true colors up the mast."[84]

It would have been hard to accuse Devo of jumping on a bandwagon. If anything, Devo *were* the bandwagon. According to cognitive science's prototype theory of categorization, for any particular category, an exemplar is (perhaps unknowingly) chosen, against which all other possible members are compared. If an individual shares enough properties with the prototype, it is accepted as a member of the category.[85] If there was a prototype new-wave band, Devo would undoubtedly have been it. In 2012, Jerry Casale provided the foreword for Daniel Bukszpan's *Encyclopedia Of New Wave*, and in surveying the movement 30 years after the fact, he could have been describing his own band.

"New wave. What was so new about it? As the ballyhooed countdown to 1980 approached, there was a coked-up excitement in popular culture that rivaled the booze-filled abandon of the 1920s and the explosive, drug-driven culture and music wars of the Vietnam era." These bands were not only looking forward to a better a future but also finding optimism in the past. "New wave's newness was mostly a repackaged vision of the future promised in America's post-

World War II exuberance. A future that had since been buried by harsh political and economic blows dealt globally and domestically, might now finally be delivered."

This worldview—which conveniently looked past the strife of the past two decades—was wholesome enough to appeal to Middle America yet exciting enough to seem trailblazing. "The new-wave juggernaut was a music marketer's wet dream. Almost any act that was releasing material could be wrapped in new wave's glitz." While Devo used this façade as a means to subversively deliver their politically motivated messages, many of the bands that followed went no more than skin deep. "Unlike the messy business of dealing with English and American punks' nihilistic, grimy, class-conscious realities," Jerry wrote, "new-wave artists were mainly clean-scrubbed, camera-ready chipmunks ready to jerk and twitch as the TV cameras rolled."[86]

Devo's concept of subversion from the inside dovetailed with new wave's commercial appeal. For better or worse, they would be seen as the quintessential new-wave band, but they would disavow the label just as they had punk. "Some people say we're new wave," Mark said in 1978, "but if we are, we're the only thing new about it. We've got a vision."[87]

"There's no such thing as new wave," Seymour Stein would finally admit in 2006. "That was new wave at the time. Right now there's another new wave. Go to Coney Island, you'll see all the new waves you want." To Stein, the phrase was no more than a marketing term. "The abundance of good music has never been the problem. It's how actively—and properly—it's pursued and signed and promoted." His intentions were undoubtedly respectable. "I was trying to get this music that I thought was great and make it as acceptable as I could to critics," he said. Ultimately, however, he too would disown the term. "That phrase means nothing to me. It was just a more acceptable term than punk to a lot of people."[88]

The label would prove useful to Devo for a while, but ultimately it would be one they found hard to shake.

CHAPTER 10
1979

Art is whatever you can get away with.
MARSHALL McLUHAN

On January 4 1979, less than a month after the second civil trial relating to the May 4 1970 shootings at Kent State began, it was announced that an out-of-court settlement had been reached. The jury was dismissed before hearing any testimony.

The plaintiffs were awarded $675,000, to be split among the nine injured and the families of the four dead. In addition to the monetary compensation, the plaintiffs asked that Governor Rhodes and the 27 National Guardsmen who were defendants in the case sign a "statement of regret." The statement read in part: "In retrospect, the tragedy of May 4 1970 should not have occurred." It also noted that students protesting the Cambodian invasion by US troops "may have believed they were right" in continuing their protests in spite of a university ban on rallies and an order for the students to disperse. The statement went on to note that those orders had been upheld as lawful by the 6th US Circuit Court of Appeals.

"Some of the guardsmen on Blanket Hill, fearful and anxious from prior events, may have believed in their own minds that their lives were in danger," it continued. "Hindsight suggests another method would have resolved the confrontation. Better ways must be found to deal with such confrontations. We devoutly wish that a means had been found to avoid the May 4 events culminating in the Guard shootings and the irreversible deaths and injuries. We deeply regret those events, and are profoundly saddened by the deaths of four students and wounding of nine others which resulted. We hope that the

258

agreement to end this litigation will help assuage the tragic moments regarding that sad day."

The plaintiffs claimed the settlement "accomplished to the greatest extent possible under present law" their main objectives, not the least of which was financial support for Dean Kahler, who has been paralyzed. The payment was distributed as follows: $350,000 to Kahler; $42,500 to Joseph Lewis; $37,500 to Thomas Grace; $27,500 to Donald MacKenzie; $22,500 to John Cleary; $15,000 each to Alan Canfora, Douglas Wrentmore, Robert Stamps, James Russell, and the families of the four students slain; and $75,000 to attorneys' fees and expenses.

Devo wasted no time in getting started on their second album. They had the material, after all, with Mark having boasted in 1977 that the band had between 60 and 85 songs to choose from for their debut. "A lot of them are fringe songs—real whacked out," he admitted. "Private. Marginally Devo." [1] Still, the number that weren't exactly private was high. According to Mark, they had 40 songs in their live repertoire—more than enough for two albums already.

Asked shortly before the new album's release whether it would be a refinement of the first, Jerry replied: "I don't know if refine would be the right word. Hopefully we didn't refine them that much. That would be probably a bad thing. It was time to get them out, you know, spring-cleaning. That's exactly what it is." [2]

Devo chose not to replicate the European adventure they had undertaken for the first album sessions but instead stayed closer to home. Fortuitously, one of the candidates from their shortlist of potential producers happened to be available—and local. "He was one of the people in the States we had thought of using from the beginning," Jerry recalled. "We knew of his work with The Beatles and Bowie. We had good examples of what he does. We had talked about Bowie and Brian [Eno], Tony Visconti, and Giorgio Moroder, and Ken was available." [3]

The London-born Ken Scott had worked as an engineer on numerous Beatles albums during the 60s, from *A Hard Day's Night* to *The White Album*, and had co-produced David Bowie's *Hunky Dory*, *Ziggy Stardust, Aladdin Sane*, and *Pin Ups* in the early 70s. Scott also knew something about the advertising jingles that Mark, in particular, was so fond of, having recorded the ubiquitous Coca-Cola ad 'I'd Like To Buy The World A Coke' in 1971. And he had just relocated to Los Angeles.

Like Eno, Scott had helped birth some of Devo's favorite records. Unfortunately, he was not initially as fond of them as they were of him. "When I first heard the band, I thought they were a load of crap," he said in 2012. "But then I saw them on *Saturday Night Live*, and that's what did it for me. Seeing them and hearing them, I got it, and I loved it."[4] After receiving a phone call from Devo's management, Scott was flown to San Francisco to see them play live and breakfasted with them the next morning.

Although Devo had been recording themselves for years back in Akron, they didn't quite feel confident enough yet to self-produce an album. It seems that this might not have been the role they wanted Scott to fill anyway. "Ken Scott is an extremely competent technician," Mark says. "We wanted to go for a sound that was very similar to our original self-recordings. We made the decision for Ken Scott on the basis that he was primarily an engineer and we felt that he could technically help us attain that."[5]

Devo had continued to make use of Chuck Statler's technical know-how with film, and they hoped Scott could offer the same guidance with recording audio. "We've learned a lot," Jerry said after the album was finished. "What we'd like to do is produce ourselves, because Devo doesn't really need production. We have our arrangements, we have the running orders, but what we need is an incredibly sophisticated engineer." (In fact, they would go on to co-produce their next album, *Freedom Of Choice*, with Robert Margouleff, who had previously worked with Stevie Wonder and was one half of the pioneering synth duo TONTO's Expanding Head Band. They would finally helm their own production on their fourth album, *New Traditionalists*.)

Ken Scott recognized in Devo a desire to increase their technical knowledge and, unlike Eno, had no real interest in imparting his own musical ideas on the band's songs. "Devo always wanted to learn," he says. "That's why they worked with each producer only once. Took what they needed and then time to move on."[6]

The sessions took place at Chateau Recorders in North Hollywood. The studio was part of a growing trend toward 'environmental recording'—an attempt to offer a comfortable, home-like feel for the client. To that end, Chateau Recorders was housed in a two-story Spanish-styled house complete with a swimming pool and small basketball court.

In addition to the more luxurious setting, Devo also had more time to record their follow up. "We only had three-and-a-half weeks to do the first one," Jerry told *Trouser Press* before the sessions began. "We're hoping for six weeks this time, so the album will have a little more variety, explore more Devo sounds."[7]

Like Eno before him, Scott was not intimidated by Devo's use of synthesizers. They were, he said, "just another instrument. It was all a matter of finding the right tones to work with." [8] In addition to the myriad of synths, the band also used three different drum kits to vary the sound between songs, and experimented with different guitar textures. They would often speak of trying to achieve a 'small' guitar sound—the very opposite of most rock bands, who are consistently attempting to make their guitars sound 'bigger.' In one instance, rather than recording the guitar through a large amplifier, as would have been common, they sent it through a pair of headphones. "I distorted it like crazy," Scott recalled, "overloading mic pre's [pre-amps] and all of that, and then we fed it out through the headphones and picked it up again through the mic ... anything that works."[9]

The sessions were largely uneventful, devoid of the rock star excesses so common at the time. But Scott also saw some similarities to another band he had recently produced, The Tubes. "They have this stage persona that makes everyone think they're totally insane, but when you get close with them ... they are very, very clever. They'd do everything they could to make people believe this persona."

Although Devo were diametrically opposed—consciously so—to the prevailing egotistical, Bacchanalian mythmaking of rock, they did have an image of their own they were interested in maintaining. Scott received a call during the sessions from the studio owner, who had an artist interested in seeing the facilities in person. Scott and the band agreed, since they weren't particularly busy that day. "It was a normal, business-like session," Scott recalled. "Sanity prevailed. Then in walks this prospective client. Mark started to sort of run around, completely ridiculous. He almost scared the guy out of the control room by appearing completely manic; that's the only way I can describe it. ... As soon as the guy left, we sat down and continued the session as normal."[10]

If Devo were surprisingly professional in the studio, they were also economical. While Scott expected the album to run up a fee of around $150,000, Devo spent less than half of that. "He just couldn't believe there was an album that cheap which he produced," the band later noted, "because he's the kind of person who likes to sit around and eat pizza in the studio at $175 an hour."[11]

While Devo were interested in preserving the sound of their demos, they were also concerned with making their second album more appealing to the airwaves. They were mostly happy with the sound of *Q: Are We Not Men?*, but they felt that the final mix prevented it from getting as much radio play as it might have, so hoped to make the follow-up more accessible to programmers. "It's got a better rhythm section," Mark told *Trouser Press*. "We're trying to hit on a number of different levels, trying to put our music in a form that will allow it to fit in on the radio without losing content." Tellingly, Devo were paying close attention to one of the radio mainstays of the time:

disco. But their interest lay more in the sounds used than anything else. "We'd like to take the electronic sounds of disco and use them to make typically Devo songs," Mark continued. "We'd be using the same palette as all the catatonic disco music, but it would be to a different end."[12] Nothing was more polarizing to the average rock music fan in mid 1979 than disco. The phrase 'disco sucks' was common on T-shirts and graffiti, and came to be taken as fact by rock fans at large. This phenomenon reached its height on the night of July 12 1979, at Comiskey Park in Chicago. The Disco Demolition Night took place during a doubleheader baseball game and involved blowing up a crate of disco records on the field. A local album-oriented rock radio station organized the event, filling the stadium beyond capacity, and the scene quickly descended into a near riot.

In any case, most of these innovations would have to wait until Devo's third album. "We don't think this is the time to make our radical move," Jerry said at the time. "I see a radical change coming about on our next album. It'll be time; it'll be the '80s." The sound of that next record, he predicted, would be "more patently electronic and more classical," with any references to rock'n'roll "even more removed. We feel this is a good thing, because it'll finally break through and take everything that's going on and synthesize it into a form that's truly Devo, rather than implicit or talked about." He also suggested that the future of Devo would be "very danceable."[13]

Duty Now For The Future opens with a short, motivational instrumental titled 'Devo Corporate Anthem,' inspired by the tune that plays before matches in the 1975 film *Rollerball*, the soundtrack to which was composed by André Previn and features futuristic Moog funk alongside classical pieces by Bach, Tchaikovsky, and Shostakovich. Mark Mothersbaugh's electronic instrumentation of Devo's corporate anthem bears little resemblance to *Rollerball*'s, which features nothing but pipe organ and sounds more like somnolent Sunday morning church music, but the parallels ran deeper than the shared name. The film is a dystopian vision of life in 2018, when the world has been divided up and is now run not by countries but by a select few companies. Bartholomew, chairman of the Energy Corporation (played by John Houseman) tells his star player, Jonathan E. (played by James Caan), that "corporate society takes care of everything. All it asks of anyone, all it has ever asked of anyone ever, is not to interfere with management decisions."[14] Devo, meanwhile, would claim that "co-operating with a large corporate body like Warner Bros is the only way to survive. ... We're trying to do what a responsible person would do in this medium: walk the tightrope. It remains to be seen how successful it is. We're Warners' rollerball team."[15]

The album's second track, 'Clockout,' is a Jerry Casale-penned, garage rock-influenced track with copious guitar riffing and hardly any synthesizer in sight until the end, where it merely provides some sound effects. Lyrically, the song appears to mock the dreary, workaday office life—one of Devo's deepest wells of inspiration. This time, they focus on the macho braggadocio of a laissez-faire middle manager as he ends his workday ("I'm afraid the future's gonna be / Maintenance free / I got the big brush for your bowl / Baby, can't you dig my plea?").

Track three is another instrumental, 'Timing X.' Again written by Mark, it is entirely electronic, save for a few notes of guitar. It clocks in at just over a minute and builds to a galloping crescendo. 'Wiggly World' begins by paraphrasing the third and first points of the Devolutionary Oath (concerning the survival of the fittest and the wearing of "gaudy colors") while the rest of the lyrics work almost as proto rap, complete with nonsensical rhyming couplets. Following the album's alternating scheme, it's another guitar-heavy track, this one co-written by Bob Mothersbaugh and Jerry Casale. The synthesizer parts peppered throughout are a perfect example of Mark's claim that he would write parts he could play "with a fist instead of fingers."[16]

'Blockhead' is the album's first instance of a seamless blend between the two previously partitioned camps of guitar and synthesizer. A sinewy synthesizer melody lays itself over the palm-muted guitar, while the addition of an extra three beats after each line of the verse (changing the song from 4/4 in the chorus to an unsettling 11/8 in the verses) helps keep things from getting too comfortable. Its restrained feel is perfectly suited to the observational tone of the lyrics. The blockhead in question, at first glance, could be a descendant of the "mongoloid" who masked his deficiencies so well that "no one knew." This year's model "never tips over" and "stands up on his own." While these lyrics could refer to another anonymous nine-to-five wage slave, it was initially inspired by another frequent source of ideas. Bob Mothersbaugh wrote the music one evening in his basement before his brother Mark stopped by to add lyrics. Bob suggested the title "after seeing a sinus spray commercial, where the congested person's head was shaped like a block before using the spray." [17] Twenty minutes later, the song was complete, with a demo recorded featuring a percussion track consisting of a chain beating against a metal pole.

While methodically avoiding most rock music clichés, Devo did break one taboo on 'Strange Pursuit,' which they would later describe as a "Devo love song." [18] Pointing more toward the synth-pop direction the band would pursue on the following year's *Freedom Of Choice*, the track features a tight, driving synth arrangement with a few buried, distorted guitar chords. Mark's increasingly impassioned vocals provide a contrasting counterpoint. The lyrics detail a possibly mutual attraction that remains unrequited ("Intersecting love lines / Drew us closer every.") Again, the song's origins are much more prosaic. Rather than being inspired by a member of the opposite sex, they were in fact derived from Japanese dolls with magnets in their mouths ("the heads either attract or repel"). [19] It's followed by 'S. I. B. (Swelling Itching Brain),' another track in the vein of 'Uncontrollable Urge,' although this time the involuntary bodily reactions are physical and not mental.

In early 1979, *Rolling Stone* posed a question of Devo: "Are we not

265

fascists?" It was an accusation that would dog the band for some time (as it had one of their musical heroes, David Bowie). Devo responded by telling the magazine that "the word fascism has zero meaning at this point, zero valence."[20] This may go some way in explaining why the album's eighth track, 'Triumph Of The Will,' shares its title with Leni Riefenstahl's 1935 film document of the previous year's Nazi Party Congress in Nuremberg, which became a key piece of propaganda for the Germans during World War II. Devo's lyrics have nothing to do with politics, but they were still eminently controversial. The first verse seems to speak to a truly uncontrollable urge ("a messy situation" of "desire for a girl"). For some, the next verse (about "the thing females ask for / When they convey the opposite") came much too close to sounding like a rapist's justification, although Jerry Casale would dub this, too, "a love song." His subsequent explanation, however, was no less crude. "Some [people] have poles and some have holes, and they're constantly in a state of agitation, going after each other or repelling each other, and it's just ... one man's statement about overcoming fear of the hole for one given night."[21]

Whatever the song's intended meaning, it did little to mitigate the Nazi comparisons. Reviewing a concert later that year, *Rolling Stone*'s Chris Morris claimed that the show "bore all the orgiastic earmarks of a Nuremburg rally for spudboys. The noisy, ebullient fans, some of whom dressed in the bright yellow Devo uniforms being sold in the lobby, screamed with glee at the group's propaganda films, aped singer Mark Mothersbaugh's twitching mock-fascist salutes during 'Praying Hands,' loudly chanted 'We are Devo!' throughout the chorus of 'Jocko Homo,' and stood in reverential silence as the 'Devo Corporate Anthem' played. About the only thing missing from the pageantry was a stage setting by Nazi architect Albert Speer."[22] In 1981, the same magazine would ask whether Devo were "Sixties Idealists or Nazis and Clowns." As far as the band was concerned, *Rolling Stone* was taking things too seriously, with Jerry noting how people were prone to taking their "satirical and ironic statements ... as serious manifestos. We said that 'Rebellion and individuality is obsolete in corporate society' and 'Your mission is to fit in.' And they were like, wow, these guys are fascists! You know, that's how *Rolling Stone* felt. Ridiculous. Clowns, Nazis, you know. While the real clowns and real Nazis were being put on the cover."[23] (On the 1979 tribute album *Devotees*, assembled from submissions sent to Los Angeles radio station KROQ and released by Rhino Records, an outfit called The Firemen recorded a version of 'Jocko Homo' renamed 'Jocko Bozo,' apparently aping this criticism. The lyrics included the lines "Funny men all / In circus suits / Acting like queers / Just for the loot.")

For all the controversy, 'Triumph Of The Will' was one of the weakest tracks on the album, a turgid song with a militaristic drumbeat that never really takes flight. The next track, 'The Day My Baby Gave Me A Surprize,' is even more opaque in its subject matter. Mark sings about receiving a note from his "honey" but never makes clear what the note says. The ambiguity only deepens when he suggests things are returning to how they were "before the accident."

The song bears some resemblance to the folk standard 'St James Infirmary Blues,' in which the narrator finds his "baby" dead in the hospital. The song was made famous by Louis Armstrong, although a version by Cab Calloway features prominently in the 1933 Betty Boop cartoon *Snow White*, which may be where Devo were exposed to it, suggesting perhaps that the surprise in the song might be that Mark's "baby" makes an unexpected recovery. Lyrical concerns aside, the song is one of the most musically accessible on the album, and was chosen to be its first single. It has a sparse verse, consisting of a minimal drumbeat and muffled, distorted guitar, and a chorus featuring a plinky synth lead, chunky synth bass, and a soaring wordless vocal.

The B-side of the single release was 'Penetration In The Centrefold,' an outtake from the band's earlier sessions with Brian Eno. It was perhaps the most sexually explicit song in a catalog rife with sexual references both subtle and not. The song documents Mark's purchase of an unnamed magazine released every "middle of the month," its composition coinciding with the first time American magazines began to show their titular subject matter in explicit detail. According to Jerry, Mark was simply "telling the news … it was just reportage."[24] The band's simple acknowledgement of pornography—something that the oversexed rock stars of the day would surely have had no use for—aligned them with the everyman. "I think it's a necessary by-product of living in a basically anti-erotic society," they told *Search & Destroy*. "People are as guilty as they've always been."[25] Furthermore, they viewed pornography as an insightful mirror held up to society. "I think porno is like a weathervane for a culture, you know?" Mark later noted. "The more interesting the porno, the more interesting the culture."[26] Some would dismiss Devo as misogynistic, but the band vehemently disagreed. "We were more like The Three Stooges," Jerry claimed. "Whenever they have girlfriends in one of their episodes they're being brow-beaten and pushed around and man-handled by the woman, you know, pussy whipped. We were passive males of tender tails in Ohio, and we were on the short end of the stick when it came to women. What we noticed in culture, though, was the complete hypocrisy where on the one hand sex is being used to sell everything, and on the other it's always being presented as bad."[27]

Back to the album, and 'Pink Pussycat' again deals in lyrical ambiguity—this time either meaningless nonsense or a thinly veiled, sexual come-on ("Pink pussycat / I'll lick you clean"). The song itself is built around a garage-rock guitar riff with additional panned guitar stabs serving as accents. The guitar is eventually doubled with synthesizer and played at a driving pace in oddly metered 11/8 time. Mark sings the entire song is a warbled falsetto, making it either cuter or creepier, depending on your interpretation. (His repeated claim of being "so stroft" is likely a reference to a popular advertising campaign for bathroom tissue.)

The updated recording of 'Secret Agent Man' remains largely unchanged from the version that appeared in *The Truth About De-Evolution* two years earlier, save for the sound quality and the absence of Jim Mothersbaugh's homebrew electronic drums. The pace is quicker, with Bob Mothersbaugh's riff more prominent, while his rare lead vocal has gained confidence as well. It serves a similar purpose as the band's version of 'Satisfaction,' although perhaps not with the same force or impact. For Jerry, the song would go a long way to explaining what Devo were all about. "It has musically and mentality-wise about zero to do with secret agents. It rewrites the spy, the all-knowing superman, the guy that saves society and lives beyond the law. Devo's restructuring it so that it's on kind of a surreal level."[28]

'Secret Agent Man' would subsequently be issued as the second single from the album, backed by an outtake from the Ken Scott sessions, 'Soo Bawlz,' which begins with a synth-heavy intro in 7/8 before becoming a more straightforward rock song in 4/4. The lyrics concern frustrated "huboons" teased by a "pretty little mongo." Originally titled 'Blue Balls,' it was supposedly renamed in honor of Jerry's then-girlfriend, Susan Massaro.

'Smart Patrol' ("patrol" being easier to sing than "proletarian") does for the band's spud philosophy what 'Jocko Homo' did for the concept of de-evolution. The lines about being "a spudboy / Looking for a real tomato" undoubtedly refer to the situation the band would have found themselves back in Akron. And for anyone who might accuse Devo of being selfish and cynical, there's the second half of the track, 'Mr DNA,' which picks up the pace after the mid-tempo first half in much the same way 'Slap Your Mammy' does after 'Gut Feeling' on the band's first album. "Wait a minute, something's wrong," they sing, before explaining how the "altruistic pervert" of the song's title is "here to spread some genes." According to Jerry, the song was about "a strain of organisms that die so that the rest of that strain can go on. So, in the human race, it would be people who sacrifice themselves through enlightened masochism so that the whole race will benefit." Later in the song we learn that Devo "must sacrifice ourselves" so that others might live. Never one to shy away from controversy, Jerry likened this process to the Jonestown Massacre: "a good example of people doing a very moral thing is lightheaded religious people getting rid of themselves. ... They had a clear vision of their destiny which was to eliminate themselves for being stupid."[29]

The album's closing track, 'Red Eye,' reads like more nonsensical schoolyard rhyming of negatives, which the narrator has chosen to escape by train. While Kraftwerk's similarly themed 'Trans-Europe Express' takes in Vienna and the Champs-Elysees, Devo's train journey reflects their more proletarian backgrounds. "Something's rotten in Idaho / And I don't know what to do." Where the Kraftwerk track is a sleek, modern marvel of German engineering with emotionless vocals and impersonal vocoder, Devo's is a frenetic, jumpy affair with the sort of bounce you would expect from an antiquated Midwestern railcar. With its pounding drums and tinny guitar riffing, the song seems to rush by in a blur before it's gone.

While *Duty Now For The Future* has come to be seen as a transitional effort, bridging the ragged exuberance of Devo's debut with the slicker and commercially minded *Freedom Of Choice*, many hardcore fans cite it as a favorite. "That's the litmus test for being a true Devotee," Mark later noted. "If you can listen all the way from 'Devo Corporate Anthem' to the end ... that's a true fan."[30]

The album's cover art features the band's new stage outfits, which they received from a fan in an odd business. Mark Rector had started one of the first skateboard safety gear companies in California, and when he showed up backstage at a club in San Francisco and saw blood pouring from Mark's knee, he offered his services. "You know, you won't be able to do that forever," he told the band. "Why don't you guys get some safety gear?" The band duly measured up for the custom-made sets of kneepads, elbow pads, and helmets they're shown wearing on the cover.[31] For the first time, the band had handed over responsibility for creating the artwork to an outsider, Janet Perr, who would go on to design similarly Day-Glo covers for Cyndi Lauper's *She's So Unusual* and The Rolling Stones' *Dirty Work*. The bold geometric shapes and primary colors used in the design would come to define the look of the coming decade. Perr placed a photograph of the band over a block of color adjustment bars, each one emblazoned with three barcodes (extending the love of superfluous UPCs that the band had first exhibited on the 'Mongoloid' / 'Jocko Homo' single). The band-members' arms are overlaid with a grid, with a series of lines and black squares covering their faces. The rectangular main image is actually a perforated 'postcard' that could be detached from the rest of the cover.

Upon the album's release, in July 1979, many reviewers noted that the band had polished their sound without really charting any new territory. For *Melody Maker*'s Ian Birch, the band were now "a universe away from what they were in the beginning," while the most striking aspect of the record was "the slickness of its sound."[32] In *The Rocket*, Karrie Jacobs wondered whether "the most insidious torment in Artist Hell is to create a first work so original and so successful that everything that follows is overshadowed by it. *Duty Now For The Future*, if isolated in vinyl history is great ... [but] Devo II is such a complacent reiteration of an album that expanded the limits of rock that it can't win."[33] Unsurprisingly, the most scathing review came courtesy of that great bastion of rock conservatism, *Rolling Stone*. After noting how most of the album's concepts had been "recycled from Frank Zappa, The Yardbirds, and other sixties avant-gardists," Dave Marsh went on to describe its "handful of original notions" as "mostly lame or fraudulent ... To say this critic despises Devo does not go nearly far enough. When I finish typing this, I'm taking a hammer to *Duty Now For The Future*, lest it corrupt anyone dumb or innocent enough to take it seriously. Shards sent on request."[34]

Only Roy Trakin, reviewing the album for *Musician*, would call *Duty Now* "an improvement over its predecessor," correctly predicting that he would be "distinctly in the minority in that opinion." He went on to suggest that the album "deepens the group's philosophy. If Devo's first album introduced us to Devo metaphysics, *Duty Now For The Future* shows us its everyday applications ... Devo's terrifying normality, its absolute banality, its celebration of the mundane, is what comes across, and this fits in perfectly with the group's notion of exaggerating the everyday until it becomes surreal." Furthermore, he saw behind this spectacle—where many others hadn't—a real substance. "What most people tend to overlook in criticizing Devo is the frighteningly absolute sincerity of the guys. They mean what they say!"[35]

One of the "dumb or innocent" that the album particularly resonated with was the 18-year-old Henry Garfield. He claimed that *Duty Now For The Future* was "a constant spin of mine in the summer of 1979."[36] Two years later Garfield would leave his native Washington DC for Los Angeles, change his surname to Rollins, and join the band Black Flag. (Rollins would later give the album its first US CD reissue on his Infinite Zero label after Warner Bros passed it over. In his liner notes, Rollins would claim that "There are two kinds of people: those who get Devo, and those who don't.")

Once again, Devo made a video to accompany the album's release, this time for 'The Day My Baby Gave Me A Surprize.' Their budget for the clip was a whopping $12,500, which enabled them to employ special effects for the first time. The video shows the band performing against a blue screen dressed in baggy gray pants cinched at the ankles and white short-sleeved shirts adorned with the *Duty Now* logo of a silhouetted man in profile in front of a beaker and a model of an atom. (They would later offer these outfits through the Club Devo catalog, which described them as "Devo's leisure fashions," and informed prospective buyers that the "shirt-jac" featured not only the Devo logo but "Pan-American golfers," "paramecium," and "atomic bombs in tailspin." The "suburban guerilla pants" have a handy "elastic ankle knit.") They also wear silver visors that completely obscure their eyes—seemingly the next logical step after cardboard 3D glasses. Bob #1 is the only member of the band shown playing a guitar; Bob #2 and Jerry Casale are positioned behind childishly small keyboards, while Alan Myers is armed with only three synth drums and a cymbal.

According to Jerry, the band had grown bored of the "band playing/visual insert" formula, and they were now ready for "more ambitious concepts." Mark had his "new-wave Charlie Chaplin" routine, and the others "projected a firmly established personae." Working with Chuck Statler, Devo had a "smooth, effective system" for making videos; now, for the first time, they had "enough money to try Chroma keys and other effects that increase costs."[37] Here, the blue-screen background eventually gives way to a dancing matrix of multicolored pixels. The effect was generated using a shortlived creation introduced in 1976 called Atari Video Music, which when connected to a stereo and a television would produce psychedelic visuals in time with the music, although according to Mark, "all it ever did was make Navajo blanket patterns."[38]

The video quickly cuts to the band in a stylized control room, this time wearing strange white caps and slightly more conventional glasses. Mark is shown talking on the phone while a crying, diapered infant is plopped into the sterile surroundings. Later, Devo are seen outside in their blue coveralls, which now disguise hunchbacks and other bulging deformities. The baby is passed around until she slips out of a one-armed band-member's grasp. She is then seen flying through the air beneath palm trees with her arms outstretched, Superman-style. Mark (now wearing a neck brace) attempts to catch her before she lands safely in a kiddie pool. "I found out it wasn't easy to make a 14-month-old baby girl fly," Jerry later recalled.

"Unfortunately, it was easy to make her cry. I attached clear mono-filament fishing line to wrist bands hidden under her red jumpsuit and stretched the line taut, up and over a support pipe in front of a large Chroma blue sweep. Against her will, she stood up straight with her hands held high while Chuck panned a camera mounted on its side from north to south. Look closely and you will see that she cries when she flips."[39] (The baby was Bob Mothersbaugh's daughter, Alex, who would subsequently appear on the cover of Devo's sixth album, *Shout*. She would also become a member of the band The Visiting Kids alongside her father and Mark's then-wife, Nancye Ferguson.)

The video ends with an animation of a hippopotamus, which opens its mouth to reveal a potato playing one of the hippo's teeth like a xylophone; another potato materializes playing a saxophone. Mark, who drew the sequence, claimed it was one of the first attempts to use animation in a rock video. Unfortunately, the potatoes came out a bit darker than he intended, making them look "vaguely cockroach-like."

Around the same time, Devo shot another very different film, *Roll Out The Barrel* (also known as *Rod Rooter's Big Reamer*), which Jerry explained was about "Devo and the record business," with Rod Rooter being "the president of the only record company left in the world."[40] The film begins with Daddy Know-It-All, head of Big Entertainment, phoning Rooter from his office. "Rod? What's this trash I hear? Nuke symbols and spring fashions make me sick," he says, referencing Devo's new stage outfits. "You left the stable door open, and now you got trouble in the barnyard. Remember, we have a deal."

Rooter, wearing an unbuttoned silk shirt with an enormous butterfly collar and vest, says he'll "straighten 'em out." Daddy Know-It-All then instructs him to get the band "back in their yellow suits like I said, or I'm gonna have to clean house."

Devo are then shown in a white, unfurnished, loft-like space in front of a giant orange ball. They are in their white shirts with "nuke symbols," black shorts, white shoes, and tall, black socks. Their faces are hidden behind silver masks that make them look not unlike the Japanese monster movie character Ultraman. They stand around a television showing medical photographs illustrating physical deformities (familiar from *My Struggle*), making comments and laughing, until their fun is interrupted by a phone call from Rod Rooter, who wants to discuss "a few problems."

The unreleased Devo track 'Midget' plays as the band enter Rooter's office. He explains that the song is by a new group called Parcheesi: "Shipped platinum. Killer. Why can't you guys cut stuff like that?"

"Well, I guess we like ideas," Bob Mothersbaugh replies.

"Yeah, well I guess we like to talk in tonnage."

Rod proposes they release "Devo dolls" and tosses a prototype action figure on the table. "I can forgive you guys for being artists," he says, chomping on a cigar, "but I can't forgive you for being stupid. I'm not telling you what to do, I'm telling you what you're doing. You're begging for the barrel room."

Devo then head to a mirrored restaurant, where Alan is teaching an old lady to play chess. When he asks how the meeting went, Jerry says he doesn't want to talk about it. "Let's just say it's hard to sit down." They discuss the new manager Rooter has assigned them, concluding that they "don't have to wear the yellow suits."

Roll Out The Barrel was clearly inspired by Devo's dealings with major record labels, and they would sum it up as an example of what can happen to a band in corporate society. "We're giving people information and letting them in on what goes on, because nobody else ever does."[41]

Rooter was a composite of every record company executive they had ever dealt with to that point. Kip Cohen's incisive remark that Devo weren't his "kind of girl" found its way into the film, as did others. "I only wrote down what executives said to us," Jerry claimed. "I didn't make up one line ... stuff like 'I can forgive you guys for being artists, but I can't forgive you for being stupid!'—that was an

275

executive explaining to us how we had to get a more commercial sound and hire this producer who was going to write a song for us."[42]

The fact that the film features no performances, with music appearing only in the background, confirms that Devo did not think of short films as mere promotional tools. *Roll Out The Barrel* would be shown during intermission on the band's upcoming tour and would also form part of their initial video release, *The Men Who Make The Music*, which was shelved by Time Life Video in 1979, after the company became aware of its anti-industry content, before eventually being issued by Warner Home Video in 1981. If Devo had previously directed their ire at the small-minded inhabitants of their native Akron, they now had a new target to attack. (Rooter would later reappear in *We're All Devo* in 1984, with his daughter Donut played by *Saturday Night Live*'s Laraine Newman, whom Mark had started dating after Devo's appearance on the show.)

Devo began their tour in support of *Duty Now For The Future* with a handful of shows in Japan in May before moving to Canada in June. They would then spend the next three months crisscrossing the United States, before finally playing Marathon '80: A New-No-Now-Wave Festival ("a preview to rock in the 80s") at the University of Minnesota's Fieldhouse (ironically in the ROTC building) in September. This was the first of their performances as Dove (The Band Of Love) and their short set would consist of easy listening versions of 'Praying Hands' and 'Shrivel-Up' as well as covers of 'Worried Man' and Bob Dylan's 'Gotta Serve Somebody,' the original version of which had been released just over a month earlier. The latter was done in the style of another festival participant, No Wave figurehead James Chance and his band The Contortions. Devo have latterly described their interpretation as a "mash-up" of Chance's 'Contort Yourself' and Dylan's song. They convincingly ape The Contortions' style while somewhat polishing the band's rough edges.

Of course, this being Devo, they took liberties with some of Dylan's lyrics, changing "high degree thief" to "high colonic freak" and "you might be a young Turk" to "some other kind of jerk." The following month, Devo would make their second national television appearance on *Don Kirshner's Rock Concert*, playing a couple of songs each from their first two albums.

A year earlier, on the European leg of their *Q: Are We Not Men?* tour, Devo had made a new fan in Stranglers vocalist and guitarist Hugh Cornwell. The Stranglers had formed in 1974 and had been associated with London's pub-rock scene before being peripherally attached with punk rock a few years later. The categorization was somewhat shaky, however, due to the band being a few years older than many of their contemporaries (drummer Jet Black was already 40 in 1978) and quite a bit more skilled and experienced, with formal backgrounds in blues, jazz, and classical music. They also blatantly violated one of the cardinal rules of punk rock by sporting facial hair: Black was often seen with a beard while keyboardist Dave Greenfield had a decidedly un-punk moustache.

Their biggest success would come in 1981 with 'Golden Brown,' a barely disguised paean to heroin. The unlikely hit not only prominently featured a harpsichord—an instrument that was probably never less cool than it was in 1981—but alternated between two difficult time signatures, 6/8 and 7/8. Cornwell was evidently already familiar with golden brown when he took in Devo's live show. "I once had a few speedballs [heroin mixed with cocaine] before going to see Devo at the Hammersmith Odeon, and thoroughly enjoyed the show," he recalled in his memoir. "I could hardly move once I had sat down in my seat, and could not believe it when Bob Mothersbaugh, the lead guitarist, jumped down from the stage and started to walk into the audience using the backs of the chairs in the stalls. What impressed me most was that he stopped directly in front of the row I was in. It was like watching a virtual reality show. When they hit the stage wearing their stripy, yellow and black costumes, it looked as if a jam-jar full of giant wasps had been emptied onto the stage. I took the Devo boys out to supper when they were in London once. They took a good look at the menu and all picked the Steak de Veau."[43]

Cornwell had also recently met the current drummer in Captain Beefheart's Magic Band, Robert Williams, after attending all three nights of a residency the group played in San Francisco. He and Williams "got on splendidly well, and spent the next couple of nights getting wrecked after the shows in his hotel room." While on hiatus from their respective bands, they reconvened in Los Angeles to record a collaborative album, *Nosferatu*, released November 1979. Cornwell convinced Williams to go into a Los Angeles studio without any songs and instead write them on the spot. After a couple of weeks of recording, Cornwell returned to the UK, leaving Williams with the task of finishing the songs. He instructed Williams to contact Bob Mothersbaugh to see if he and Mark would be interested in appearing on a song. That song became 'Rhythmic Itch,' which Mark and Bob not only played on but also co-wrote. It is also one of the few appearances that members of Devo would make on other artists' albums.

It is fitting that they appeared on a record by a member of the Magic Band, considering the sizeable influence Beefheart had exerted on Devo since their earliest days. They made no effort to hide this debt, with Jerry referring in an early interview to the "silent movement of people" affected by Beefheart's masterpiece, *Trout Mask Replica*.[44] Many journalists also made the connection, with *Melody Maker* noting that Devo's 'Satisfaction' had been rearranged "in the style of the Magic Band."[45] The comparison was most commonly made in Britain, where Beefheart was arguably better known than in his home country, thanks in no small part to the championing of him by the influential BBC DJ John Peel. Beefheart himself had an odd view of success, and his career alternated between ensuring its failure (on the complex and difficult *Trout Mask Replica*) and blatantly striving for it (on commercially oriented but unsuccessful albums like

The Spotlight Kid and *Bluejeans & Moonbeams*). When some members of the "silent movement" began to make themselves heard, Beefheart, in typically curmudgeonly fashion, let it be known he wasn't particularly flattered. The fact that they were finding success with many of his signature sounds and rhythms was a particular point of contention. He told one journalist in early 1979 that Devo "have one of my entire drum parts, obviously, in one of their songs. But why do they have to put The Rolling Stones on it?"[46]

Beefheart felt these musical homages were not being matched with a desperately needed financial boost (by the mid 70s, he was living in a trailer in the Mojave desert). "One thing about Don Van Vliet, Captain Beefheart, is that there were a lot of bands out there like Devo, the B-52's, and the Stranglers, and several other groups that were very influenced by Beefheart's music," Williams recalled. "Rather than Beefheart kind of taking that as a tip of the hat, it was more of him saying, these people are taking my music and components of my music and they're making a lot of money with it and I'm not making any money with my music, and I think I should get paid and I should make some money off of it too. He alienated a lot of fans because of that, where he could have capitalized on that by perhaps going on tour with one of them. If Captain Beefheart had opened for Devo, I don't know how well it would have gone over with the audience, but he would have gotten a ton of exposure, because Devo was playing in front of thousands and thousands of people."[47]

By the dawn of the 80s, as this new breed of bands was exhibiting his influence, Beefheart was positioning himself for a last-ditch effort to capitalize on it. A 1980 television report from around the time of his penultimate album, *Doc At The Radar Station*, went so far as to call him "the father of the new wave" (even as Beefheart himself is shown playing some distinctly not-new-wave-approved harmonica).[48] This new angle didn't provide any inroads to the charts, however, and after one final album, Beefheart would pull the plug on his music career altogether to take up painting full time. According to Magic Band bassist Eric Drew Feldman, Beefheart's prestigious gallery representative told him he had to pick one or the other. "You'll never be respected as an artist," Michael Werner told him, "you'll be a musician that paints. If you want to be a painter you have to stop doing music."[49]

In 1979, *Rolling Stone* writer Langdon Winner noted that in the decade since *Trout Mask Replica* was released, "the vast majority of rock'n'roll fans have found it to be completely unlistenable. No record alienates the ear of modern America faster than Beefheart's magnum opus." Winner also suggested that most musicians felt the same way. "With the exception of a few punk rock guitarists who have imitated *Trout Mask Replica* licks, most rock'n'roll performers have ignored his work."[50]

With Beefheart little more than a musical footnote in his own country, many listeners had little or no reference points for Devo's music. Even the mainstream music press would strain to find precedents, usually reverting to 60s rock as a point of comparison. The *Rolling Stone* review of the band's first album had drawn comparisons to The Velvet Underground and The Byrds, while *Melody Maker*'s J.B. had suggested it reminded him of "an updated and mutated version of The Yardbirds," although he admitted that was "just a thought and not a cast-iron reference point."[51]

Devo ushered in the 80s in an enviable position. They spent the last night of 1979 playing the 13,500-capacity Long Beach Arena in their adopted home of Southern California (a venue that usually hosted FM-stapes like REO Speedwagon, Jethro Tull, Cheap Trick, and Blue Öyster Cult). They had taken time out of the recording of their third album to play the handful of dates at the end of the year before resuming work on what was to be the biggest album of their career. They were also afforded the luxury of opening the show with the third and final performance of their alter egos, the Christian soft-rock group Dove, performing Devo songs in a faux sincere style reminiscent of The Osmonds. They were outfitted for the occasion in transparent green visors, which they wore with "double-knit mustard colored suits, pasted-on sideburns, white shoes and belts, and lime green, jersey-knit wide collar shirts."[52] Devo's two sets bookended a performance by up-and-coming Los Angeles punk band X, who were still a few months away from issuing their first album.

Devo had clearly been impatient for the new decade to arrive. They had taken to characterizing themselves as "an 80s industrial band" long before the decade began, and the newspaper advertisements for their New Year's Eve show boldly proclaimed: "THE 80s ... WE'RE FOR IT!" They had completed an amazing transformation during the course of the 70s, from the germination of an idea to a scruffy art project to a powerful, innovative, and successful rock band that others would look to for inspiration. Their ambitions and abilities were expanding, and the general public would soon find themselves ready to embrace their unique blend of music, technology, and convoluted message in a way that nobody could have foreseen. Their challenge for the next decade was to maintain that position. In many ways, it would be a much harder proposition.

EPILOGUE
THE 80s

By the dawn of the new decade, it appeared that popular culture had slowly come around to Devo's way of thinking. They had once explained their ambition by noting how, having first talked about being "Ohio's version of The Residents," they then thought what they were doing was "bigger and stronger than that, so we decided to give it the acid test, which is to put it out there in the public and see how far we could take it."

"It's easy to be artsy and obscure and tedious, and it's easy to be gutless and poppy, but it's very hard to have a valid aesthetic and be popular," Jerry said. "We saw Bowie do it up through *Diamond Dogs* as well as Roxy Music and Kraftwerk. We respected those people because they had a great fine line between art and pop commerce."[1]

The Residents themselves had begun to question their theory of obscurity, and would eventually discard it, although they continued to maintain their anonymity. Hardy Fox would subsequently explain how, instead of recording music that they never planned to release, the group had latterly realized that "even though that changes what you might do, all it does is add a different factor to that. That is, you're consciously aware that you're doing something that you're not going to release. So maybe, you would do something ... BECAUSE you're not going to release it. Then in some ways, it becomes the same thing again. It's like the other side, that whole thing about one man's ceiling is another man's floor."[2] Former Residents fan club president Uncle Willie puts it more bluntly in his book, *Uncle Willie's Highly Opinionated Guide To The Residents*: "The Residents dumped the theory once the media started to notice them."[3] To drive the point home, in

October 1980 (just five months after the release of Devo's breakthrough album, *Freedom Of Choice*), The Residents issued an album of 40 one-minute-long tracks with the revealing title *Commercial Album*. The liner notes explained their rationale:

Point One: Pop music is mostly a repetition of two types of musical and lyrical phrases: the verse and the chorus.

Point Two: These elements usually repeat three times in a three-minute song, the type usually found on Top 40 radio.

Point Three: Cut out the fat, and a pop song is only one minute long. Then, record albums can hold their own Top 40; twenty minutes per side.

Point Four: One minute is also the length of most commercials, and therefore their corresponding jingles.

Point Five: Jingles are the music of America. (To convert the jingles to pop songs, program each song to repeat three times.)[4]

The band then purchased 40 one-minute ad spots on the San Francisco radio station KFRC-AM. Jay Clem made explicit what the title implied when he noted how "the conception, execution, and marketing of the LP was intended to be more commercial than anything we've done so far. ... Because the album has 40 cuts we wanted to premiere on a Top 40 station, and we have also pressed 40,000 copies of the album."[5] By having the entirety of the album played on a commercial radio station—but doing so under the pretenses of advertising rather than art—the band intentionally blurred the distinction between the two. While the album sold in respectable numbers, it was critically panned, marking a shift from the widespread praise for their earlier albums.

A few years later, the group's commercial aspirations appeared to have hit a dead end. When Devo's manager, Elliot Roberts, told them he was looking for some similarly minded artists to sign, Mark suggested The Residents, and took Roberts and his partner Billy

Gerber to see the group perform in Pasadena on their *Mole Show* tour. Mothersbaugh immediately knew he'd made a mistake. "It really looked like a high-school production," he recalled. "There were people with cardboard things where the craft paper was peeling off of the front thing cos it wasn't tacked down right ... and I was sitting there thinking, wow, this is the dinkiest thing they've ever done. It wasn't like their videos, 'cos their videos were kind of scary." Mothersbaugh's manager was predictably nonplussed. "And all I remember is Elliot ... walking up to me and saying, don't ever recommend another band to me."[6]

Others would prove more successful. Gary Panter was a Los Angeles-based artist whose turn-of-the-decade illustrations in punk fanzine *Slash* (including the flat-topped, freckled, muscle-shirted Jimbo) and his iconic logo of a shrieking, spike-haired head for The Screamers earned him the title King of Punk Art. Panter also designed album covers for Ralph Records, including the *Subterranean Modern* compilation, Renaldo & The Loaf's *Songs For Swinging Larvae* (1981), and three of the label's *Buy Or Die* samplers. In 1979, Panter wrote an 18-point manifesto, dubbed 'Rozz-Tox,' which he placed, point by point, over several months in the personal ads of the *LA Reader*. The manifesto argued that artists should relinquish outmoded ideas of themselves as bohemian rebels and embrace the potential in willingly participating in a capitalist marketplace and reaching a wider audience. In 1980, the entire Rozz-Tox Manifesto was included in the Ralph Records catalog. Many of its points read like a Devo manifesto, right down to the choice of words:

Item 1: The avant-garde is no corpus. It merely lies in shock after an unfortunate bout with its own petard. It feigns sleep but one eye glitters and an involuntary twitch in the corner of the mouth belies a suppressed snicker. The giggle of coming awake at one's own funeral dressed in atomic TV beatnik furniture. A mutant with a mission.

Item 9: It is unfortunate and unacceptable what vile and lazy do-nothings are given unwarranted credence for mouthing such foul and mean clichés as "rip-off" and "sell-out." They have no understanding of our economy and the time it takes society to go. Confess and shut up! Capitalism good or ill is the river in which we sink or swim. Inspiration has always been born of recombination.

Item 10: In a capitalistic society such as the one in which we live, aesthetics as an endeavor flows thorough a body which is built of free enterprise and various illnesses. In boom times art may be supported by wildcat speculation or by excess funds in form of grants from the state or patronship as a tax write-off. Currently we are suffering from a lean economy. By necessity we must infiltrate popular mediums. We are building a business-based art movement. This is not new. Admitting it is.

Item 11: Business. 1. To create a pseudo-avant-garde that is cost effective. 2. To create merchandising platforms on popular communications and entertainment media. 3. To extensively mine our recent and ancient past for icons worth remembering and permutating: recombo archaeology.

Item 13: Market saturation was reached in the sixties—everyone knows that. Fine Elitist Art is of diminishing utility. There is not more reward for maintaining or joining an elite and sterile crew.

Panter would later work as a set designer on *Pee Wee's Playhouse* (for which Mark Mothersbaugh composed the theme song), winning three Emmy Awards in the process. By contrast, in 1986, Residents/Cryptic Corporation 'spokesman' Homer Flynn would note: "The Residents' primary interest has always been more or less to do what they want to do, and if that means being a cult band, that's OK. If it came out to being grossly popular, that would kind of be OK too."[7]

As other bands began to take a more favorable view of consciously

285

penetrating the mainstream, Devo's subversive idea of abandoning rebellion to work within the system came to resemble not so much a challenging artistic stance as simply selling out. Their inspiration, Andy Warhol, had left his career as a commercial illustrator to work in the art world, where his paintings of Campbell soup cans and sculptures of Brillo boxes provided a commentary on the world he had left behind. Devo made this journey in reverse, leaving the insularity of the art world for the big business of popular music. Their attempts to provide a critique of that business (while simultaneously paying their bills) was often misinterpreted.

"We liked to cross the line between art and outright advertising," Mark said in 1988. "We made fun of it by being both subversive and being part of it all and just climbing right into the middle of it all." While this strategy may have worked for an artist like Warhol, whose critics commended him for his insightful critiques, Devo would quickly find that the world of rock criticism was a far different animal. "The mythology that the press preferred to present about Devo is that we were incredibly clever, incredibly devious, incredibly deliberate and self-aware," Jerry added. The suggestion was that Devo were "playing a game on the music business, hoodwinking them, playing a prank on them."[8]

In addition to accusations of selling out, many of the new bands that looked to Devo for inspiration would also come under fire for offering nothing to match the perceived 'substance' of rock music from the 60s and 70s. A spate of 'haircut' bands—exemplified by the ridiculously coiffed British quartet A Flock Of Seagulls—would be summarily dismissed for valuing style over any trace of substance. Devo didn't fit quite so neatly into this categorization, having since their inception characterized themselves as a political band (and their haircuts were nothing special). Their strain of political commentary (mostly found in Jerry Casale's songs rather than Mark Mothersbaugh's) was of a twisted and submerged variety not readily apparent to the casual listener. (Only in 2006—26 years after its release—would Mark reveal that 'Whip It' was in fact a letter of encouragement to the unpopular, embattled US President, Jimmy Carter. "We really saw 'Whip It' as kind of a Dale Carnegie, 'You can do it' kind of thing," he said.[9])

Jumping on this new trend was made even easier by advances in technology. Relatively affordable and reliable synthesizers and drum machines would gradually make their way onto the market, and all of a sudden their ease of use made guitars seem like a hassle. Mute Records founder Daniel Miller bought his first synthesizer in 1977 and released the groundbreaking 'Warm Leatherette' as The Normal the following year. "The thing that pissed me off about punk was you had to learn three chords to be in a punk band," he said. "If you had a synthesizer, all you had to do was press one key with a finger."[10] The Human League's Philip Oakey echoed that sentiment. "Usually, with a synthesizer, you can get it to do something for you—you don't have to be manually good at all. That was why we turned to them in the first place, 'cos no one could learn how to do the guitars. It just hurts your hand. So we use these things. You can press a switch on them and they'll do things for about ten minutes. It's quite interesting."[11] The young Oakey sounded like a kid in a candy shop as he described his surprise at the sort of sounds mysteriously and effortlessly produced by his new acquisitions. The Human League would refine their sound with each subsequent release; their third album, *Dare*, would go triple platinum, while the single 'Don't You Want Me' would top the charts in both the USA and the UK in 1981. The synthesizer's ease of use would reach its tipping point in 1983 with the release of Yamaha's groundbreaking DX7, the first commercially successful digital synth.

Meanwhile, as music videos began to attract more attention, an increasing number of bands embraced the form, even as it became more of a marketing vehicle and less of an art form in its own right. Mike Nesmith (formerly of The Monkees) premiered his *PopClips* television show in late 1980, a year before an entire channel dedicated to music videos—MTV—was unveiled. Devo found themselves disappointed by the unsurprisingly commercial turn the form had taken. "What we had been doing all along turned into something called 'promo videos'—baby pictures for record companies," Mark said.[12]

Although Devo were initially embraced by MTV, their videos would later be shunned for their subversive messages. The donut and French fry from Jerry Casale's 1972 essay 'Polymer Love' would reappear ten years later in their video for 'That's Good,' a seemingly innocuous clip of the band performing on a soundstage with SMPTE color bars flashing behind them. A minute into the clip, we see an animated French fry screw itself into the hole of a frosted donut, followed by a shot of a flesh-and-blood—and apparently naked—ecstatic-looking woman. Thirty seconds later, the French fry reappears, but this time it breaks in two, and the woman casts her gaze down disappointedly. MTV refused to air the video. Jerry Casale later recalled receiving a phone call from the network's co-founder, John Sykes, who told him: "I know what you're trying to do." After that, Casale added, "MTV turned their backs on Devo."[13]

While Devo may not have considered themselves part of the new wave genre, they did recognize their influence on others. "Even in The Cars, who were just basically a get-down-and-rock'n'roll group, the additions of little fetish synthesizer lines and keyboard breaks and so on are reminiscent of Devo," Jerry suggested in 1980. "The B-52's also. I certainly don't think they could have come along and do what they do unless we laid over the barbed wire first." Devo also saw themselves in a musician whose 1979 single 'Cars' would reach the top ten in the USA and hit number one in the UK. "There's Gary Numan, with his presentation of Man: kind of robotic, kind of cold and analytical, with a lack of black roots, rock'n'roll, jerking your pelvis," Jerry continued. "The whole presentation he made was like Devo. A cold, scientific, pure, new aesthetic."[14]

Even former Kent Staters Chris Butler and Chrissie Hynde would be drawn into this environment. Butler's new project started as something of a lark. The Waitresses only became a band when Antilles

Records, a subsidiary of Island Records, wanted to issue his song 'I Know What Boys Like.' He assembled a band to record a B-side, and the single was a surprise hit. The Waitresses eventually released two full albums, a Christmas single (another unexpected hit), and even the theme song to TV high school comedy *Square Pegs* (on which Devo would coincidentally appear in 1983). "I was grateful that the music business cracked open for a second and let all kinds of new stuff come on the scene," Butler later recalled, before summing up the genre's lifespan as "bigger than a minor musical-historical blip, but smaller in that the open door did not stay open for long."[15] Hynde, meanwhile, would find longer-lasting success after relocating to London in 1973. Her band, The Pretenders, released a platinum-selling debut in 1979 (on Sire Records), while the single 'Brass In Pocket' became a UK number one. Despite numerous line-up changes, they would be one of most enduring of the crop of bands to emerge at the cusp of the decade.

While Devo rejected every rock music cliché promoting the rebellious, bohemian vision of artist as truth-teller in a dishonest world, they instead devised a position that turned the equation on its head. The ideal of the artist as functioning outside of society, and therefore freed of its constraints, was declared obsolete. While punk had superficially rejected the leftover trappings of the hippies, its rebellion was cut fundamentally from the same cloth. Johnny Rotten's war cry of "Destroy" was deemed as hopelessly misguided as hippie icon Timothy Leary's motto, "Turn on, tune in, drop out." While Devo selectively took cues from both camps—the band's formation symbolically equidistant between the Summer of Love and punk's year zero—they largely adopted their own novel approach. Devo instead presented themselves as a Platonic ideal of conformity: The Men In The Gray Flannel Suits of the 21st century. This exaggerated vision of lockstepped obedience was as unrealistic as the idea of rock star as Romantic hero. Devo avoided the trap of pure parody by couching their own fiercely held beliefs behind an absurdist presentation. In championing a Warhol-like vision of artificiality, Devo freed themselves to make more honest music than nearly anyone else at the time, addressing concerns that were previously outside the purview of the medium. The ideal of authenticity so beloved of the baby-boomer rock musicians of the 60s (itself directly influenced by the self-reported travails of blues, country, and folk musicians) was, by its very definition, unattainable for those born into the relative affluence and prosperity of postwar Middle America. Devo found more inspiration in Warhol's credo that the superficial is more interesting than the authentic ("It's not what you are that counts, it's what they think you are"). Like Kiss (a band that championed the hedonistic excesses of the 70s as much as Devo disdained them), Devo almost never appeared in public out of character. They tightly controlled all the information, personal or otherwise, that they released (as de facto band spokesmen, Mark and Jerry were almost always the only members to give interviews). Just how much of this information was true—and how much was intentional exaggeration, however—is, of course, open to conjecture (and probably missing the point).

Meanwhile, their extensive plundering of sources far outside the stifling confines of rock music—including conceptual art, collage, and advertising—expanded the vocabulary of popular music in the coming decade. This intellectual and artistic curiosity provided one of the last much-needed doses of fresh ideas periodically required to save rock music from its perpetual Ouroboros. As these concepts became widely adopted in the 80s, they helped to make that decade one of the last times that rock music would embody such a forward thinking, adventurous spirit.

By then, however, the vision that Devo had pursued in the 70s had become reality, and their innovations were now so commonplace that they were easy to overlook. While the general public had spent the preceding decade giving up on the promise of the 60s, Casale, Mothersbaugh, and the rest of the band had done so in the span of a few short seconds on May 4 1970. Devo had been so far ahead of their time that the world would spend the next ten years catching up. As the decade wore on, they soldiered on with their attempts to balance their concerns of art and commerce. But as their interests (and those of the world at large) shifted in favor of the latter, they came to be seen as simply another contender in a rapidly overcrowded fray making them truly the pioneers who got scalped.

After creating *Partially Buried Woodshed* on the Kent State campus in January 1970, artist Robert Smithson intended his work to stand undisturbed until it would naturally deteriorate and symbolically return to the land. But when Smithson died in a plane crash while surveying sites for a future work in Texas on July 20 1973, his widow, Nancy Holt, began to reconsider this position. As it turns out, the university's president at the time was making plans to raze the piece, unaware of the school's investment in it. A battle over the artwork's fate began, and it was only saved by the intervention of the University Arts Commission.

The following year, half of the structure was destroyed by fire. A mangled Pepsi can containing kerosene was found inside. Again, the university lobbied to demolish what remained of the artwork, while Holt argued to let it stand. A pragmatic decision was finally reached, in the interest of safety, to simply remove any 'debris' that fell to the ground. Grounds crews would routinely carry away the rotting or charred wood that separated from the structure. When a new stadium was built on campus, the crumbling woodshed, including the 'MAY 4 KENT 70' graffiti, was clearly visible from one of the access roads to the new building. The university's solution was to landscape the area with large trees to obscure the woodshed from view.

As the years went on, fewer pilgrimages were made, and as the Woodshed was out of sight it remained largely out of mind. It wasn't until February 1984 that anyone realized that nothing but the concrete foundation remained.

291

ENDNOTES

INTRODUCTION

1 *The History Of Rock And Roll* (Warner Home Video 1995)

PROLOGUE

1 Harvey Rice, *Sketches Of Western Reserve Life* (Kessinger Publishing 2005)
2 'The Cuyahoga River Watershed,' Kent State University, November 1 1968
3 Michael Scott, *The Plain Dealer*, June 22 2009
4 *Time*, August 1 1969

CHAPTER 1: 1970–71

0 William Butler Yeats, 'The Second Coming,' *Michael Robartes And The Dancer* (Cuala Press 1920)
1 Chris Ziegler, *Obey Clothing*
2 Thomas Wictor
3 Frank Mullen, *Ink 19*, May 2000
4 avclub.com, October 17 2006
5 may4.org, February 23 2010
6 Matt Peters, *The Burr*, Spring 2005
7 Matt Peters, *The Burr*, Spring 2005
8 KZSU Radio, Stanford University, 2002
9 Robert Lewis, truthtribunal.org/testimonials, May 3 2010
10 Rob Warmowski, warmowski.wordpress.com
11 Robert Lewis, 'Some Thoughts On Devo: The First Postmodern Band' PDF (2006)
12 Rob Warmowski, warmowski.wordpress.com
13 Robert Lewis, 'Some Thoughts On Devo: The First Postmodern Band' PDF (2006)
14 Robert Lewis, 'Some Thoughts On Devo: The First Postmodern Band' PDF (2006)
15 may4.org, February 23 2010
16 Mark Rudd, *Underground: My Life*

With SDS And The Weathermen (William Morrow, 2009)
17 SDS *New Left Notes*, April 24 1969
18 *The Report Of The President's Commission On Campus Unrest* (US Government 1970)
19 hibbleton.com/interviews/
20 lynda.com, July 23 2010
21 Travis Atria, *Thriller*, February 2 2010
22 Patrick Hickey Jr, *Review Fix*, June 30 2010
23 Chris Wade, *Hound Dawg #6*, April 2010
24 Vivien Goldman, *Melody Maker*, January 1980
25 Matt Peters, *The Burr*, Spring 2005
26 hibbleton.com/interviews/
27 Author's interview, April 4 2012
28 *Search & Destroy #3*, 1977
29 Julie Grant, WSKU.org, April 6 2005
30 Samuel Lipsman, Edward Doyle, et al, *Fighting for Time* (Boston Publishing Company 1983)
31 Ashley Kahn, et al (eds), *Rolling Stone: The Seventies* (Little, Brown 1998)
32 Gerald Casale, truthtribunal.org/testimonials, May 3 2010
33 Ashley Kahn, et al (eds), *Rolling Stone: The Seventies* (Little, Brown 1998)
34 Robert Lewis, truthtribunal.org/testimonials, May 3 2010
35 Robert Lewis, truthtribunal.org/testimonials, May 3 2010
36 Chris Butler, truthtribunal.org/testimonials, May 3 2010
37 Robert Lewis, truthtribunal.org/testimonials, May 3 2010
38 Chris Butler, truthtribunal.org/testimonials, May 3 2010

39 Gerald Casale,
    truthtribunal.org/testimonials,
    May 3 2010
40 Matt Peters, *The Burr*, Spring 2005
41 Allen Ginsberg, *Berkeley Barb*,
    November 19 1965
42 Daniel Odier, *The Job: Interviews with
    William S. Burroughs* (Penguin 1989)
43 Dorothy Shinn, 'Robert Smithson's
    Partially Buried Woodshed,'
    robertsmithson.com
44 Brian L. Knight, *Vermont Review*,
    August 5 2003
45 Wil Forbis, *Acid Logic: A Decade Of
    Humorous Writing On Pop Culture,
    Trash Cinema, And Rebel Music*
    (AuthorHouse 2008)
46 Gerald Casale,
    truthtribunal.org/testimonials,
    May 3 2010
47 Chris Willman, *Spin*, August 2010
48 *Youngstown Vindicator*, November 2
    1971
49 *The Artist Formerly Known as Captain
    Beefheart* (BBC 1997)
50 Langdon Winner, *Rolling Stone*,
    May 14 1970
51 *Modesto Bee*, May 10 1970
52 *Nixon: A Presidency Revealed* (History
    Channel 2007)
53 Jimmy McDonough, *Shakey*
54 Simon Reynolds, *Totally Wired*
55 Rob Warmowski,
    warmowski.wordpress.com
56 John Robb, *Clash*, June 2010
57 *Krautrock: The Rebirth Of Germany*
    (BBC 2004)
58 Jonathan Valania, *Phawker*, June 27
    2008
59 Nick Spacek, *The Pitch*, May 5 2010
60 Alex Pasternack, *Motherboard*,
    December 8 2011
61 Sam Inglis, *Sound On Sound*, August
    2010
62 Trevor Pinch and Frank Trocco,
    Analog Days
63 *Mystery In Space* vol1 #50 (DC
    Comics March 1959)
64 D.M. Collins, *Nuclear Rays From My*

    Halogen Haze, June 12 2001
65 songfacts.com, December 2003
66 *Island Of Lost Souls* (Criterion DVD
    2011)
67 Jon Savage, *Sounds*, May 1978

CHAPTER 2: 1972–73

0   Oscar Wilde, 'The Critic As Artist,'
    Intentions (1891)
1   Robert Lewis,
    truthtribunal.org/testimonials,
    May 3 2010
2   Bob Lewis, *Los Angeles Staff*, July 14
    1972
3   Jerry Casale, *Los Angeles Staff*, July
    14 1972
4   Magdalena Sinclair, *Ann Arbor Sun*,
    February 1971
5   Peter Margasak, *Chicago Reader*,
    June 2 2005
6   Robert Lewis, 'Some Thoughts On
    Devo: The First Postmodern Band'
    PDF (2006)
7   Abe Peck, *Rolling Stone*, January 25
    1979
8   Liner notes to Devo, *Q: Are We Not
    Men? A: We Are Devo!* CD (Warner
    Bros 1978)
9   Nic Harcourt, *DEVO: Origins—
    SXSW Music 2009*
10 *The History Of Rock And Roll* (Warner
    Home Video, 1995)
11 Simon Reynolds, *Rip It Up & Start
    Again*
12 Paul Oliver, *Blues Fell This Morning*
13 *Reality Never Applied to Me*
    (GlamourPuss Productions 2009)
14 *It's Everything, And Then It's Gone*
    (PBS 2003)
15 Sam Adams, avclub.com, June 30
    2010
16 Sam Adams, avclub.com, June 30
    2010
17 numbersband.com
18 Edward Dorn, *Gunslinger*
19 Kurt Hemmer (ed), *Encyclopedia Of
    Beat Literature* (Facts On File 2007)
20 Edward Dorn, *Gunslinger*
21 M.T. Laverty, *Trouser Press*, April 1978

22 Lynn Van Matre, *Chicago Tribune*, December 30 1978
23 Joel Francis, *Daily Record*, July 23 2010
24 Steve Olson, *Juice* #53, 2001
25 Simon Reynolds, *Totally Wired*
26 Aaron Williams *De-evolve*, 1992
27 *New Vinyl Times* vol1 #11, 1980
28 Robert Lewis, 'Some Thoughts On Devo: The First Postmodern Band' PDF (2006)
29 Ayisha Khan, *Distorted*, June 16 2010

CHAPTER 3: 1974

0 Alfred Jarry, 'Twelve Theatrical Topics,' *Selected Works* (Grove Press 1965)
1 B.H. Shadduck, *Jocko-Homo Heavenbound* (Jocko-Homo Publishing 1924)
2 *Search & Destroy* #7, 1978
3 Jaan Uhelszki, *TONEAudio* #26, 2009
4 Kyle Schlesinger, *Chicago Review*, Summer 2004
5 Edward Dorn, *Green Poems* (Zephyrus Image 1974)
6 *Search & Destroy* #7, 1978
7 Greg Armbruster, *Keyboard Wizards*, Winter 1985
8 Video interview by Dan Bailey, June 1988
9 *Search & Destroy* #2, 1977
10 Jerry Casale, audio commentary on *DEVO: The Complete Truth About De-evolution* (Rhino, 1993)
11 *Synth Britannia* (BBC, 2009)
12 Liner notes to Silver Apples, *Silver Apples* liner notes (Kapp Records, 1968)
13 Richard Kostelanetz, *The Fillmore East: Recollections Of Rock Theater* (Shirmer 1995)
14 Clemens Breznikar, *It's Psychedelic Baby!*, March 2 2012
15 John Pareles, *New York Times*, November 1 2010
16 Richard Henderson, *The Wire* #303, June 2009

17 David Goggin, *Faces of Music*
18 Chris Willman, *Spin*, August 2010
19 Dusty Wright, *Culture Catch*, September 27 2005
20 Oscar Kiss Maerth, *The Beginning Was the End* (Michael Joseph 1973)
21 *Search & Destroy* #2, 1977
22 Interview by Martin Perlich, May 2 1979
23 Michael Goldberg, *New Times*, October 30 1978
24 Simon Reynolds, *Totally Wired*
25 *The History Of Rock And Roll* (Warner Home Video 1995)

CHAPTER 4: 1975

0 Alfred Jarry, 'Twelve Theatrical Topics,' *Selected Works* (Grove Press 1965)
1 Jason Prufer, *Kent Patch*, August 7 2011
2 *Search & Destroy* #3, 1977
3 *The History Of Rock And Roll* (Warner Home Video 1995)
4 Jason Prufer, *Kent Patch*, August 7 2011
5 Pat Gleeson, *Synapse*, May/June 1978
6 Alex Brunelle and Tom Chiki, boojiboysbasement.com, 2005
7 Joel Francis, *Daily Record*, July 23 2010
8 David Goggin, *Faces Of Music*
9 Kent Carmical, *Premier Guitar*, October 2010
10 Thomas Wictor, *In Cold Sweat*
11 Jason Prufer, *Kent Patch*, August 7 2011
12 Michael Norman, blog.cleveland.com, December 4 2007
13 D.B. Keeps, *CLE* #3, Summer 1979
14 Trevor Pinch and Frank Trocco, *Analog Days*
15 Peter Watrous, *New York Times*, May 31 1993
16 Maura Kelly, *The Believer*, September 2005
17 Jesse Thorn, *Maximum Fun*, June 17 2010

18 Charlotte Pressler, *CLE* #1, Winter 1977
19 John Gorman with Tom Feran, *The Buzzard*
20 Gerald V. Casale, liner notes to *Devo Live: The Mongoloid Years* (Rykodisc 1992)
21 Joe Garden, theonion.com, July 9 1997
22 Maura Kelly, *The Believer*, September 2005
23 John Gorman with Tom Feran, *The Buzzard*
24 Maura Kelly, *The Believer*, September 2005
25 Chris Willman, *Spin*, August 2010
26 Gerald V. Casale, liner notes to *Devo Live: The Mongoloid Years* (Rykodisc 1992)
27 Lucy R. Lippard (ed), *Dadas On Art: Tzara, Arp, Duchamp, And Others* (Prentice-Hall 1971)
28 Hans Richter, *Dada: Art And Anti-Art* (Thames & Hudson 1997)
29 Leah Dickerman (et al), *Dada: Zurich, Berlin, Hannover, Cologne, New York, Paris* (National Gallery of Art, Washington, 2005)
30 Walter Serner, *Letzte Lockerung: Manifest Dada* (Paul Steegemann 1920)
31 Hans Richter, *Dada: Art And Anti-Art* (Thames & Hudson 1997)
32 *Tid För Design: Showroom* (STV2 November 8 2005)
33 Robert Motherwell, *The Dada Painters And Poets: An Anthology* (Belknap 1989)
34 Ian Birch, *Melody Maker*, February 25 1978
35 Robert Motherwell, *The Dada Painters And Poets: An Anthology* (Belknap 1989)
36 Joe Garden, theonion.com, July 9 1997
37 Simon Reynolds, *Rip It Up & Start Again*
38 Hans Richter, *Dada: Art And Anti-Art* (Thames & Hudson 1997)

CHAPTER 5: 1976

0   R. Buckminster Fuller, *Ideas and Integrities: A Spontaneous Autobiographical Disclosure* (McMillan 1969)
1   Chuck Terhark, *City Pages*, September 29 2004
2   songfacts.com, December 2003
3   William McKeen (ed), *Rock And Roll Is Here To Stay*
4   Leah Pietrusiak, *Time Out Chicago*, April 28 2005
5   David Wolinksky, avclub.com, June 7 2007
6   Chris Riemenschneider, *Minneapolis Star-Tribune*, July 6 2010
7   songfacts.com, December 2003
8   Stephen Fortner, *Keyboard Magazine*, September 2010
9   Chris Riemenschneider, *Minneapolis Star-Tribune*, July 6 2010
10 Jaan Uhelszki, *TONEAudio* #26, 2009
11 Dan Collins, *LA Record*, November 4 2009
12 Tim Holmes, *New York Rocker*, January 1979
13 Rob Warmowski, warmowski.wordpress.com
14 Jon Savage, *Sounds*, May 1978
15 Ian Birch, *Melody Maker*, February 25, 1978
16 Lynn Van Matre, *Chicago Tribune*, December 30 1978
17 *Jazz & Pop*, March 1971
18 *Jazz & Pop*, March 1971
19 Robert Barry, thequietus.com, May 11 2011
20 Stephen Ronan, *Mondo 2000*, February 1993
21 Richard Gehr, *Spin*, April 1986
22 Jason Gross, furious.com/perfect, March 1999
23 Richard Gehr, *Spin*, April 1986
24 residents.com
25 *Mole Show / Whatever Happened To Vileness Fats?* (Ralph Records 1984)
26 *Mole Show / Whatever Happened To Vileness Fats?* (Ralph Records 1984)

27 Mark Prindle, markprindle.com, 2005

28 Richard Gehr, *Spin*, April 1986

29 Interview by Martin Perlich, May 2 1979

30 Liner notes to The Residents, *Eskimo* (Ralph Records 1979)

31 Greg Armbruster, *Keyboard Wizards*, Winter 1985

32 lynda.com, July 23 2010

33 Dave Segal, *The Stranger*, November 3 2009

34 Gerald V. Casale, liner notes to *Devo Live: The Mongoloid Years* (Rykodisc 1992)

35 Mary Harron, *Melody Maker*, May 26 1979

36 *Search & Destroy #2*, 1977

37 Thomas Wictor, *In Cold Sweat*

38 Neil Gladstone, *CMJ New Music Monthly*, August 2000

39 *The History Of Rock And Roll* (Warner Home Video 1995)

40 Matt Fink, *Under The Radar*, July 28 2010

41 3 Jonathan Valania, *Phawker*, June 27 2008

42 Ryan Todd, *KDViations*, Winter 2006

43 *Devo: The Men Who Make The Music* (Warner Home Video 1981)

44 Tom Wolfe, *New York Magazine*, August 23 1976

45 Brad Warner, suicidegirls.com, November 11 2009

46 Tom Wolfe, *New York Magazine*, August 23 1976

47 Michael Goldberg, *Rolling Stone*, December 10 1981

48 Douglas Vuncannon, *Independent Weekly*, December 13 2006

49 *It's Everything, And Then It's Gone* (PBS 2003)

50 Robert Christgau, *The Village Voice*, April 17 1978

51 David Goggin, *Faces of Music*

52 Andy Gray, *Tribune Chronicle*, August 21 2008

53 *It's Everything, And Then It's Gone* (PBS 2003)

54 Lester Bangs, *The Village Voice*, October 24 1977

55 Cheetah Chrome, *A Dead Boy's Tale; From The Front Lines Of Punk Rock* (Voyageur Press 2010)

56 Gerald V. Casale, liner notes to *Devo Live: The Mongoloid Years* (Rykodisc 1992)

57 *It's Everything, And Then It's Gone* (PBS 2003)

58 Cheetah Chrome, *A Dead Boy's Tale; From The Front Lines Of Punk Rock* (Voyageur Press 2010)

59 Gerald V. Casale, liner notes to *Devo Live: The Mongoloid Years* (Rykodisc 1992)

CHAPTER 6

0 Christopher Butler, *After The Wake: An Essay On The Contemporary Avant-Garde* (Oxford University Press 1980)

1 Matt Fink, *Under The Radar*, July 28 2010

2 Rich Frank, *CMJ*, 1979

3 Jon Savage, *Sounds*, May 1978

4 Ian Birch, *Melody Maker*, February 25 1978

5 Melissa Parker, *Smashing Interviews Magazine*, September 2 2010

6 Thomas Wictor, *In Cold Sweat*

7 *The History Of Rock And Roll* (Warner Home Video 1995)

8 Jon Allan, liner notes to *The Day the Earth Met the Rocket From the Tombs* (Smog Veil Records 2002)

9 Simon Reynolds, *Totally Wired*

10 ubuprojex.net

11 *Search & Destroy #3*, 1977

12 Deanna R. Adams, *Rock'n'Roll And The Cleveland Connection*

13 Anthony Dhanendran, pennyblackmusic.com, August 20 2005

14 Graham Reid, *Elsewhere*, August 7 2007

15 Bret Miller, *Highwire Daze*, September 18 2006

16 Dusty Wright, *Culture Catch*,

September 27 2005

17 Jason Gross, furious.com/perfect, October 2010

18 ubuprojex.net

19 Jason Gross, furious.com/perfect, October 2010

20 Jason Gross, furious.com/perfect, October 2010

21 *Search & Destroy #3*, 1977

22 Jason Gross, furious.com/perfect, October 2010

23 Sigmund Freud, *The Psychology of Love* (Penguin Classics 2007)

24 Sigmund Freud, *Civilization And Its Discontents* (Norton 2010)

25 Pat Gleason, *Synapse*, May/June 1978

26 D.X. Ferris, *Cleveland Scene*, August 17 2005

27 Frank Mullen, *Ink 19*, May 2000

28 ubuprojex.net

29 Greg Shaw, *Who Put The Bomp*, July–August 1970

30 James Wolcott, *The Village Voice*, August 18 1975

31 Roman Kozak, *Billboard*, November 20 1976

32 Legs McNeil and Gillian McCain, *Please Kill Me*

33 Legs McNeil and Gillian McCain, *Please Kill Me*

34 Jean Encoule, *trakMARX #6*, September 2002

35 Greg Shaw, *Bomp! #17*, November 1977

36 Craig Bromberg, *The Wicked Ways of Malcolm McLaren*, (HarperCollins 1989)

37 Jon Savage, *England's Dreaming*

38 Richard Hell, richardhell.com

39 *The Great Rock'n'Roll Swindle* (Virgin Films 1980)

40 Patrick Emery, *I-94 Bar*, July 8 2008

41 Nic Harcourt, *DEVO: Origins— SXSW Music 2009*

42 Matt Fink, *Under The Radar*, July 28 2010

43 Ronald Binder, hotrails.co.uk

44 Mark E. Waterbury, *Music Morsels*,

November 2002

45 Jeff Schwachter, *Atlantic City Weekly*, August 11 2005

46 Simon Reynolds, *Totally Wired*

47 Andy Warhol and Pat Hackett, *Popism: The Warhol Sixties* (Harcourt Brace Jovanovich 1980)

48 Byron Coley, *York Rocker*, January 1979

49 maxskansascity.com, July 10, 2009

50 Nader Sader, *Mean Magazine*, June/July 2006

51 Alan Vega, press release for *Station*, 2007

52 David Nobahkt, *Suicide: No Compromise* (SAF 2005)

53 *Electric Independence*, vice.com, April 21 2010

54 D.X. Ferris, *Cleveland Scene*, August 17 2005

CHAPTER 7

0 William Goldman, *Adventures In The Screen Trade: A Personal View Of Hollywood And Screenwriting* (Warner Books 1983)

1 *The Tubes Project* (TBC)

2 Ian Cranna, *Smash Hits* vol1 #14, June 14–27 1979

3 Denyse Beaulieu, *Surfin' Bird #1*, November 1978

4 music.com *Living Legends*, 2000

5 Pete Feenstra, *Get Ready To Rock*, June 2007

6 M.T. Laverty, *Trouser Press*, April 1978

7 Jonathan Valania, *Phawker*, June 27 2008

8 Rich Frank, "CMJ Interview: Devo" *CMJ*, 1979

9 Andy Gill, *NME*, December 9 1978

10 Ian Cranna, *Smash Hits* vol1 #14, June 14–27 1979

11 Nic Harcourt, *DEVO: Origins— SXSW Music 2009*

12 Matt Diehl, *Room 100*, February 20 2007

13 Rob Hughes and Stephen Dalton, bowiewonderworld.com

14 Sam Adams, avclub.com, June 30
    2010
15 *Electric Independence*, vice.com, April
    21 2010
16 Rob Hughes and Stephen Dalton,
    bowiewonderworld.com
17 *BAM*, December 3 1982
18 Frank Mullen, *Ink 19*, May 2000
19 Julian Myers, *Frieze*, March 3 2007
20 Tosh Berman, *Support The
    Revolution* (ICA 1993)
21 Ed McCormack, *Gallery & Studio*
22 Tim Burrows, *Daily Telegraph*, May
    17 2007
23 Nic Harcourt, *DEVO: Origins—
    SXSW Music 2009*
24 *Billboard*, October 28 2006
25 Richard Henderson, *The Wire #303*,
    June 2009
26 Matt Diehl, *Room 100*, February 20
    2007
27 Matt Diehl, *Room 100*, February 20
    2007
28 Greg Prato, *MTV Ruled the World*
29 Richard Henderson, *The Wire #303*,
    June 2009
30 *The Cockettes* (Grandelusion 2002)
31 *The Cockettes* (Grandelusion 2002)
32 Adam Block, *The Advocate*, January
    3 1989
33 Greg Prato, *Grunge Is Dead*
34 Mark Spitz and Brendan Mullen,
    We Got The Neutron Bomb
35 James Stark, *Punk '77*
36 Mikel Toombs, *Slash* vol1 #10, May
    1978
37 Jon Savage, *Melody Maker*, January
    6 1979
38 Richard Henderson, *The Wire #303*,
    June 2009
39 Mark Spitz and Brendan Mullen,
    We Got The Neutron Bomb
40 Author's interview, June 7 2012
41 Abe Peck, *Rolling Stone*, January 25
    1979
42 Author's interview, June 7 2012
43 Thomas Wictor, *In Cold Sweat*
44 David Byrne, *How Music Works*
    (McSweeney's 2012)

45 Doug Gordon, ttbook.org, October
    15, 2006
46 Mark Mothersbaugh, audio
    commentary on *DEVO: The Complete
    Truth About De-evolution* (Rhino,
    1993)
47 Dusty Wright, *Culture Catch*,
    September 27, 2005
48 Simon Reynolds, *Totally Wired*
49 Jon Savage, *Sounds*, May 1978
50 Dan Collins, *LA Record*, November
    4 2009
51 D.J. Johnson, *Cosmik Debris #7*,
    December 1995
52 *Fresh Air* (WKSU-FM 1979)
53 James Stark, *Punk '77*
54 James Stark, *Punk '77*
55 James Stark, *Punk '77*
56 Sheldon Renan, *An Introduction To
    The American Underground Film* (E.P.
    Dutton 1967)
57 William C. Wees, *Breakaway: Films
    By Bruce Conner 1958–2004*
    (Northwest Film Forum, November
    11 2010)
58 cinemad.com, 2009
59 *Breakaway: Films By Bruce Conner
    1958–2004* (Northwest Film Forum,
    November 11 2010)
60 Jesse Thorn, *Maximum Fun*, June 17
    2010
61 Danny Sofer and Doug Lynner,
    Synapse vol1 #5, January/February
    1977
62 Ira Robbins, *Trouser Press*, January
    1979
63 Steve Anker, Kathey Geritz, Steve
    Seid (eds), *Radical Light: Alternative
    Film & Video In The San Francisco
    Bay Area 1945–2000* (University of
    California Press 2010)
64 Simon Reynolds,
    totallywiredbysimonreynolds.blogsp
    ot.com
65 Max Dax and A.J. Samuels,
    Electronic Beats, January 12 2012
66 Isabelle Corbisier, *Music For
    Vagabonds: The Tuxedomoon Chronicles*
    (OpenMute 2008)

67 Michael Snyder, *San Francisco Chronicle–Examiner*, December 14 1980
68 V. Vale, *Slash* vol2 #6, June 1979
69 Michael Snyder, *San Francisco Chronicle–Examiner*, December 14 1980
70 Susan Klein, *BAM*, October 10, 1980
71 Eric Cecil, wfmu.org, May 17 2012
72 Simon Reynolds, totallywiredbysimonreynolds.blogspot.com
73 Rory Phillips, erolalkan.co.uk
74 Joseph Kelner and James Munves, *The Kent State Coverup* (Harper & Row 1980)
75 Dan Collins, *LA Record*, November 4 2009
76 John Tobler, *Zigzag*, January 1978
77 Jonathan Valania, *Phawker*, June 27 2008
78 Stanley Mieses, *Melody Maker*, May 20 1978
79 Nic Harcourt, *DEVO: Origins— SXSW Music 2009*

CHAPTER 8

0 Robert Motherwell (ed), *The Dada Poets And Painters: An Anthology* (George Wittenborn, 1951)
1 *The Artist Formerly Known as Captain Beefheart* (BBC 1997)
2 Kevin E.G. Perry, drownedinsound.com, June 15 2010
3 Rose Dennen, *Big City Redneck*
4 Joe Garden, theonion, July 9 1997
5 Whitney Matheson, *USA Today*, March 23 2009
6 Rose Dennen, *Big City Redneck*
7 Wil Forbis, *Acid Logic*
8 Whitney Matheson, *USA Today*, March 23 2009
9 Jonathan Valania, *Phawker*, June 27 2008
10 Ian Birch, *Melody Maker*, February 25 1978
11 *The Tomorrow Show* (NBC June 25 1980)

12 *Krautrock: The Rebirth of Germany* (BBC 2004)
13 *Krautrock: The Rebirth of Germany* (BBC 2004)
14 *Fresh Air* (WKSU-FM 1979)
15 D. Strauss, *Electronic Musician*, August 1 2004
16 Author's interview, March 3 2012
17 Michael Davis, *Keyboard Wizards*, Winter 1985
18 Mark Cunningham, *The Mix*, September 1994
19 Andy Gill, *Mojo*, June 1995
20 Cole Springer, *Trouser Press*, January 1979
21 Andreas Trolf, fecalface.com, January 3 2008
22 Stanley Mieses, *Melody Maker*, May 20 1978
23 Stephen Fortner, *Keyboard Magazine*, September 2010
24 Andrew Perry, *Mojo*, August 2010
25 Sara Jayne Crow, *Flavorwire*, March 31 2009
26 Andrew Perry, *Mojo*, August 2010
27 Stanley, *Crossfire*, July 10 2010
28 Andreas Trolf, fecalface.com, January 3 2008
29 Cole Springer, *Trouser Press*, January 1979
30 Jonathan Valania, *Phawker*, June 27, 2008
31 Jon Savage, *Sounds*, May 1978
32 Ian MacDonald, *NME*, December 16 1972
33 Ian MacDonald, *NME*, December 23 1972
34 Ian MacDonald, *NME*, April 28 1973
35 Sam Adams, avclub.com, June 30 2010
36 *Search & Destroy* #2, 1977
37 John Doran, thequietus.com, January 6 2010
38 *Kraftwerk & The Electronic Revolution* (Prism Films 2008)
39 Lester Bangs, *Creem*, September 1975
40 Wolfgang Flür, *I Was A Robot* (Sanctuary 2000)

41 *Search & Destroy* #3, 1977
42 billboard.com, October 28 2006
43 *Krautrock: The Rebirth Of Germany* (BBC 2004)
44 *Krautrock: The Rebirth Of Germany* (BBC 2004)
45 *Kraftwerk & The Electronic Revolution* (Prism Films 2008)
46 Jean François Bizot, *Actuel Magazine/Radio Nova*, November 1991
47 Doug Lynner and Bryce Robbley, *Synapse*, September/October 1976
48 *Kraftwerk & The Electronic Revolution* (Prism Films 2008)
49 Jonathan Valania, *Phawker*, June 27 2008
50 Kris Needs, *Zigzag* #85, July 1978
51 Ian Birch, *Melody Maker*, February 25 1978
52 Allan Jones, *Melody Maker*, March 13 1978
53 moshcam.com, May 13 2012
54 *If It Ain't Stiff* (BBC 2007)
55 *If It Ain't Stiff* (BBC 2007)
56 *If It Ain't Stiff* (BBC 2007)
57 *Fresh Air* (WKSU-FM 1979)
58 Jimmy McDonough, *Shakey*
59 Jimmy McDonough, *Shakey*
60 *Neil Young: Don't Be Denied* (BBC 2008)
61 Sylvie Simmons, *Neil Young: Reflections in Broken Glass* (Canongate 2001)
62 *DEVO: The Complete Truth About De-evolution* (Rhino Home Video 1993)
63 *Human Highway* (Shakey Pictures 1982)
64 Jimmy McDonough, *Shakey*
65 *Innerview* (KMET-FM 1980)
66 Stanley, *Crossfire*, July 10 2010
67 Andy Spade, *Index*, 2002

CHAPTER 9

0   Kurt Vonnegut, *Mother Night* (Fawcett Publications 1961)
1   *DEVO: The Complete Truth About De-evolution* (Rhino Home Video 1993)
2   *DEVO: The Complete Truth About De-*
evolution (Rhino Home Video 1993)
3   *Fresh Air* (WKSU-FM 1979)
4   *DEVO: The Complete Truth About De-evolution* (Rhino Home Video 1993)
5   Simon Reynolds, *Totally Wired*
6   Simon Reynolds, *Totally Wired*
7   Rob Warmowski, warmowski.wordpress.com
8   Eldon Garnet, *Impulse Archeology* (University of Toronto Press 1995)
9   Matt Fink, *Under The Radar*, July 28 2010
10 Joe Velazquez, *Spin*, October 1988
11 Michael Goldberg, *New Times*, October 30 1978
12 Christopher Petit, *Melody Maker*, November 25 1978
13 Paul Barrel, *Innocent Words*, October 2 2010
14 Rob Warmowski, warmowski.wordpress.com
15 lynda.com, July 23 2010
16 Gerald V. Casale, *Optic Music*, August 1984
17 *Adventures Of The Smart Patrol* (Inscape CD-ROM 1996)
18 Alex Pasternack, *Motherboard*, December 8 2011
19 Bobzilla, *LAist*, April 17 2010
20 Eldon Garnet, *Impulse Archeology* (University of Toronto Press 1995)
21 David Goggin, *Faces of Music*
22 Alex Pasternack, *Motherboard*, December 8 2011
23 Dave Fudger, *Sounds*, July 5 1978
24 Jas Obrecht, *Guitar Player*, July 1981
25 Brandon Lieberman, unknown publication, February 1 1985
26 Pete Feenstra, *Get Ready To Rock*, 2007
27 Michael Goldberg *New Times*, October 30 1978
28 Ryan Todd, *KDViations*, Winter 2006
29 Brad Warner, suicidegirls.com, November 11 2009
30 Dave Segal, *The Stranger*, November 3 2009
31 Jas Obrecht, *Guitar Player*, July 1981

32 Interview by Martin Perlich, May 2 1979
33 Video interview by Dan Bailey, June 1988
34 Gordon Ornelas, Cynthia Connolly, Chris Bald, Jessie Q, *W.D.C. Period* #18, 1989
35 Cole Springer, Ira Robbins, Steven Grant, *Trouser Press*, January 1979
36 J.B., *Melody Maker*, September 2 1978
37 Tom Carson, *Rolling Stone*, November 30 1978
38 Andy Gill, *NME*, December 9 1978
39 Lester Bangs, unpublished profile
40 Michael Davis, *Keyboard Wizards*, Winter 1985
41 Christopher Petit, *Melody Maker*, November 25 1978
42 Denyse Beaulieu, *Surfin' Bird* #1, November 1978
43 Ayisha Khan, *Distorted Magazine*, June 16 2010
44 *Backstage Pass* (1981)
45 Scion ART, 2010
46 Allan Jones, *Melody Maker*, March 13 1978
47 Robert Christgau, *The Village Voice*, 1981
48 *Night Flight* (ATI Video January 3 1989)
49 John Soeder, *The Plain Dealer*, October 15 2008
50 *American Bandstand* (Dick Clark Productions June 21 1980)
51 Robert Christgau, "*The Village Voice*, April 17 1978
52 *If It Ain't Stiff* (BBC 2007)
53 Robert Christgau, *The Village Voice*, April 17 1978
54 Isabelle Corbisier, *Music for Vagabonds: The Tuxedomoon Chronicles* (OpenMute 2008)
55 Bret Miller, *Highwire Daze*, September 18 2006
56 Phil Freeman, *The Wire* #272, October 2006
57 Wayne Bledsoe, *Knoxville News Sentinel*, March 21 2008

58 Stephen Ronan, *Mondo 2000*, February 1993
59 Graham Reid, *Elsewhere*, August 7 2007
60 Phil Freeman, *The Wire* #272, October 2006
61 Greg Shaw*Bomp!* #17, November 1977
62 Clinton Heylin, *From The Velvets To The Voidoids*
63 *Two In The Wave* (Films à Trois 2010)
64 Jean-Luc Godard, *Introduction à une véritable histoire du cinéma* (Editions Albatros 1980)
65 Clinton Heylin, *From The Velvets To The Voidoids*
66 Liner notes to *New Wave Rock'n'Roll: Get Behind It Before It Gets Past You* (Sire 1977)
67 *The History Of Rock And Roll* (Warner Home Video 1995)
68 *The History Of Rock And Roll* (Warner Home Video 1995)
69 Gordon Ornelas, Cynthia Connolly, Chris Bald, Jessie Q, *W.D.C. Period* #18, 1989
70 Paul Barrel, *Innocent Words*, October 2 2010
71 Russell A. Trunk, *Exclusive Magazine*
72 Rose Dennen, *Big City Redneck*
73 Cameron Crowe, *Rolling Stone*, July 26 1979
74 *DEVO: The Complete Truth About De-evolution* (Rhino Home Video 1993)
75 Andy Gray, *Tribune–Chronicle*, August 21 2008
76 Legs McNeil and Gillian McCain, *Please Kill Me*
77 Author's interview, August 18 2012
78 *Punk's Not Dead* (Aberration Films/Red Rover Films 2007)
79 *Fresh Air* (WKSU-FM 1979)
80 Thurston Moore and Byron Coley, *No Wave: Post-Punk. Underground. New York. 1976--1980* (Abrams Image 2008)
81 Josh Frank with Charlie Buckholtz, *In Heaven Everything Is Fine: The*

Unsolved Life Of Peter Ivers And The Lost History Of New Wave Theatre (Free Press 2008)

82 *The Decline Of Western Civilization* (Spheeris Films 1981)

83 Greil Marcus, *Lipstick Traces*

84 Sting, *Broken Music: A Memoir* (Dial Press 2005)

85 James Hampton, *Categories & Concepts: Theoretical Views & Inductive Data Analysis* (Academic Press 1993)

86 Gerald Casale, Daniel Bukszpan, *The Encyclopedia Of New Wave* (Sterling 2012)

87 Denyse Beaulieu, *Surfin' Bird #1*, November 1978

88 Nader Sader, *Mean Magazine*, June/July 2006

CHAPTER 10

0 Marshall McLuhan, *Understanding Media: The Extensions Of Man* (McGraw–Hill 1964)

1 *Search & Destroy #2*, 1977

2 *The Dr Demento Show* (KMET July 8 1979)

3 Regan McMahon, *BAM*, May 18 1979

4 Ken Scott and Bobby Owsinski, *Abbey Road To Ziggy Stardust*

5 Jon Young, *Trouser Press*, September 1979

6 SH Forums, July 2 2007

7 Cole Springer, "YES!" *Trouser Press*, January 1979

8 Ken Scott and Bobby Owsinski, *Abbey Road To Ziggy Stardust*

9 Barbara Schultz, *Mix*, February 22 2010

10 Rick Clark, *Mix*, October 1 2004

11 Eldon Garnet, *Impulse Archeology* (University of Toronto Press 1995)

12 Jon Young, *Trouser Press*, September 1979

13 Jon Young, *Trouser Press*, September 1979

14 *Rollerball* (United Artists 1975)

15 Abe Peck, *Rolling Stone*, January 25 1979

16 Simon Reynolds, *Rip It Up & Start Again*

17 Alex Brunelle, boojiboysbasement.com

18 Eldon Garnet, *Impulse Archeology* (University of Toronto Press 1995)

19 Eldon Garnet, *Impulse Archeology* (University of Toronto Press 1995)

20 Abe Peck, *Rolling Stone*, January 25 1979

21 Interview by Martin Perlich, May 2 1979

22 Chris Morris, *Rolling Stone*, September 6 1979

23 *Plan B #23*, July 2007

24 *Plan B #23*, July 2007

25 *Search & Destroy #3*, 1977

26 Dan Collins, *LA Record*, November 4 2009

27 *Plan B #23*, July 2007

28 Regan McMahon, *BAM*, May 18 1979

29 Interview by Martin Perlich, May 2 1979

30 George Petros, *Seconds #4*, 1986

31 Alex Pasternack, *Motherboard*, December 8 2011

32 Ian Birch, *Melody Maker*, June 9 1979

33 Karrie Jacobs, *The Rocket*, August 1980

34 Dave Marsh, *Rolling Stone*, September 20 1979

35 Roy Trakin, *Musician*, September 1979

36 Henry Rollins, *LA Weekly*, July 7 2001

37 Gerald V. Casale, *Optic Music*, August 1984

38 *DEVO: The Complete Truth About De-evolution* (Rhino Home Video 1993)

39 Gerald V. Casale, *Optic Music*, August 1984

40 Jon Young, *Trouser Press*, September 1979

41 Rich Frank, *CMJ*, 1979

42 Frank Mullen, *Ink 19*, May 2000

43 Hugh Cornwell, *A Multitude Of Sins: Golden Brown, The Stranglers &*

Strange Little Girls (HarperCollins 2004)
44 *Search & Destroy #3*, 1977
45 Allan Jones, *Melody Maker*, March 13 1978
46 Byron Coley with Robert Carey, *New York Rocker*, January 1979
47 Author's interview, August 14 2012
48 *Channel 7 Eyewitness News* (KABC-TV 1980)
49 *The Artist Formerly Known As Captain Beefheart* (BBC 1997)
50 Greil Marcus (ed), *Stranded*
51 J.B., *Melody Maker*, September 2 1978
52 Cary Darling, *Billboard*, November 22 1980

EPILOGUE
1 Tim Noakes, *Social Stereotype*, July 23 2009
2 Jason Gross, furious.com/perfect, March 1999
3 Uncle Willie, *Uncle Willie's Highly*

Opinionated Guide To The Residents (Cryptic Corporation 1993)
4 Liner notes to The Residents, *Commercial Album* (Ralph Records 1980)
5 Jack McDonough, *Billboard*, November 15 1980
6 Richard Henderson, *The Wire #303*, June 2009
7 Richard Gehr, *Spin*, April 1986
8 Joe Velazquez, *Spin*, October 1988
9 *To The Best Of Our Knowledge* (Public Radio International October 15 2006)
10 *Synth Britannia* (BBC 2009)
11 *Synth Britannia* (BBC 2009)
12 Nick Spacek, *The Pitch*, May 5 2010
13 *The History Of Rock And Roll* (Warner Home Video 1995)
14 Cindy Lamm and Bart Mann, *BAM*, November 7 1980
15 oldschool.tblog.com, February 25 2012

BIBLIOGRAPHY

BOOKS
Adams, Deanna R. *Rock'n'Roll And The Cleveland Connection* (Kent State University Press, 2002)
Anderson, Maggie, and Alex Gildzen (eds) *A Gathering Of Poets* (Kent State University Press, 1992)
Aust, Stefan (translated by Anthea Bell) *Baader-Meinhof: The Inside Story Of The R.A.F* (Oxford University Press, 2009)
Austerlitz, Saul *Money For Nothing: A History Of The Music Video From The Beatles To The White Stripes* (Continuum, 2007)
Baker, Grover 'Monkey Biz-ness (Down In Tennessee)' *Music Reference Services Quarterly*, Vol. 10(2) 2006
Bangs, Lester *Psychotic Reactions And*

Carburetor Dung (Alfred A. Knopf, 1987)
Berman, Tosh *Support The Revolution* (Institute of Contemporary Art, 1993)
Booji Boy *My Struggle* (Neo Rubberband, 1978)
Breakaway: Films by Bruce Conner: 1958–2004 (Northwest Film Forum; presented by the Sprocket Society and Third Eye Cinema, Seattle, Washington, November 11, 2010)
Bürger, Peter *Theory Of The Avant-Garde* (University of Minnesota Press, 1984)
Bussy, Pascal *Kraftwerk: Man, Machine And Music* (SAF, 1993)
Cateforis, Theo *Are We Not New Wave? Modern Pop At The Turn Of The*

1980s (University of Michigan Press, 2011)

Cope, Julian *Japrocksampler: How the Post-war Japanese Blew Their Minds On Rock'n'Roll* (Bloomsbury, 2007)

Cornwell, Hugh *A Multitude Of Sins: Golden Brown, The Stranglers & Strange Little Girls* (HarperCollins, 2004)

Cracknell, Robert *The Lonely Sense: The Autobiography Of A Psychic Detective* (Anomalist Books, 2011)

Davis, Adam, and Kate Schaefer *Art Terrorism In Ohio: Cleveland Punk, The Mimeograph Revolution, Devo, Zines, Artists' Periodicals, And Concrete Poetry, 1964–2011* (Division Leap Gallery, 2011; published in conjunction with the exhibition of the same name)

Dellinger, Jade, and David Giffels *We Are DEVO!* (SAF, 2003)

Dickerman, Leah, et al *Dada: Zurich, Berlin, Hannover, Cologne, New York, Paris* (National Gallery of Art, Washington, 2005)

Dorn, Edward *Gunslinger* (Duke University Press, 1995)

Flür, Wolfgang *Kraftwerk: I Was A Robot* (Sanctuary, 2000)

Fredman, Stephen, and Michael Duncan *Semina Culture: Wallace Berman & His Circle* (Santa Monica Museum of Art, 2005)

Gendron, Bernard *Between Montmartre And The Mudd Club* (University of Chicago Press, 2002)

Goggin, David *Faces Of Music: 25 Years Of Lunching With Legends* (Course Technology PTR, 2005)

Gorman, John, with Tom Feran *The Buzzard: Inside The Glory Days Of WMMS And Cleveland Rock Radio—A Memoir* (Gray & Company, 2007)

Greil Marcus *Lipstick Traces: A Secret History Of The 20th Century* (Harvard University Press, 1990)

Heylin, Clinton *From The Velvets To The Voidoids: The Birth Of American Punk Rock* (Chicago Review Press, 1993)

Heylin, Clinton *Babylon's Burning: From Punk To Grunge* (Canongate, 2007)

Hughes, Robert *The Shock Of The New* (Alfred A. Knopf, 1980)

Johnson, Alastair *Zephyrus Image: A Bibliography* (Poltroon Press, 2003)

Kahn, Ashley, Holly George-Warren, and Shawn Dahl (eds) *Rolling Stone: The Seventies* (Little, Brown, 1998)

Kossy, Donna *Strange Creations: Aberrant Ideas Of Human Origins From Ancient Astronauts To Aquatic Apes* (Feral House, 2001)

Kostelanetz, Richard *The Fillmore East: Recollections Of Rock Theater* (Shirmer, 1995)

Larson, Edward J. *Trial And Error: The American Controversy Over Creation And Evolution* (Oxford University Press, 2003)

Lippard, Lucy R. (ed) *Dadas On Art: Tzara, Arp, Duchamp And Others* (Prentice-Hall, 1971)

McDonough, Jimmy *Shakey: Neil Young's Biography* (Random House, 2002)

McKeen, William (ed) *Rock And Roll Is Here To Stay: An Anthology* (W.W. Norton, 2000)

McNeil, Legs, and Gillian McCain *Please Kill Me: The Uncensored Oral History Of Punk* (Penguin, 1996)

Maerth, Oscar Kiss (translated by Judith Hayward) *The Beginning Was The End* (Michael Joseph, 1973)

Miller, Carol Poh, and Robert A. Wheeler *Cleveland: A Concise History, 1796–1996* (Indiana University Press, 1997)

Motherwell, Robert *The Dada Painters And Poets: An Anthology, Second Edition,* (Belknap Press, 1989)

Oliver, Paul *Blues Fell This Morning: Meaning In The Blues* (Cambridge University Press, 1990)

Palmer, Myles *New Wave Explosion: How Punk Became New Wave, Became The 80s* (Proteus, 1981)

Pinch, Trevor, and Frank Trocco *Analog Days: The Invention And Impact Of*

The Moog Synthesizer (Harvard University Press, 2002)

Prato, Greg *MTV Ruled The World: The Early Years Of The Music Video* (Greg Prato, 2010)

Reynolds, Simon *Rip It Up And Start Again: Postpunk 1978–1984* (Penguin, 2005)

Reynolds, Simon *Totally Wired: Post-punk Interviews And Overviews* (Soft Skull Press, 2009)

Richter, Hans *Dada: Art And Anti-Art* (Thames & Hudson, 1997)

Rombes, Nicolas *A Cultural Dictionary Of Punk: 1974–1982* (Continuum, 2009)

Savage, Jon *England's Dreaming: Anarchy, Sex Pistols, Punk Rock, And Beyond* (St Martin's, 2002)

Scott, Ken, and Bobby Owsinski *Abbey Road To Ziggy Stardust: Off-The-Record With The Beatles, Bowie, Elton & So Much More* (Alfred Music Publishing Co, 2012)

Seabrook, Thomas Jerome *Bowie In Berlin: A New Career In A New Town* (Jawbone Press, 2008)

Shadduck, B. H. *Jocko-Homo Heavenbound* (Jocko-Homo Publishing Co, 1924)

Shapiro, Peter (ed) *Modulations—A History Of Electronic Music: Throbbing Words On Sound* (Caipirinha Publications, 2000)

Shaw, Suzy, and Mick Farren *Bomp!*

Saving The World One Record At A Time (American Modern, 2007)

Sheppard, David *On Some Faraway Beach: The Life And Times Of Brian Eno* (Chicago Review Press, 2009)

Spitz, Marc, and Brendan Mullen *We Got The Neutron Bomb: The Untold Story Of LA Punk* (Three Rivers Press, 2001)

Stark, James *Punk '77: An Inside Look At The San Francisco Rock'n'Roll Scene* (RE/Search Publications, 1999)

Uncle Willie *Uncle Willie's Highly Opinionated Guide To The Residents: 1972–1992: A Survey Of Two Decades Of Anonymous Fame* (Cryptic Corporation, 1993)

Wald, Elijah *How The Beatles Destroyed Rock'n'Roll: An Alternative History Of American Popular Music* (Oxford University Press, 2009)

Wictor, Thomas *In Cold Sweat: Interviews With Really Scary Musicians* (Limelight Editions, 2001)

Wolfe, Tom *From Bauhaus To Our House* (FSG, 1981)

WEBSITES
Booji Boy's Basement boojiboysbasement.com/
Devo Live Guide huboon.com/index.html
Devo-Obsesso! devo-obsesso.com/
Ronald Cole's Devo Site forte-intl.com/~ronald/devo/index.html

SELECTED DISCOGRAPHY

SINGLES
'Mongoloid' / 'Jocko Homo' (Booji Boy Records 7033-14A, USA, March 1977; Stiff Records DEV1, UK #51, February 1978). Produced by Devo.

'(I cån't gèt mé nö) SÅTISFACTIÖN' / 'SLÖPPY (I såw my baby getting)'

(Booji Boy Records 72843-1/75677-2, USA, September 1977; Stiff Records DEV2, UK #41, March 1978). Produced by Devo.

(Warner Bros also released the Brian Eno-produced version of 'Satisfaction' as a single in 1978)

'Be Stiff' / 'Social Fools' (Stiff Records BOY2, UK #71, July 1978). A-side produced by Brian Eno; B-side produced by Devo.

'Come Back Jonee' / 'Social Fools' (Warner Bros WBS 8745, USA, August 1978; Virgin Records VS 223, UK #60, August 1978). Produced by Brian Eno.

'The Day My Baby Gave Me A Surprize' / 'Penetration In The Centrefold' (Warner Bros Pro-S-813, USA, June 1979; Virgin Records VS 265, UK, June 1979). A-side produced by Ken Scott; B-side produced by Brian Eno.

'Secret Agent Man' / 'Soo Bawlz' (Warner Bros WBS 49028, USA, 1979, August 1979; Virgin Records VS 280, UK, August 1979). Produced by Ken Scott.

ALBUMS
Q: Are We Not Men? A: We Are Devo! (Warner Bros BSK 3239, USA #78, August 1978; Virgin Records V2106, UK #12, September 1978). Produced by Brian Eno. Engineered by Konrad Plank. Recorded October 1977–February 1978 at Conny's Studio, Köln, Germany, except 'Shrivel-Up' and 'Come Back Jonee,' recorded at Different Fur Studios, San Francisco, California with Patrick Gleeson. Mixed at Conny's Studio.
A1 Uncontrollable Urge (M. Mothersbaugh) 3:08
A2 (I Can't Get No) Satisfaction (M. Jagger/K. Richard) 2:38
A3 Praying Hands (G. Casale/M. Mothersbaugh) 2:47
A4 Space Junk (G. Casale/M. Mothersbaugh) 2:13
A5 Mongoloid (G. Casale) 3:42

A6 Jocko Homo (M. Mothersbaugh) 3:38 //
B1 Too Much Paranoias (M. Mothersbaugh) 1:56
B2 Gut Feeling / (Slap Your Mammy) (M. Mothersbaugh/B. Mothersbaugh, G. Casale) 4:54
B3 Come Back Jonee (G. Casale/M. Mothersbaugh) 3:46
B4 Sloppy (I Saw My Baby Gettin') (M. Mothersbaugh/B. Mothersbaugh/G. Casale/G. Jackett) 2:37
B5 Shrivel-Up (G. Casale/M. Mothersbaugh/B. Mothersbaugh) 3:05

Duty Now For The Future (Warner Bros BSK 3337, US #73, July 1979; Virgin Records V 2125, UK #49, July 1979). Produced and engineered by Ken Scott. Recorded September 1978–January 1979 at Chateau Recorders, North Hollywood, California.
A1 Devo Corporate Anthem (M. Mothersbaugh) 1:14
A2 Clockout (G. Casale) 2:45
A3 Timing X (M. Mothersbaugh) 1:11
A4 Wiggly World (B. Mothersbaugh/G. Casale) 2:42
A5 Blockhead (B. Mothersbaugh/M. Mothersbaugh) 2:58
A6 Strange Pursuit (G. Casale/M. Mothersbaugh) 2:42
A7 S.I.B. (Swelling Itching Brain) (M. Mothersbaugh) 4:28
B1 Triumph Of The Will (M. Mothersbaugh/G. Casale) 2:16
B2 The Day My Baby Gave Me A Surprise (M. Mothersbaugh) 2:41
B3 Pink Pussycat (M. Mothersbaugh/B. Mothersbaugh) 3:08
B4 Secret Agent Man (P. Sloan/S. Berri, Arr. by M. Mothersbaugh) 3:35
B5 Smart Patrol / Mr. DNA (G. Casale, M. Mothersbaugh/G. Casale) 6:02
B6 Red Eye (M. Mothersbaugh/G. Casale) 2:51

COMPILATIONS

Be Stiff EP (Stiff Records ODD1, UK, 1978)
A1 Jocko Homo
A2 (I Can't Get Me No) Satisfaction
A3 Be Stiff
B1 Mongoloid
B2 Sloppy (I Saw My Baby Getting)
B3 Social Fools

The Akron Compilation (Stiff Records GET3, UK, June 1978). A-side listed as 'TIRESIDE'; B-side as 'PLATESIDE'
A1 Jane Aire & The Belvederes 'When I Was Young'
A2 Tin Huey 'Chinese Circus'
A3 Rachel Sweet 'Truckstop Queen'
A4 The Bizarros 'Nova'
A5 The Waitresses 'The Comb'
A6 Rubber City Rebels 'Rubber City Rebels'
B1 The Waitresses 'Slide'
B2 Jane Aire & The Belvederes 'I'm An Actress'
B3 Sniper 'Love Is Making Me Bleed'
B4 Idiots Convention 'Mephistopheles' Passion'
B5 Rachel Sweet 'Tourist Boys'
B6 Terraplane 'A Beer And A Cigarette'
B7 Chi Pig 'Apu-Api (Help Me)'
B8 The Waitresses 'Clones'

KROQ.FM Devotees Album (Rhino Records RNSP 301, USA, 1979)
A1 Knife Lust 'Shrivel Up'
A2 Jupiter 'Mongoloid'
A3 The View 'Uncontrollable Urge'
A4 The Firemen 'Jocko Bozo'
A5 The Deadliners 'Mongoloid'
A6 The Bakersfield Boogie Boys 'Okie From Muskogee'
B1 Lonnie & The Devotions 'Jocko Homo'
B2 The Doguloids 'Blockhead'
B3 The Touch Tone Tuners 'Jocko Homo'
B4 Y-22 'Music Inspired By Space Junk'
B5 The Sordese 'Mongoloid'
B6 Bohonian Plimquins 'Gut Feeling'

Be Stiff Tour (Stiff Records ODD2, UK, 1979)
A1 Lene Lovich & The Musicians Union 'Be Stiff'
A2 Mickey Jupp & The Cable Layers 'Be Stiff'
A3 Wreckless Eric & The Four Rough Men 'Be Stiff'
B1 Rachel Sweet & The Records 'Be Stiff'
B2 Jona Lewie & Two's Company 'Be Stiff'
B3 Lene Lovich, Mickey Jupp, Wreckless Eric, Rachel Sweet, and Jona Lewie 'Be Stiff (Chorus)'

Hardcore Devo, Vol. 1: 1974–1977 (Rykodisc RCD 10188, USA, August 1990)
1 Mechanical Man (M. Mothersbaugh) 4:20
2 Auto Modown (G. Casale) 2:01
3 Space Girl Blues (G. Casale) 1:50
4 Social Fools (G. Casale) 3:37
5 Soo Bawls (M. Mothersbaugh) 2:40
6 (I Can't Get No) Satisfaction (M. Jagger/K. Richard) 2:58
7 Jocko Homo (M. Mothersbaugh) 2:53
8 Golden Energy (M. Mothersbaugh) 2:27
9 Buttered Beauties (G. Casale/M. Mothersbaugh) 3:37
10 Midget (G. Casale/B. Mothersbaugh) 2:37
11 I'm A Potato (G. Casale/B. Casale) 2:35
12 Uglatto (G. Casale) 1:58
13 Stop Look and Listen (M. Mothersbaugh) 2:31
14 Ono (G. Casale, M. Mothersbaugh) 2:44
15 Mongoloid (G. Casale) 3:32

Hardcore Devo, Vol. 2: 1974–1977 (Rykodisc RCD 20208, USA, August 1991)
1 Booji Boy's Funeral (M. Mothersbaugh) 1977 3:59

307

2 Can U Take It? (G. Casale) 1974 3:00
3 Bamboo Bimbo (G. Casale/M. Mothersbaugh) 1975 3:16
4 A Plan For U (G. Casale) 1974 3:11
5 The Rope Song (G. Casale/B. Lewis) 1974 3:21
6 Goo Goo Itch (M. Mothersbaugh) 1976 2:17
7 Be Stiff (G. Casale/B. Lewis) 1974 3:19
8 All Of Us (G. Casale) 1974 4:53
9 Baby Talkin' Bitches (G. Casale/M. Mothersbaugh) 1975 2:25
10 I Need A Chick (G. Casale/P. Gregg) 1974 2:51
11 U Got Me Bugged (M. Mothersbaugh) 1975 2:45
12 Chango (G. Casale/M. Mothersbaugh) 1975 3:10
13 Fraulein (M. Mothersbaugh) 1975 3:06
14 Dogs Of Democracy (M. Mothersbaugh) 1976 3:25
15 "37" (G. Casale/M. Mothersbaugh) 1975 2:57
16 Bottled Up (G. Casale) 1976 2:21
17 Working In The Coal Mine (A. Toussaint) 1977 3:13
18 I Been Refused (G. Casale) 1974 3:32
19 Fountain Of Filth (G. Casale/B. Casale) 1977 3:09
20 Clockout (G. Casale) 1976 3:09
21 Let's Go (M. Mothersbaugh) 1977 2:42

Devo Live: The Mongoloid Years (Rykodisc RCD 20209, USA, October 1992). Tracks 1–9 recorded at Max's Kansas City, New York, May 1977; tracks 10–13 recorded at the Crypt, Akron, Ohio, December 1976; tracks 14–17 recorded at WHK Radio, Cleveland, Ohio, October 1975.

1 Satisfaction (I Can't Get No) (M. Jagger/K. Richard) 3:18
2 Too Much Paranoias (M. Mothersbaugh) 2:20

3 Praying Hands (G. Casale/M. Mothersbaugh) 4:10
4 Uncontrollable Urge (M. Mothersbaugh) 3:21
5 Mongoloid (G. Casale/M. Mothersbaugh) 3:26
6 Smart Patrol / Mr. DNA (G. Casale, M. Mothersbaugh/G. Casale) 8:02
7 Gut Feeling / Slap Your Mammy (M. Mothersbaugh/B. Mothersbaugh/G. Casale) 4:43
8 Sloppy (M. Mothersbaugh/B. Mothersbaugh/G. Casale/G. Jackett) 2:42
9 Come Back Jonee (G. Casale/M. Mothersbaugh) 4:00
10 Clockout (G. Casale) 2:40
11 Soo Bawlz (M. Mothersbaugh) 3:50
12 Space Junk (G. Casale/M. Mothersbaugh) 2:31
13 Blockhead (B. Mothersbaugh/M. Mothersbaugh) 3:11
14 Subhuman Woman (G. Casale/B. Lewis) 4:42
15 Bamboo Bimbo (G. Casale/M. Mothersbaugh) 3:21
16 Beulah (G. Casale) 3:13
17 Jocko Homo / I Need A Chick (M. Mothersbaugh, G. Casale/P. Gregg) 12:31

Recombo DNA (Rhino Handmade RHM2 7718, USA, May 2000)
A1 Recombo DNA (Demo) 2:06
A2 The Words Get Stuck In My Throat (Live) 5:27
A3 Sloppy (I Saw My Baby Gettin') (Demo) 2:17
A4 Be Stiff (Alternate Mix) 2:43
A5 Pink Pussycat (Demo) 4:08
A6 Goo Goo Itch (Alternate Version) 2:25
A7 Strange Pursuit (Demo) 2:31
A8 The Day My Baby Gave Me A Surprise (Demo) 3:32
A9 Bushwhacked (Prosthetic Version) 4:40
A10 Girl U Want (Demo / Alternate Version) 2:59

A11 Turn Around (Demo / Alternate Version) 2:12
A12 Snowball (Demo / Alternate Version) 2:49
A13 Luv & Such 2:53
A14 Gates Of Steel (Demo / Alternate Version) 3:28
A15 Planet Earth (Demo / Alternate Version) 3:16
A16 Whip It (Demo / Alternate Version) 2:38
A17 Cold War (Demo / Alternate Version) 2:33
A18 Time Bomb 3:13
A19 That's Pep (Demo / Alternate Version) 2:31
A20 Make Me Dance (Labeled 'Make Me Move')2:16
A21 Gotta Serve Somebody (Live) Performed by Dove, The Band Of Love 6:30
A22 I Saw Jesus 1:30
A23 Psychology Of Desire (Demo) 4:23
A24 Pity You (Demo) (Labeled 'You Say You Got A Problem') 2:54
B1 Beautiful World (Demo) 3:41
B2 Race Of Doom (Demo) 3:43
B3 I Desire (Demo) 3:18
B4 Big Mess (Demo) 2:48
B5 The 4th Dimension (Alternate Version / Rough Mix) 4:19
B6 Here To Go (Alternate Version / Rough Mix) 3:18
B7 Some Things Don't Change (Rough Mix) 2:55
B8 Big Adventure (Rough Mix) 2:45
B9 No Noise (Rough Mix) 2:49
B10 Love Is Stronger Than Dirt 2:11
B11 Faster And Faster 2:49
B12 Modern Life 3:04
B13 The Only One (Demo) Vocal by Toni Basil 4:06
B14 Baby Doll (Demo) 3:36
B15 Some Things Never Change (Demo) 5:27
B16 Plain Truth (Demo) 3:59
B17 Happy Guy (Demo) 3:32
B18 Somewhere With Devo (Studio Version / Demo) 18:22

VIDEO COLLECTIONS
The Men Who Make The Music
(VHS/Beta, Warner Home Video IN 24029, USA, 1981). Directes by Chuck Statler & Gerald V. Casale. Includes music videos, *Roll Out The Barrel*, clips from *In The Beginning Was The End: The Truth About De-Evolution*, and concert footage taped at the Starwood, Hollywood, October 1978; Walker Arts Center, Minneapolis, November 1978; and the Budokan, Tokyo, May 1979.

We're All Devo! (VHS/Beta/Video-8, Sony Pictures Home Entertainment, 1983; laserdisc, RCA Videodiscs 12232, 1984; VHS, Rhino Home Video RNVD 1941, 1990). Directed by Gerald V. Casale. 54 minutes. Includes music videos and clips from *Human Highway* and *In The Beginning Was The End: The Truth About De-Evolution*.

The Complete Truth About De-Evolution (Laserdisc, Voyager, 1993; DVD, Rhino Records, 2003.) 90 minutes. Includes music videos, clips from *Human Highway*, and the full *In The Beginning Was The End: The Truth About De-Evolution*.

INDEX

Unless otherwise stated, words in *italics* indicate album titles; words in 'quotes' indicate song titles.

After The Heat, 198
Agora Ballroom (venue), 16, 72, 167
Akeley, Carl, 82
Akron Art Institute, 143, 147
Akron Compilation, The, 242
Aladdin Sane, 260
Aleph (film), 171
'Allison' (poem), 143
Allison (film), 101
A&M Records (label), 158, 164, 195
Ambient 1: Music For Airports, 198–9
American Bandstand (TV show), 241
American Civil Liberties Union (ACLU), 80
American Dream, The (artwork), 118
Amon Düül, 52–3, 203–4
Angley, Ernest, Reverend, 234
'Animal Speaks, The,' 72
Ann Arbor Film Festival, 101, 147, 158
'Another World,' 211
Antilles Records (label), 289
Apocalypse Now (film), 217
Armstrong, Louis, 267
ARP Odyssey (synthesizer), 93, 131, 174
Arp, Hans, 111
Artaud, Antonin, 178, 247
Arthur J. & The Gold Cups, 227
Ash Ra Tempel, 198
Atari Video Music system, 273
'Auto Modown,' 47, 48, 91
Autobahn, 88, 168, 208–9
'Autumn's Child,' 91
Avengers, The, 11, 175

Aykroyd, Dan, 147, 214, 225

Baader, Andreas, 53
Baby Sex, 127, 128
'Bamboo Bimbo,' 109
Bangs, Lester, 139–40, 154–5, 238
Barbie (doll), 65
Barclay James Harvest, 247
Barger, Ed, 55, 56–7, 107
Barrett, K.K., 174
Bartos, Karl, 88, 205
Basil, Toni, 168–9, 170–1, 172, 184, 215, 227
Bauhaus (movement), 135–6
BBC, the, 146
'Be Stiff,' 229–30, 236
Be Stiff (EP), 230–1
Be Stiff Route 78 Tour, 230
Beach Boys, The, 88, 169, 243
Bean News (magazine), 85
Beatles, The (aka The White Album), 259
Beatles, The, 25, 33, 55, 92–3, 104, 119, 123–4, 129, 232, 247, 259–60
'Because,' 123
Beck, Jeff, 103
Beetle Beat, The, 92–3
Before & After Science, 198
Beginning Was The End, The (book), 93–7
Belushi, John, 225, 250
Bender, Ariel, 104
Bent, Rod, see Welch, Ward
Berman, Wallace, 169–70, 171, 184
Berry, Chuck, 210, 236
Berry, Fred, 169
Bertholf, Robert, 73, 74, 84
Bessy, Claude 'Kickboy Face,' 255
Bewlay Brothers (company), 222–3
Beyond The Unknown (comic book), 57
B-52's, 187, 279, 288
Biafra, Jello, 176, 254
Bib Le Flambeur (film), 246
Biggs, Ronnie, 195

Binder, Ronald, 159
Bingenheimer, Rodney, 173
Bizarros, The, 139, 241
Black Flag, 272
Black Panther Party, 30, 46
Black Sabbath, 210
Black, Jet, 277
Blackwell, Chris, 194, 222
'Blank Generation,' 157
Blank Generation, 247
'Blockhead,' 264–5
Blondie, 155, 175, 253, 255
'Blue Balls,' see 'Soo Bawlz'
Blue Öyster Cult, 159, 244, 280
Blue Velvet (film), 217, 219
Bluejeans & Moonbeams, 194, 279
Blues Brothers, The (film), 214, 250
Blues Fell This Morning (book), 71
Bob #1, see Mothersbaugh, Bob
Bob #2, see Casale, Bob
Bohn, Roger, 105–6, 107, 108
Bomp Records (label), 181–2, see also Who Put The Bomp (magazine)
Bonnie & Clyde (film), 146
Boogie Boy, 102–3, see also Booji Boy
Booji Boy Records (label), 144, 178, 181, 211
Booji Boy, 9, 11, 102–3, 114, 120, 121–2, 123, 138, 141, 174, 216, 218, 220, 227, 228, 239, 250, 252, see also Mothersbaugh, Mark
Bookchin, Murray, 63
Bowie, David, 49, 87, 100, 155, 160, 167–8, 172, 190–2, 194, 198, 199, 201, 202, 203, 213, 222–3, 242, 259–60, 266, 282
Bowie, Zowie, 190
'Boy Named Sue, A,' 80
Bozzio, Terry, 159–60
Brakha, Moshe, 180–1
Brand X, 228
Brandt, Elmer, 138

Branson, Richard, 194, 195–7, 223–4, 228, 229
'Brass In Pocket,' 289
Breakaway (film), 171
Breathless (film), 246
Bringing It All Back Home, 24
Brown, David, 176
Brown, James, 169, 179
Brown, Steven, 186, 187, 189, 243
Bryan, William Jennings, 80, 81
Buchla, Don, 35–6, 56
Buckley, Tim, 128
Buffalo Springfield, 215
Buggs, The, 92–3
Bukszpan, Daniel, 256
Buñuel, Luis, 118
Burger King (restaurant chain), 235
Burroughs, William S., 45, 49, 170, 239
Butler Act, the, 79–81
Butler, Chris, 42, 43, 44, 71, 172, 241–2, 288–9
Butler, John Washington, 79
Buy Or Die (album series), 284
Buzz Clic, see Brandt, Elmer
'Bye Bye Johnny,' 236
Byrd, Joseph, 90
Byrds, The, 280
Byrne, David, 72, 171, 179, 186, 243

Cage, John, 150
Cahiers du Cinéma (magazine), 245
California Institute of the Arts (CalArts), 35, 38
Calloway, Cab, 267
Can, 198, 205, 207, 210
'Can U Take It,' 57, 91
'Can't Buy Me Love,' 124
Canterbury, Robert, 42
Capitol Records (label), 253
Captain Beefheart, 48–9, 72, 91, 104, 125–6, 127, 128, 149, 165, 194–5, 210, 278–80
Carroll, Lewis, 67
Cars, The, 225, 255, 288

Carson, Johnny, 21
Carter, Jimmy, 254, 287
Casale, Bob (aka Bob #2),
75, 76, 98, 132, 177,
179, 196, 250, 273
Casale, Jerry, as
Chinaman, 12, 102,
106, 121, 122, 239;
early life and influences,
23–5, 33, 47, 59, 60,
99–100, 129, 168, 172;
first musical
experiments, 47–9, 57,
72–3, 74; interest in
filmmaking, 170–1; at
Kent State, 27–9, 30,
39, 41–2, 43, 44,
45–6, 51, 52, 71, 101,
180; meeting Mark
Mothersbaugh, 49,
69–71, 76; move to
California, 62–3;
playing and recording
with Devo, 75–7, 86,
93, 97–8, 108, 110,
114, 117–18, 119, 133,
140, 141, 144, 145,
152, 158, 163, 172,
179, 186, 202, 206,
214, 222, 228–9, 249,
250, 259, 260, 263,
266, 273, 286, 288;
other works, 134;
teaching, 99; writing
and songwriting, 47–8,
50, 64–5, 68–9, 93,
146, 169, 229, 235,
236, 239, 256–7, 264,
274, 286, 288
Cash, Johnny, 80, 218
'Cathy's Clone,' 165
CBGB, 8, 139, 142, 155,
156, 157, 159, 160,
161, 162, 175, 182,
247
Chabrol, Claude, 245,
246
Chance, James, 276
'Charlie Brown,' 26
Chateau Recorders
(studio), 261
Cheap Trick, 280
Cheetah Chrome, 140–1,
147–8, 253
Chinaman, 12, 102, 106,
121, 122, 239, see also
Casale, Jerry
Christmas Wishes, 144

Chroma keys (video
technique), 273, 274
Chrysalis, The (book), 82
Civilization & Its
Discontents (book),
152
Clapton, Eric, 103, 179,
209
Clark, Dick, 129, 241
Clean Water Act, 21
Clear Spot, 165
Cleaveland, Moses,
General, 19
Clem, Jay, 130, 283
'Clockout,' 264
'Cloud Pump,' 111
Clown, The, 102, 103, see
also Mothersbaugh,
Bob
Club Devo (catalog), 272
Cluster & Eno, 198
Cluster, 198, 203, 204
Coasters, The, 26
Cockettes, The, 174, 186
Cohen, Kip, 158, 164, 165,
166, 167, 275
Coleman, Harry S., 28–9
Coley, Byron, 161
Collins, Phil, 228
Coltrane, John, 127
'Come Back Jonee,' 186,
202, 219, 236, 252;
video for, 13, 251
Commercial Album, 283
Completion Backward
Principle, The, 166
Concept (event), 143
Confrontation At Kent State
(film), 101
Conner, Bruce, 171,
183–5, 186, 189
'Contort Yourself,' 276
Contortions, The, 276
Cook, Paul, 195
Cooper, Alice, 175
Coppola, Francis Ford, 219
Cornwell, Hugh, 277–8
Costello, Elvis, 197, 211,
214, 249, 256
Cotten, Michael, 165
Coxe, Simeon, 89
Cramps, The, 162, 172
Crazy Horse, 220
Creative Arts Festival, see
Kent State University
Creem (magazine), 154
Cristgau, Robert, 139, 238,
240, 241–2

Crocus Behemoth, 148,
152, see also Thomas,
David
Crosby Stills Nash &
Young, 46, 51
Crosby, David, 46, 51
CROSSROADS (film),
185–6
Crowley, Peter, 161
Crypt, the (venue), 138–9,
140, 142, 149
Cuyahoga River, 19, 20,
149
Czukay, Holger, 198, 199,
207

Daalder, Rene, 176
Dada and Dadaism, 52, 85,
110–15, 170, 171, 251
Damned, The, 211, 214
Dangerhouse Records
(label), 176
Dare, 287
Dark Side Of The Moon,
194
Darwin, Charles, and
Darwinism, 50, 81, 83
Dassin, Jules, 246
Davis, Dennis, 168
'Day My Baby Gave Me A
Surprize, The,' 267;
video for, 14, 272
Dayho Electronics (store),
47, 91
de Gaulle, Charles, 29
Dead Boys, The, 139,
140–1, 142, 147, 159,
172, 242, 247, 248,
253
Dead Kennedys, The, 176,
254
Deathstyles (film), 101
Decline Of Western
Civilization, The (film),
255
Demy, Jacques, 246
De-evolution (concept of),
46, 49, 64, 65, 75, 84,
87, 97, 122–3, 133,
141, 151, 144, 181,
226, 240–2, 269
'Devo Corporate Anthem,'
263, 266, 270
Devo Featuring Johnny
Rotten, 195–6
Devo 'leisure fashions,' 16,
272–3
Devo Live: The Mongoloid

Years, 109, 140
Devo 2.0, 232
Devotees, 267
Diamond Dogs tour, 100,
171, 282
Dick, Nigel, 242
Dickies, The, 254
Dictators, The, 156
Diddley, Bo, 73
Different Fur Studios, 185,
186, 202, 236
Dinger, Klaus, 206–7,
210–11
Dirksen, Dirk, 183
Dirty Work, 271
disco, 56, 89, 173, 263
Disney, Walt, 38, 107, 123
DMZ, 253
Doc At The Radar Station,
270
Doe, John, 173–4
Don Kirshner's Rock
Concert (TV special),
277
Dont Look Back (film), 125
'Don't You Want Me,' 287
Dorn, Ed, 73–4, 84–5, 98,
272
Dove (The Band Of Love),
276, 280–1
Dr Demento Show, The, 81
draft lottery, 25, 34
Du Plenty, Tomata, 174,
175–6, 177
Dunn, Ged, 156
Durrett, Richard, 90
Dury, Ian, 211
Duty Now For The Future,
artwork, 270–1;
recording sessions,
259, 261–3; release
and promotion, 271–2,
276–8; response to,
270, 271–2, 280;
songs, 263–7, 268–9
DX-7 synthesizer, 287
Dylan, Bob, 24, 29, 125,
178, 235, 276–7

Eagles, 75
Easy Rider (film), 169
Ed Sullivan Show, The (TV
show), 25, 33, 55, 124,
232
'Editions Of You,' 78
'Electricity,' 91
Ellington, Duke, 119
Ellul, Jacques, 63

Encyclopedia Of New Wave (book), 256–7

Eno, Brian, 78, 150, 186, 191–2, 197–202, 211, 213, 223, 225, 229, 233, 235, 242, 259, 267

Ensslin, Gudrun, 53

Ernest Angley Hour, The (TV show), 234

Eskimo, 129–30

Esleben-Schneider, Paul, 199

'Evolution Mama,' 81

Fabulous Four Skins Sing Songs Of Medicine And Med School, The, 144

Faulkner, William, 244

Faust, 194, 204

'Feel In My Heart,' 153

Feldman, Eric Drew, 280

Female Trouble (film), 102

Ferguson, Nancy, 274

Ferlinghetti, Lawrence, 182

Fieger, Doug, 253

Fier, Anton, 72

15-60-75, *see* Numbers Band, The

Filo, John, 44, 51

Firemen, The, 267

Firestone, Rod, 142, 151, 253, *see also* Welch, Ward

First Issue, 234

Five Easy Pieces (film), 169

Flamin' Groovies, The, 181

Flintstones, The (TV show), 168, 191

Flock Of Seagulls, A, 286

Floh De Cologne, 204

Flossy Bobbitt, 55, 75

Flür, Wolfgang, 88, 178, 206

Flynn, Homer, 127–8, 244, 285

Fonda, Peter, 169

For Your Pleasure, 78

400 Blows, The (film), 247

'Frankie Teardrop,' 162

'Fraulein,' 92

Freak Out, 129

Freedom Of Choice, 260, 265, 270, 283

Freud, Sigmund, 50, 152, 233

Fripp, Robert, 191, 242, 254

Froese, Edgar, 191

Frost, Robert, 35

Futurama (TV show), 49

Garcia, Jerry, 81

Garfield, Henry, 272

Garr, Teri, 171

Gear, Tommy, 174, 175

Geduldig, Bruce, 187

'Gegen, Ohne, Für Dada,' 111

General Boy, 32, 122, 134, 151, 227, 240, *see also* Mothersbaugh, Robert, Sr

Generation X (band), 173

Gerber, Billy, 283–4

Germs, The, 176

Geza X, 254

Ghoulardi, 59, 126

Gibson Ripper (guitar), 12–13

Gildzen, Alex, 143

Gill, Andy, 166, 238

Ginsberg, Allen, 45, 49, 143, 170, 182

Gleeson, Patrick, 185–6, 202, 236

'Go Go Go,' 236

'God Save The Queen,' 210

Godard, Jean-Luc, 245, 246

'Golden Brown,' 277

Golden Palominos, The, 72

Gorman, John, 105, 108, 110

'Gotta Serve Somebody,' 276

Grateful Dead, 36, 249

Great Rock'n'roll Swindle, The (film), 158

Green, Al, 255

'Green Poems' (poem), 85

Greenfield, Dave, 277

Gregg, Peter, 27, 47, 75, 91, 98

Griffith, Andy, 34

Grisman, David, 81

Groening, Matt, 49

Gropius, Walter, 135–6

Grundy, Bill, 212

Gunslinger (book), 73–4, 85

Guru Guru, 204

'Gut Feeling,' 235, 269

Gysin, Brion, 49

Half-Mute (album), 187

'Halleluhwah,' 210

Hamilton, Kipp, 153

Hancock, Herbie, 185

Hansa Studios, 198

Hard Day's Night, A (album), 260

Hard Day's Night, A (film), 124

Hardcore Devo, 47, 57, 93, 230, 231, 235

Harmonia, 198, 203

Harris, George, 45, 174, *see also* Hibiscus

HAZMAT suits, 9, 130, 161, 221, 249

Head (film), 169

Hearpen Records (label), 72

'Heart Of Glass,' 255

Hearthan Records (label), 145

Hell, Richard, 157, 158, 178, 211, 229, 247–8, 252

Hell's Angels, 45, 155

Hendrix, Jimi, 103, 209, 215, 230

Herber, Lewis, *see* Bookchin, Murray

'Here Comes Peter Cottontail,' 76, 77

Herrick, Rensselaer R., Mayor, 19

'Hero,' 210–11

"Heroes", 190, 198

'Hey Hey, My My (Into The Black),' 219–20, 221

'Hey Hey, My My (Out Of The Blue),' 221

'Hey Joe' / 'Piss Factory' (single), 145

Hibiscus, 174–5, 186–7, *see also* Harris, George

Hicks, Sue K., 80

Hitler, Adolf, 66–7, 68, 73, 85, 129

Hoffman, Samuel, Dr, 91–2

'Holidays In The Sun,' 235

Holmstrom, John, 156–7

Holt, Nancy, 46, 291

'Hong Kong Garden,' 213

Hooker, John Lee, 24

Hopper, Dennis, 169, 171, 216–17, 219

Houston, Penelope, 11, 175

'How Many Ropes Must A Poor Monkey Climb Before He Can Sleep In His Tree?,' 216

Howlin' Wolf, 127

Hughes, Howard, 74

Hughes, Langston, 35

Human Highway (film), 216–20

Human Issue (magazine), 27

Human League, The, 287

Hunky Dory, 260

Hunter, Ian, 232

Hüsker Dü, 254

Hütter, Ralf, 88, 205–7, 208

Hy Maya, 150

Hynde, Chrissie, 34, 39, 40, 43, 288–9

Hynde, Terry, 72

'I Been Refused,' 47, 91

'(I Can't Get Me No) Satisfaction,' 178–9, 181, 212, 215, 231, 238, 249, 252, 269, 278; video for, 12, 174, 226–7

'(I cån't gèt mé nö) SÅTISFACTIÖN' / 'SLÖPPY (I såw my baby getting)' (single), 178–81, 212

'I Know What Boys Like,' 289

'I Need A Chick,' 47, 91, 109

'I Want To Hold Your Hand,' 232

'I'd Like To Buy The World A Coke,' 260

Idiot, The, 167

Idol, Billy, 173

In The Beginning Was The End: The Truth About De-Evolution (film), 120–2, 143, 145, 147, 158, 181, 183, 203, 213, 242, 250, 269

Ingham, Jonh, 157

Institute For Defense Analyses (IDA), 28

Iron Eyes Cody, 21

Island Of Dr Moreau, The (book), 59

Island Of Lost Souls (film),
59–60
Island Records (label),
194, 222, 289
Isolar II tour, 190
Ivers, Peter, 255

Jackett, Gary 'General,' 62,
104, 121, 180
Jagger, Mick, 231–2
James Gang, The, 27, 75
Jarry, Alfred, 79, 101, 148
Jethro Tull, 280
Jetsons, The (TV show),
168, 191
Jett, Joan, 173
Jihad Jerry & The
Evildoers, 47
Jimmy Bell's Still In Town,
72
'Jocko Bozo,' 267
'Jocko Homo,' 15, 108,
109, 120, 122–3, 140,
141, 145, 173, 174,
200, 201, 250, 266,
267, 269; video for, 226
'Jocko Homo' / 'Mongoloid'
(single), 144–6, 181,
212, 271
Jocko-Homo Heavenbound
(pamphlet), 7, 81–4,
120
'Joeboy The Electronic
Ghost' / 'Pinheads On
The Move' (single), 187
'Johnny B. Goode,' 236
Jones, Davy, 169
Jones, Jim, Reverend, 97
Jones, Steve, 195, 212
Journey Through The Past
(film), 215, 218
Jungle Jim, 102, 103, *see
also* Mothersbaugh, Jim
Jupp, Mickey, & The Cable
Layers, 230
Just A Gigolo (film), 192
'Just What I Needed,' 255

Kaczynski, Ted (aka The
Unabomber), 63, 64
Kaprow, Allan, 35, 36, 38
Kaye, Lenny, 154
Ken (doll), 65
Kennedy, John F., 25, 97,
121, 137, 183, 237
Kent State University, 19,
25–6, 28, 29, 31, 32,
34, 36, 38–51, 69, 71,

75, 97, 147, 180, 291;
Commuter's Cafeteria,
27, 42, 62; Creative
Arts Festival, 35, 74,
77, 84–5, 91, 117,
123, 132; Hi-Y (club),
23; May 4 1970
shootings and aftermath
30, 38–52, 62, 99,
104, 105, 190, 258–9,
291; Tuesday Cinema
(club), 101–2
Kentucky Fried Chicken
(restaurant chain), 165
KFRC-FM (radio station),
283
Kidney, Robert, 71–2, 73
King Cobra, 138, 139–40,
142, *see also* Rubber
City Rebels, The
King Crimson, 242
King Jr, Martin Luther, 25
Kinks, The, 103
Kirk, Grayson, 20
Kirkland, Sally, 216
Kiss, 18, 102, 108, 237,
238, 240, 290
Knack, The, 253
Knebworth Festival, 15,
228–9
Koons, Jeff, 189
Kraftwerk 2, 208
Kraftwerk, 208
Kraftwerk, 88, 108, 168,
198, 199, 203, 204,
205–7, 208, 270, 282
Krause, Alison, 43, 44, 45,
101, 143
Krauss, Scott, 149
krautrock, 52, 168, 194,
198, 203–7, 208,
210–11
'Krautrock,' 204
Kristal, Hilly, 155, 172
KROQ (radio station), 267
KTTV (TV station), 126
Ku Klux Klan, 130, 216
Kurzwellen, 207

Laban, Rudolph, 111, 112
LaBaye 2x4 (guitar), 10
'Land Of 1,000 Dances,'
129, 130
Lang, Fritz, 123, 240
Laughner, Peter, 148
Laughton, Charles, 59
Lauper, Cyndi, 271
Leary, Timothy, 289

Led Zeppelin, 55, 128,
209, 233
Lennon, John, 33, 55, 66,
232
Les Rallizes Dénudés,
54–5
Lessing, Doris, 240
Lester, Richard, 124
Letze Lockerung (Dada
maninfesto), 111, 112
Levene, Keith, 197
Lewie, Jona, & Two's
Company, 230
Lewis, Bob, early life and
influences, 25–7, 47,
48; at Kent State, 26–7,
40–3, 49–50, 52;
managing Devo, 103,
131, 223–6; move to
California, 62; playing
and recording with
Devo, 74–5, 76; writing
and songwriting, 63–4,
65, 91, 98, 229
Lick My Decals Off, Baby,
125–6
Lie: The Love & Terror Cult,
92
'Like A Hurricane,' 221
'Like A Rolling Stone,' 235
Lindsay-Hogg, Michael,
124
'Little Johnny Jewel, Part
One' / 'Little Johnny
Jewel, Part Two'
(single), 145
Little Red Book, The (book,
aka Quotations *From
Chairman Mao Tse-
Tung*), 66
Lloyd, Richard, 162
Lolita (book), 48
Lookout Management
(company), 225
Looney Tunes, 248
Los Angeles Staff
(newspaper), 62, 63,
65, 75
Low, 87, 160, 198
Lowe, Nick, 211
Lugosi, Bela, 60
Lunine, Mike, 25
Lust For Life, 87, 167
Lux Interior, 162
Lydon, John, 72, 183, 195,
196–7, 210–11, 220,
223, 235, 248, 289
Lynch, David, 219, 255

Mabuhay Gardens (venue),
9, 10–11, 12, 182,
183, 184, 185, 186,
187, 188, 190, 195,
219, 243
'MacArthur Park,' 89
MacDonald, Ian, 204
Maerth, Oscar Kiss, 94,
120
Magic Band, The, 125,
278, *see also* Captain
Beefheart
Magma, 244
Magnum, Jeff, 253
Man Who Fell To Earth, The
(film), 192
Manowar, 156
Manson, Charles, 92, 97,
180
Mao Tse-Tung, 66, 68, 121
Mapplethorpe, Robert, 145
Marcheschi, Cork, 90
Marcus, Greil, 255
Marcuse, Herbert, 38
Margouleff, Robert, 260–1
Marley, Bob, 72, 179
Marsh, Dave, 154–5, 244,
271
Marshall, Ann, 171
Martin, George, 124
Martin, Mary, 175
Marx, Karl, 50
Massaro, Susan, 269
Max's Kansas City (venue),
8, 160, 161, 190, 232,
251
Max's Kansas City 1976
(aka *New York New
Wave*), 161
May 4 1970 shootings,
see Kent State
University
Mayberry R.F.D. (TV
show), 34
MC5, 147, 155
McClure, Michael, 170,
185
McCluskey, Andy, 88
McCormack, Ed, 171
McDonald's (restaurant
chain), 122, 123, 165,
235
McLaren, Malcolm, 29,
157–8, 195, 210, 249
McMahon, Ed, 217
McNeil, Legs, 156–7, 248
'Meadow Meal,' 204
Meat Loaf, 238

313

'Mechanical Man,' 92, 122
Meet The Residents, 129
Mein Kampf (book), 67
Meinhof, Ulrike, 53
Mellotron, 55, 124
Melody Maker (magazine), 196, 197, 203, 244
Melville, Jean-Pierre, 246
Men Who Make The Music, The (video compilation), 134, 276
Mer Records (label), 145
Metropolis (film), 123, 240
Meyer, Russ, 118
Michaels, Lorne, 248
'Midget,' 275
Midnight Special (TV show), 88
Mieczkowski, Ed, 143
Miller, Daniel, 287
Miller, Jeffrey, 42, 43, 44, 51
Mine Is Not A Holy War, 47
Missing Persons, 159
'Mr DNA,' 269
'Mr Jingeling,' 76
Mitchell, Joni, 225, 251
Mizutani, Takashi, 55
Moebius, Dieter, 198
Mole Show tour, 284
Monkees, The, 169, 287
'Mongoloid,' 78, 146, 184, 187, 215; video for, 184–5
Moog (synthesizers), 36, 56–7, 90, 93, 106, 138, 207, 220, 263
'Moonage Daydream,' 50
Mooney, Malcolm, 207
Moroder, Giorgio, 259
Morris, Kenny, 212
Mothers Of Invention, The, 129
Mothersbaugh Sr, Robert, 32, 55, 122, 134, 151
Mothersbaugh, Alex, 274
Mothersbaugh, Bob (aka Bob #1), early musical experiences, 75, 86, 103–4, 131; at Kent State, 40, 41; playing and recording with Devo, 93, 121, 132, 139, 161, 199, 223, 229, 233, 235, 249, 269, 277; songwriting, 264, 265, 278

Mothersbaugh, Jim, 8, 34, 86–7, 88, 93, 98, 103, 118, 131, 144, 269
Mothersbaugh, Mark, as Booji Boy, 9, 11, 102–3, 122, 141; early life and influences, 32–4, 35, 44, 59–60, 84, 92, 136, 165, 180; first experiments with synthesizers, 55–7, 76, 93, 138; as Gorj, 70–1; at Kent State, 34–6, 55–6, 70–1; meeting Jerry Casale, 49, 69–71, 76; playing and recording with Devo, 74–7, 86, 87, 91–2, 103–4, 108–9, 121, 132, 134, 140, 141, 143–4, 150, 166, 173, 179, 191, 200, 201–2, 203, 213–14, 218, 219–21, 228, 229, 232, 233, 234, 235, 250, 252, 260, 262–3, 266, 267, 270, 273, 286; as Poot Man, 70; other work, 120, 151; trip to Jamaica, 195–7; writing and songwriting, 66–9, 92–3, 98–9, 146, 239, 259, 265, 268, 278, 285
Mothersbaugh, Mary, 41, 180
Mott The Hoople, 104, 232
Mottram, Eric, 49–50, 57, 98
MOVIE, A (film), 183
MTV, 118, 143, 188, 287–8
Muddy Waters, 24
Murphy, Turk, 81
Music Machine, The, 149
Mutato Muzika (company), 33
'My Head Is My Only House Unless It Rains,' 165
My Life In The Bush Of Ghosts, 186
My Struggle (book), 66–7, 71, 77, 98, 99, 216, 230, 239–40, 275
Myers, Alan, 89, 131–2, 181, 250, 273, 275
Myers, Michael, 85

Myers, Richard (aka Dick), 40, 101
Mystery In Space (comic book), 57
National Association of Broadcasters (NAB), 126
National Guard, 41–3, 45, 50, 63, 78, 91, 101, 190, 258
Neu! '75, 210–11
Neu!, 168, 198, 204, 205, 206–7, 210–11
Never Mind The Bollocks, Here's The Sex Pistols, 195
New Traditionalists, 261
new wave, 91, 153, 175, 209, 220, 244–5, 248, 253, 254–7, 279, 288
New Wave Rock'n'Roll: Get Behind It Before It Gets Past You, 247–8
New Wave Theatre (TV show), 255
New York Dolls, 155, 157, 175, 210, 244
Newman, Laraine, 276
Newsmith, Mike, 287
Nicholson, Jack, 169
Nieberger, Colin, 31
1910 Fruitgum Company, The (band), 237
Nixon, Richard, 38–9, 51, 62–3, 121, 162, 237
NME (magazine), 196, 204
No Wave, 276
Noir Kakadu (ballet), 112
NON, 189
Normal, The, 287
'Norwegian Wood,' 104
Nosferatu, 278
Not Available, 130
Nouvelle Vague (movement), 245
Now It Can Be Told: DEVO At The Palace 12/9/88, 97
Now, 165
Nuggets: Original Artyfacts From The First Psychedelic Era 1965–68, 154–5, 245
Numan, Gary, 240, 288
Numbers Band, The, 6, 71–2, 75, 76, 97
Nuns, The, 182, 183

Oakey, Phil, 287
Oberheim, Tom, 90
Oblique Strategies, 192, 201–2
Oh, No! It's Devo, 102
'Ohio,' 51–2
Ohio Express, The, 237
Oldfield, Mike, 194
Olener, Jeff, 182
Oliver, Paul, 71
'Once In A Lifetime,' 171
One From The Heart (film), 219
'1-2-3 Red Light,' 237
Ono, Yoko, 147
Ork Records (label), 145, 211
Ork, Terry, 145
Osmonds, The, 280
Our Trip (film), 171
'Paint It Black,' 104, 179
Palm Casino Revue, The (show), 175
Panter, Gary, 284, 285
'Paperback Writer,' 124
Parcheesi, 275
Partially Buried Woodshed (artwork), 6, 36, 46, 291
Pas De Trois (film), 171
Patti Smith Group, 155, see also Smith, Patti
Pauline, Mark, 189
Pee Wee's Playhouse (TV show), 285
'Penetration In The Centrefold,' 267
Pennebaker, D.A., 125
'Penny Lane,' 124
Pere Ubu, 72, 145, 148–54, 160, 172, 241, 242, 243, 244
Perloff, Marjorie, 74
Perottet, Suzanne, 111
Perr, Janet, 271
Pet Sounds, 243
Peter & The Wolf, 190
Petty, Tom, & The Heartbreakers, 228
Philly Dogs tour, 100
'Pinheads On The Move,' 187
Pin Ups, 260
Ping Pong Match, The (film), 171
Pink Flamingos (film), 102, 104, 175

'Pink Pussycat,' 131, 268
Pirate's Cove, the (venue), 148–9, 152
Pitney, Gene, 164
'Plan For U, A,' 93
Plank, Konrad 'Conny,' 198–9
Plank's (studio), 198–9, 202, 210, 229–30, 233
'Pocket Calculator,' 88
'Poème Simultané,' 111
Pollard, Joe, 88
'Polymer Love' (essay), 64, 98, 288
Pop, Iggy, 87, 139, 160, 167, 168–9, 172, 190, 197, 205, 207
PopClips (TV show), 287
Population: 1 (film), 176
'Positively 4th Street,' 235
post-punk, 146, 209
Potter, Charles Francis, Reverend, 82
Powell, Mike, 55
'Powerhouse,' 92
'Praying Hands,' 233, 266, 276
Presley, Elvis, 24, 247
Pretenders, The, 289
'Pretty Vacant,' 157
Principle, Peter, 187
'Private Secretary,' 76
Public Image Ltd, 197, 210–11, 234
Public Image, The (book), 197
Punk (magazine), 156
punk, 83, 115, 142, 145, 148, 155–8, 160, 168, 171, 173–4, 176, 178, 182, 186, 187–9, 197, 205, 209–10, 214, 215, 219, 220, 227, 235, 242–3, 244–5, 247, 248, 249, 253–5, 256, 257, 277, 287, 289
'Purple Haze,' 230
Puttin' Out Is Dreamsville (musical), 175
Pynchon, Thomas, 239

Q: Are We Not Men? A: We Are Devo!, artwork, 236–7; recording sessions, 198–203, 233, 235; release and promotion, 226–7, 232, 249–51, 277; response

to, 237–9, 262, 280; songs, 233–6
Queen City Records (pressing plant), 144

Radio Birdman, 253
'Rain,' 124
'Rainy Day Women #12 & 35,' 24
Ralf und Florian, 208
Ralph Records (label), 129, 187, 284
Ramones, 133, 139, 155, 157, 160, 163, 175, 197, 247, 248, 252, 253
Rappleyea, George, 80
Ravenstine, Allen, 150–1, 152
'Recombo DNA,' 158–9
Recombo DNA, 158
'Readers vs. Breeders' (essay), 63–4, 98
Red Army Faction, 53–4
'Red Eye,' 270
Reid, Jamie, 29
Reininger, Blaine, 186, 243
Reisman, Rod, 75, 76, 86
'Religion I' / 'Religion II,' 234
Renaldo & The Loaf, 284
REO Speedwagon, 280
Reserve Officers' Training Corps (ROTC), 30, 39, 40–1, 45, 50, 276
Residents, The, 126–30, 187, 243, 244, 282–3, 285
'Revolution,' 66
Reymann, Marty, 55, 56–7
Rhodes, Jim, Governor, 41, 45, 63, 78, 105, 174, 190, 258
'Rhythmic Itch,' 278
Richter, Hans, 111, 112, 115
Riefenstahl, Leni, 266
Rififi (film), 246
Rimbaud, Arthur, 247
'Ring My Bell,' 89
Rivers, Johnny, 121
Rivette, Jacques, 245
Robbins, Terry, 30, 31
Roberts, Elliot, 225, 232, 248–9, 250, 251, 283–4
Robinson, Dave, 194, 211–12, 213, 214–15

Rock'n'Roll High School (film), 252
Rocket From The Tombs, 147, 148
Rocket To Russia, 247
Rod Rooter's Big Reamer (film), see Roll Out The Barrel
Rodriguez, Chi Chi, 230, 236–7
Roedelius, Hans-Joachim, 198, 203
Roessler, Paul, 174, 176, 177, 178
Rohmer, Éric, 245
Roland (instrument manufacturer), 131
Roll Out The Barrel (film), 274–6
Rollerball (film), 263–4
Rolling Stone (magazine), 69, 106, 177, 238, 265–7, 271, 280
Rolling Stones, The, 24, 33, 103–4, 114, 169, 179, 231, 249, 271, 279
Rollins, Henry, 272
Roosevelt, Theodore, 82
'Rope Song, The,' 47, 48, 91
Rother, Michael, 198, 206–7, 211
Rothwell III, Craig Allen, 227–8, see also Spazz Attack
Rotten, Johnny, see Lydon, John
Roxy Music, 78, 150, 197, 212, 282
Rozz-Tox Manifesto, 284–5
Rubber City Rebels, The, 142, 172, 241, 253, see also King Cobra
Rubin, Jerry, 30
Rudd, Mark, 28, 29, 30
Rudge, Peter, 231, 232
Runaways, The, 173
Rust Never Sleeps (album), 220
Rust Never Sleeps (film), 221
Ryser, Scott, 188–9, 190

'St James Infirmary Blues,' 267
Saints, The, 247, 248
Sat Sun Mat, 34

Satisfied Mind, The, 24
Satrom, Leroy, 39, 40, 41
Saturday Night Live (TV show), 15, 147, 168–9, 225, 232, 248–51, 260, 276
Savage, Jon, 60, 176
Scene, The (magazine), 148
Schacht, Janis, 253
Schaeffer, Pierre, 207
Scheuer, Sandra, 44–5
Schlesinger, Karl, 85
Schlesinger, Leon, 248
Schmidt, Irwin, 205, 207
Schmidt, Peter, 201
Schneider, Florian, 88, 199, 207
Schnitzler, Conrad, 203
Schroeder, William, 45, 61
Schwartz, Les, 224–5
Schwartzmiller, Donald L., 40
Scopes, John T., 80, 81
Scott, Ken, 259–60, 261, 262, 269
Scott, Raymond, 92
Screamers, The, 174, 175–8, 284
SDS-V (electronic drum kit), 89
Search & Destroy (magazine), 148, 152, 182, 184
'Secret Agent Man,' 121, 269; video for, 226
Secret Museum Of Mankind, The (book), 92
Seidel, Wolfgang, 207–8
Sellers, Peter, 124
Semi-Hard (pamphlet), 86
Semina (journal), 170
Sender, Ramon, 185
Serner, Walter, 110, 111–12, 113
77 Sunset Strip (TV show), 33
Severin, Steve, 212–13
Sex Pistols, 157–8, 186, 195, 196, 211, 212, 219, 235, 249
Shadduck, Bertram Henry, 81–4, 94, 120
Shakey, Bernard, 215, see also Young, Neil
Shapiro, David, 29

Shaw, Greg, 154, 157, 181, 245
She's So Unusual, 271
Shelly's (magazine), 98
Shinn, Dorothy, 37, 46
Shock Theater (TV show), 59, 126
Shoes, The, 181
'Shrivel-Up,' 186, 202, 236, 276
'S. I. B. (Swelling Itching Brain),' 265
Sick Fucks, The, 175
Silver Apples Of The Moon, 35
Silver Apples, 89–90
Silverstein, Shel, 80
Sinclair, Magdalene, 66
Sioux, Siouxsie, 212
Siouxsie & The Banshees, 212
Sire Records (label), 186, 247–8, 253, 289
Sirius (journal), 112
sitar, 103–4
Skylab (space station), 234–5
'Slap Your Mammy,' 235, 269
Slash (fanzine), 284
'Sloppy (I Saw My Baby Gettin'),' 180, 181
'Smart Patrol,' 136–7, 161, 269
Smiling Dog Saloon, 105, 107, 110
Smith, Patti, 145, 147, 154, 155, 245
Smithson, Robert, 6, 35, 36, 37–8, 46, 291
Snow White (film), 267
Snyder, Tom, 197
'Social Fools,' 230
Soft Machine, 55, 244
Some Girls, 249
Songs For Swinging Larvae, 284
'Soo Bawlz,' 269
'Space Girl Blues,' 57, 91
'Space Junk,' 234–5
'Space Man' (poem), 27
Spark, Muriel, 197
Spazz Attack, 227, 252
Speer, Albert, 266
Spencer-Brown, G., 63
Spheeris, Penelope, 255
Spiral Jetty (artwork), 35
'spud' (concept), 77,

137–8, 160, 269
Spungen, Nancy, 253
Square Pegs (TV show), 289
Stalling, Carl, 92
Star Wars (film), 221
Starwood, the (venue), 166, 167, 168–9, 173, 174
Statler, Chuck, 71, 117–18, 120, 122, 227, 252, 260, 273–4
Stein, Seymour, 247, 252–4, 257
Stewart, Charlotte, 219
Stiff Records (label), 194, 211–12, 213, 214–15, 230–1, 238, 242, 256
Stiv Bators, 139, 142
Stockhausen, Karlheinz, 207
Stockwell, Dean, 171, 215, 216–17, 219
Stokes, Carl, Mayor, 20
Stooges, The, 139, 147, 149, 155, 156, 210
Stranglers, 277, 279
'Strawberry Fields Forever,' 124
Students for a Democratic Society (SDS), 27–8, 29, 30–1, 38, 39, 46, 52
Subotnick, Morton, 35–8, 185
'Subterranean Homesick Blues,' 29, 125
Subterranean Modern, 284
Suicide, 162
Summer, Donna, 89
Sun Ra, 106–7, 108, 109, 110, 242, 249
Sweet, Rachel, 230
Sykes, John, 288
Sylvain, Sylvain, 157
Synare, 89
Syndrum, 88–9
synth pop, 265
synthpunk, 174, 188

'Taboo Of Virginity, The' (essay), 152
Taeuber, Sophie, 112
Tago Mago, 210
'Take Me To The River,' 255
Talking Heads 77, 247
Talking Heads, 72, 155,

163, 179, 243, 247, 248, 253, 255
Tamblyn, Russ, 171, 216, 219
T.A.M.I. Show, The (TV special), 169
Tangerine Dream, 191, 194, 203–4
Television, 145, 155, 162, 182, 243
Teter, Holbrook, 85
Third Reich 'n Roll, 129, 130
'30 Seconds Over Tokyo' / 'Heart Of Darkness' (single), 145
Thomas, David, 72, 148, 149, 152–3, 243–4
Thomas, Pete, 249
3D glasses, 122, 123, 180, 221, 249, 273
Three Stooges, The, 119, 148, 250, 268
'Timing X,' 264
Tin Huey, 242
Today (TV show), 157, 212
Tomorrow Show, The (TV show), 197
Tone Float, 208
Tong, Winston, 187
TONTO's Exploding Head Band, 261
'Too Much Paranoias,' 201, 235
'Town Without Pity,' 164
Tracks & Traces, 198
'Trans-Europe Express,' 270
'Triumph Of The Will,' 266–7
Trouser Press (magazine), 237, 261–2
Trout Mask Replica, 278, 280
Truffaut, François, 245, 247
Tubes, The, 138, 164, 165–6, 262
Tubular Bells, 194
Tupperwares, The, see Screamers, The
Tuxedomoon, 186–8, 189, 243
Twin Peaks (TV show), 219
Twisted Sister, 156
Tzara, Tristan, 111, 112–13, 114, 115, 194

'U Got Me Bugged,' 92–3
Ubu Roi (play), 148
Umbrellas Of Cherbourg, The (film), 246
Uncle Lou, 242
Uncle Willie, 282
Uncle Willie's Highly Opinionated Guide To The Residents (book), 282–3
'Uncontrollable Urge,' 201, 232, 233, 265–6
Unfaithful Wife, The (film), 246
Unit Services (store), 120, 144
United States Of America, The (band), 90

Vale, V., 182, 186
Van Vliet, Don, see Captain Beefheart
Vance, Tommy, 210
Vecchio, Mary Ann, 44, 51
Vega, Alan, 162
Velvet Underground & Nico, The, 119, 192
Velvet Underground, The, 54, 147, 152, 156, 192, 244, 280
Verlaine, Tom, 243
Vicious, Sid, 140, 195, 253
Vietnam War, 27, 28, 29, 34, 39, 53, 56, 101, 152, 256
Vileness Fats (film), 128–9, 130
Virgin Records (label), 194–5, 223–4, 228, 232
Visconti, Tony, 87, 259
Visions Of Excess, 72
Visiting Kids, The, 274
Vonnegut, 222, 239
Vox Continental (organ), 33

Waitresses, The, 172, 288–9
Wakabayashi, Moriaki, 54
Walsh, Joe, 26–7, 75
Walt Disney Records (label), 233
'Waltz, The' (poem), 7, 85
War Of The Gargantua (film), 153, 219
Ward, Anita, 89
Warhol, Andy, 35, 64, 119,

147, 160, 187, 286, 290
'Warm Leatherette,' 287
Warner Bros (label), 72, 92, 126, 128, 222–5, 226, 232, 236, 248, 252, 254, 264, 272
Warner Bros Album, The, 128
Watergate scandal, 62, 97
Waters, John, 102, 118, 174
Waybill, Fee, 164, 165, 166
'We Stole This Riff,' 128
We Have Come For Your Children, 253
Weathermen, The (aka Weather Underground), 29–30, 31, 52
Webb, Bob, 41
Webber, Rachel, 188
Weber, Fred, 75, 76–7, 86
Weinzierl, John, 52–3
Weiss, Jon, 107

Welch, Ward, 138, 139, 140–1, 142, see also Firestone, Rod
Wells, H.G., 59
We're All Devo (film), 276
Whatever Happened To Vileness Fats? 129, see also Vileness Fats (film)
When Pigs Fly: Songs You Never Thought You'd Hear, 52
'Whip It,' 89, 159, 174, 212, 287
Whisky A Go-Go, the (venue), 173, 176, 253
White Castle (restaurant chain), 236
White Panther Party, 66
'White Punks On Dope,' 138, 164
'Who Do You Love?,' 73
Who Put The Bomp (magazine), 154
Whole Earth Catalog, The (book), 63

'Wholelottadick,' 128
'Wiggle Worm,' 75
'Wiggly World,' 264
Williams, Robert, 278
Winterland Ballroom (venue), 186, 195
Witthüser & Westrupp, 204
Wizard Of Oz, The (film), 219
WMMS (radio station), 105–6, 107, 117, 242
'Woe-Is-Uh-Me-Bop,' 125
Wolfe, Tom, 135–6, 137
Wonder Woman (comic book), 7, 57–8, 59, 60
Wonder, Stevie, 260
'Words Get Stuck In My Throat,' 153
World Of Rubber (museum), 8, 120
World War I, 110, 113, 115
World War II, 32, 52–3, 90, 115, 257, 266
'Worried Man' (aka

'Worried Man Blues), 218, 276
Wreckless Eric, 211, 230
Wright, Tim, 172
Wulff, Käthe, 111
X (band), 173, 281
Yardbirds, The, 280
Yeats, William Butler, 23, 35
Young Girls Of Rochefort, The (film), 246
Young Loud & Snotty, 247
Young, Neil, 51–2, 215–17, 219–21, 225, 249
Zappa, Frank, 129, 159, 165, 240, 249, 271
Ze Whiz Kidz, 175
Zephyrus Image (press), 7, 85, 86
Ziggy Stardust, 260

ACKNOWLEDGEMENTS

THANK YOU
Alex Brunelle, Holger Czukay, Adam Davis at Division Leap, Larry DeMellier, Alex Gildzen, Robert Kidney, Janet Macoska, Richard Peterson, Paul Roessler, Janis Schacht, Norman Seeff, James Stark, Seymour Stein, Morton Subotnick, Robert Williams, Tom Seabrook and all at Jawbone, and the San Francisco, Oakland, and Berkeley public libraries.

PICTURE CREDITS
The photographs used in this book came from the following sources, and we are grateful for their help. **Jacket front** Eric Blum/Michael Ochs Archives/Getty Images. **Jacket back** Richard Peterson. **2** Richard Peterson. **6** *Partially Buried Woodshed* courtesy of Kent State University Libraries Special Collections and Archives. **15-60-75** David King. **7** *Wonder Woman* © DC Comics. All rights reserved. Used with permission. *The Waltz* courtesy of Division Leap. **8** Ebet Roberts/Redferns/Getty Images. **9** *Booji Boy* Eric Blum/Michael Ochs Archives/Getty Images. *Mabuhay* James Stark. **10** *Bob #1* James Stark. **11** *Both images* Richard Peterson. **12** *Backstage* James Stark. *Downtown* Janet Macoska. **13** *Akron* Janet Macoska. *Cowboys* Richard Peterson. **14** *Beach* Norman Seeff. **15** *Knebworth* Gus Stewart/Redferns/Getty Images. *SNL* NBC Universal/Getty Images. **16** *Jerry* Tom Hill/WireImage/Getty Images. *Planking* Richard Peterson.

MILLION DOLLAR
BASH: BOB DYLAN,
THE BAND, AND THE
BASEMENT TAPES
by Sid Griffin

ISBN 978-1-906002-05-3

HOT BURRITOS:
THH TRUE STORY OF
THE FLYING BURRITO
BROTHERS
by John Einarson with
Chris Hillman

ISBN 978-1-906002-16-9

BOWIE IN BERLIN:
A NEW CAREER IN A
NEW TOWN
by Thomas Jerome
Seabrook

ISBN 978-1-906002-08-4

TO LIVE IS TO DIE:
THE LIFE AND DEATH
OF METALLICA'S
CLIFF BURTON
by Joel McIver

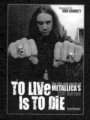

ISBN 978-1-906002-24-4

MILLION DOLLAR
LES PAUL: IN SEARCH
OF THE MOST
VALUABLE GUITAR IN
THE WORLD
by Tony Bacon

ISBN 978-1-906002-14-5

THE IMPOSSIBLE
DREAM: THE STORY
OF SCOTT WALKER
AND THE WALKER
BROTHERS
by Anthony Reynolds

ISBN 978-1-906002-25-1

JACK BRUCE:
COMPOSING
HIMSELF: THE
AUTHORISED
BIOGRAPHY
by Harry Shapiro

ISBN 978-1-906002-26-8

FOREVER CHANGES:
ARTHUR LEE AND THE
BOOK OF LOVE
by John Einarson

ISBN 978-1-906002-31-2

RETURN OF THE
KING: ELVIS PRESLEY'S
GREAT COMEBACK
by Gillian G. Gaar

ISBN 978-1-906002-28-2

A WIZARD, A TRUE
STAR: TODD
RUNDGREN IN THE
STUDIO
by Paul Myers

ISBN 978-1-906002-33-6

SEASONS THEY
CHANGE: THE STORY
OF ACID AND
PSYCHEDELIC FOLK
by Jeanette Leech

ISBN 978-1-906002-32-9

WON'T GET FOOLED
AGAIN: THE WHO
FROM LIFEHOUSE TO
QUADROPHENIA
by Richie Unterberger

ISBN 978-1-906002-35-0

THE
RESURRECTION OF
JOHNNY CASH:
HURT, REDEMPTION,
AND AMERICAN
RECORDINGS
by Graeme Thomson

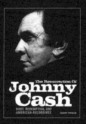

ISBN 978-1-906002-36-7

CRAZY TRAIN: THE
HIGH LIFE AND
TRAGIC DEATH OF
RANDY RHOADS
by Joel McIver

ISBN 978-1-906002-37-4

JUST CAN'T GET
ENOUGH:
THE MAKING OF
DEPECHE MODE
by Simon Spence

ISBN 978-1-906002-56-5

GLENN HUGHES:
FROM DEEP PURPLE
TO BLACK COUNTRY
COMMUNION
by Glenn Hughes

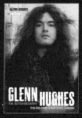

ISBN 978-1-906002-92-3

ENTERTAIN US:
THE RISE OF NIRVANA
by Gillian G. Gaar

ISBN 978-1-906002-89-3

MIKE SCOTT:
ADVENTURES OF A
WATERBOY
by Mike Scott

ISBN 978-1-908279-24-8

SHE BOP: THE
DEFINITIVE HISTORY
OF WOMEN IN
POPULAR MUSIC
by Lucy O'Brien
Revised Third Edition

ISBN 978-1-908279-27-9

SOLID
FOUNDATION: AN
ORAL HISTORY OF
REGGAE
by David Katz
Revised and Expanded
Edition

ISBN 978-1-908279-30-9

READ & BURN:
A BOOK ABOUT WIRE
by Wilson Neate

ISBN 978-1-908279-33-0

BIG STAR: THE STORY
OF ROCK'S
FORGOTTEN BAND
by Rob Jovanovic
Revised & Updated
Edition

ISBN 978-1-908279-36-1

RECOMBO DNA

THE STORY OF DEVO
OR HOW THE 60s BECAME THE 80s

KODAK SAFETY FILM